Contents

3 Editorial: More of the same in these last days

7 *John A. Davies*, Solomon in the Gospels and Acts—Saint or Sinner?

23 *Nickolas A. Fox*, The mechanisms of unity: The social identity-forming power of the eucharist

37 *Francis Otobo*, The Holy Spirit and Luke's infancy narrative: Reading a legitimatory role

57 *Patrick Cole*, Global evangelism in Jesus' Temple destruction/ last times discourse in Luke-Acts and in synoptic tradition: Confluence, congruence, intertextual linkages, and connective shaping

93 *James R. Harrison*, 'Wonders in the heaven above' (Acts 2:19): The Graeco-Roman portent mentality and terata in Luke-Acts

117 *Christoph Stenschke*, Human flourishing and the Paul of the book of Acts

131 *Andrew Stewart*, Herod Agrippa II: The embodiment or extinction of Israel's hope?

Book Reviews

145 Walter Ameling, Hannah M. Cotton, Werner Eck et al. (eds.), *Corpus Inscriptionum Iudaeae / Palaestinae*

146 Folker Siegert, Johann Maier, Frieder Lötzsch (eds.), *Rechtsgeschichtlicher Kommentar zum Neuen Testament Band I: Einleitung, Arbeitsmittel und Voraussetzungen*

148 Richard Bauckham, *"Son of Man," Volume 1: Early Jewish Literature*

151 Udo Schnelle, Manfred Lang (Hrsg.), *Texte zum Matthäusevangelium Teilband 2: Matthäus 11–28. Neuer Wettstein: Texte zum Neuen Testament aus Griechentum und Hellenismus Band I/1.2*

152 Nathan C. Johnson, *The Suffering Son of David in Matthew's Passion Narrative*

154 Gene L. Green, *Vox Petri: A Theology of Peter*

157 Michael F. Bird, *A Bird's-Eye View of Luke and Acts: Context, Story, and Themes*

159 Jenny Read-Heimerdinger, *Luke in His Own Words: A Study of the Language of Luke-Acts in Greek*

161 Chris Seglenieks, *Johannine Belief and Graeco-Roman Devotion: Reshaping: Devotion for John's Graeco-Roman Audience*

More of the same in these last days

As this eighth issue of *JGAR* goes to press, the 'anguish on the earth among nations' (Luke 21:25) is patent. In both rumour and reality 'nation [is] raised up against nation, and kingdom against kingdom' (Luke 21:10). After all, Jesus' words were simply a description of a constant feature of human history. Why should we be surprised that one human ideology clashes with another over and again, and then now? After rival ideologues cancel conversation or compromise, isn't it entirely regular that force, violence, and bloodshed soon follow?

According to the apocalyptic prophet from Nazareth, this cosmic turmoil constantly stirred up by the beastly kingdoms biting and devouring one another (cf. Dan 7:1–8, 17) provides the background for the persecution of God's people:

> they will lay their hands on you and persecute you. They will hand you over to the synagogues and prisons, and you will be brought before kings and governors because of my name. (Luke 21:12)

Again, why should we be surprised that as human ideology continues its long march through human institutions, it also tramples upon God's people?

Even in a formerly freedom-loving nation such as Australia, Christian institutions and activities are now seriously under threat, as the talking-classes and power-brokers seek to curtail the freedom of religion and its speech. Jesus' warning is once again ever so timely.

But no matter what mouth or muscle might make cause to calumniate and cancel, the ideologues have set themselves an impossible task. Jesus' warning was actually a promise of good things to come. For sure, the warning was severe. Who wants to hear of a world in which the people of the Prince of Peace must steel themselves whenever they recall his words?

> You will even be betrayed by parents, brothers, relatives, and friends. They will kill some of you. You will be hated by everyone because of my name, ... (Luke 21:16–17a).

And yet, this hostility will not have the ultimate victory. It is simply the world's means to the Kingdom's ends, for:

> ... not a hair of your head will be lost. By your endurance, you will take hold of your souls (Luke 21:17b–18).

As others 'faint from fear and expectation of the things that are coming on the world' (v.25), those with their eyes fixed upon the coming of the Son of Man to his glory are to 'stand up and lift your heads, because your redemption is near' (v.28).

Whatever the current form the cosmic turmoil might take, this is still the world in which a man has risen from the dead. And since the risen Christ's outpouring of the Spirit of God on the Day of Pentecost, this is still the arena in which his people bear him witness:

> This will give you an opportunity to bear witness. Therefore make up your minds not to prepare your defence ahead of time, for I will give you such words and a wisdom that none of your adversaries will be able to resist or contradict. (Luke 21:13–15).

And so, even in the present context—perhaps especially in this present context—, Gospels and Acts research must also continue to stand up, lift the head, endure, bear witness.

This eighth edition of *JGAR* throws a narrative arc from Solomon to Agrippa II, from 'Solomon in all his glory' (ἐν πάσῃ τῇ δόξῃ αὐτοῦ; Matt 6:29; Luke 12:27), to Agrippa II 'with all [his] fantasy' (μετὰ πολλῆς φαντασίας; Acts 25:23). As always, the outward display of human majesty was meant to impress and overwhelm. But what is the reality behind this glitter and bling? Perhaps for Solomon, his robes took on the afterglow of his father David, who was promised a son who would reign over God's eternal kingdom. For those who knew the story, the robes of Agrippa II were a stark reminder of that fateful morning when his father's robes, made wholly of silver, caught the sun so 'miraculously' (θαυμασίως) that the crowd cried out, 'It's the voice of a god and not of a man!'. When he then suddenly died, it was interpreted as an act of God's judgement in the wake of such pretension (Josephus, *Ant.* 19:343–350; Acts 12:20–23). As Nebuchadnezzer also had had to learn (Dan 4), 'all the inhabitants of the earth are nothing', and '[the Lord's] dominion is an everlasting dominion, and his kingdom is from generation to generation'. Despite their outward appearances and inner pretensions, the kings of this earth must regain their sanity by acknowledging the Lord of Heaven. In the midst of the beastly kingdoms, staggering around in their madness, the gospel mission continues to offer a movement towards a better mind.

At the beginning of this 'narrative arc', **John A. Davies** pays careful attention to the interweaving of the biblical accounts, Old Testament and New, asking: How do the Gospels and Acts view King Solomon? Is he the flawed king of the book of Kings, responsible for the dissolution of the kingdom of Israel? Or is he the idealised figure of Chronicles? Set over against the glorious yet flawed king Solomon, Jesus is great David's greater son and heir whose work is not for his own aggrandisement, but makes him worthy of the worship of the nations.

Once this great Son exceeds king David by rising from the dead to the right hand of the Father, made 'both Lord and Christ' (Acts 2:36), the Spirit of God is poured out as the great sign of the last days. Meditating on the historical trajectory accessed through the Gospel of Mark, Paul's first letter to the Corinthians, and the early second-century *Didache*, **Nickolas Fox** explores the Lord's Supper as an intersection of cultural memory, common meal, shared ritual, and the dysphoric experience drawing together both Christ and his people. Always operating within the differences and divisions of the wider world, 'these elements combine to create a new social universe for the participant'. The unity both expressed in and facilitated by that common meal which became one of the 'iconic rituals in the Christian church throughout the millennia', is forged by a common experience of the Spirit of God.

Poured out on believing individuals drawn from any of the categories that otherwise divide human beings one from another, the Spirit of Jesus now becomes an active force amongst human beings for the common good. Recognising the Holy Spirit as 'a strong theme in Luke-Acts', **Francis Otobo** focuses upon Luke's infancy narrative, in which 'the main human characters are filled with the Holy Spirit before they carry out specific tasks'. Introducing a pattern that becomes 'programmatic for the rest of Luke-Acts', the Spirit 'legitimat[es] the various human characters and their participation in the divine purpose'.

With meticulous attention to the details of Luke 21:5–36 in relation to the Synoptic parallels, **Patrick Cole** puzzles over the absence of a command to evangelise the nations equivalent to Mark 13:10. By adding his own distinctive eyewitness material into the discourse, and also the ascension accounts (Luke 24:44–49//Acts 1:6–9) as a 'narrative hinge' between his two volumes, Luke 'locat[es] the Lord's global evangelism command within Old Testament prophecies pointing to Jesus as the Servant Saviour "light to the Gentiles"'. Fuelled by the Spirit of God, the gospel goes into the nations by means of Christ's people participating in the divine purpose to bring that light into the darkness of the world of the beasts.

As Luke narrates the events of the Day of Pentecost that launched this cosmic mission, he adapted a citation from LXX Joel 2:30 to refer to 'wonders from the heavens above' (Acts 2:19). **James R. Harrison** explores this adaptation against the backdrop of Jewish and Graeco-Roman literary accounts of prodigies and portents, assisted by two case studies from Acts: Luke's supra-cephalic fire portents (Acts 2:3) and the meteorite statue from heaven in the temple of Artemis (19:35). Luke's narrative would not only resonate with Graeco-Roman auditors, but out of the similarities to their own traditions the distinctives of Luke's message to the nations emerges. Breaking beyond the constriction of portents to the Roman rulers, Luke brings out the cross-cultural significance of Pentecost. Although indigenous gods such as Artemis may still pose a threat to the Christian mission, Luke exposes their ultimate powerlessness.

This new movement that began sweeping through the nations was a force for good and a recipe for a better world. Contributing to the wider discussions on 'human flourishing', **Christoph Stenschke** focuses on the portrait of Paul revealed in his various speeches in the book of Acts, seeking for 'clues pointing to his view of the essential ingredients to human flourishing'. Speaking into this contemporary discussion of 'the good life' and the quest for human satisfaction and fulfilment, a bold alternative emerges—as radical today as it was to the ancient world. Akin to Jesus' own viewpoint on human life in the Beatitudes, Paul promises human flourishing through 'being aligned with the salvific purposes of the living and faithful God who is revealed through his Son Jesus'.

Since the gospel of Jesus Christ calls upon individuals of all races, sexes, and stations in life to embrace him and so benefit personally from those salvific purposes brought through the forgiveness of sins, there is nobody whose life could not be turned around by the Spirit of God and, in that realignment, begin to flourish. But what about the beastly power-brokers themselves, who are so often intoxicated with their own 'glory' and 'fantasy', as if their god-given role for the common good is a signal of their own personal greatness rather than a supreme indicator of the Lord's common grace?

Openness to all is anchored in the gospel movement in its earliest years. Against the scholarship that seeks to collectivise the Herods into a literary representation of hostility to God, **Andrew Stewart** draws out the individual features of Agrippa II apparent in the account of Paul standing before Festus in his company. Not only does this 'representative of the covenant nation of Israel [... display] an openness to Paul's gospel', but Paul's words show the openness of the gospel even to the king. Paul 'demonstrates his enduring commitment to preaching the gospel to Jewish people'—a crucial part of his 'Jew-first-and-also-for-the-Greek' strategy with which he fulfilled his commission as apostle to the Gentiles. Even king Agrippa could take his part in God's purposes. Perhaps he would. Perhaps he even did?

There are the two brackets to *JGAR* 8's narrative arc: two flawed kings, both situated within the wider purposes of God the Father that centre upon God the Son and are brought about through God the Spirit. And enclosed by those brackets: there is the gospel that continues to go out to the divided nations as this world's only true hope. Prefigured. Celebrated. Legitimated. Commanded. Demonstrated. And as an outcome of these essays: there is a challenge for readers of and researchers into the Gospels and Acts in 'these last days'.

> [29] Then he told them a parable: "Look at the fig tree, and all the trees. [30] As soon as they put out leaves you can see for yourselves and recognize that summer is already near. [31] In the same way, when you see these things happening, recognize that the kingdom of God is near. [32] Truly I tell you, this generation will certainly not pass away until all things take place. [33] Heaven and earth will pass away, but my words will never pass away.
>
> [34] "Be on your guard, so that your minds are not dulled from carousing, drunkenness, and worries of life, or that day will come on you unexpectedly [35] like a trap. For it will come on all who live on the face of the whole earth. [36] But be alert at all times, praying that you may have strength to escape all these things that are going to take place and to stand before the Son of Man." (Luke 21:29–34)

Stand in order to endure. Endure in order to stand.

Peter G. Bolt
Executive Editor
September 2024

Solomon in the Gospels and Acts—Saint or Sinner?

JOHN A. DAVIES

Abstract

How do the Gospels and Acts view King Solomon? Is he the flawed king of the book of Kings, responsible for the dissolution of the kingdom of Israel? Or is he the idealised figure of Chronicles? From Jesus' teaching recorded in Matthew and Luke, and other material (and omissions) in the Gospels and Acts, we learn something more of the character and ministry of Jesus and the values of his Kingdom by way of comparison and contrast with Solomon and his achievements.

How do the writers of the Gospels and Acts regard King Solomon? There is just a handful of explicit references to Solomon in these five New Testament books. Of these mentions, two are in Matthew's genealogy of Jesus (Matt. 1:6–7); there are two pairs of synoptic parallels where Solomon is mentioned in Jesus' teaching (Matt. 6:29 // Luke 12:27; Matt. 12:42 // Luke 11:31); there are three references to 'Solomon's portico' in the temple precincts (John 10:23; Acts 3:11; 5:12); and there is one reference to Solomon as the builder of the first temple (Acts 7:47). Beyond these there is no mention of Solomon in the rest of the New Testament. He is not among the heroes of faith in Hebrews 11 which includes such marginal characters as Samson and Jephthah. As we shall see below, there are a number of other passages in the Gospels and Acts evocative of Israel's third king, the son and successor of David and the builder of Israel's temple.

Solomon is sometimes considered a 'type' of Christ with the expectation that a 'type' has to be a largely positive figure to be worthy of comparison with Jesus. Whether or not we use the language of 'type' (τύπος, Rom. 5:14), there is both comparison and contrast between Solomon and Jesus in the New Testament.

Solomon in the Old Testament

The portrayal of Solomon in the Old Testament is far from straightforward.[1] While the Primary History (Joshua—Kings) and the later Chronicles have rather different portraits of Solomon, in both of these his forty-year reign in some senses represented the high point of Israel's history.

---

1 For general treatments of the characterisation of Solomon in the Old Testament and later tradition, see Handy, 'Solomon'; Brueggemann, *Solomon*; Verheyden (ed.), *Figure*; Herbst, *Development*.

Following the conquest of Canaan, the turmoil of the period of the Judges, and Saul's troubled reign, there had been (according to Kings) a struggle to consolidate the unity of the tribes under king David as well as a time of dynastic rivalry. Solomon, with the ailing David's blessing, and with some palace intrigue, emerged as the winner (1 Kgs 1).

Solomon's reign is said to be marked by peace and security (4:24–25 [Heb. 5:4–5]). His trading empire and political influence were extensive (4:21,24 [Heb. 5:1,4]. He accrued large quantities of gold, silver, and other precious items (9:14,28; 10:2,10,11,14,21,22). Solomon enjoyed a cooperative relationship with his near neighbours, such as Hiram of Tyre (5:1–12), and a favourable reputation with those further abroad like the queen of Sheba (10:1–13). It is for his 'wisdom', a royal enterprise (Prov. 20:26; 25:2; 31:1), that Solomon is best remembered. When invited, he had prayed for a 'listening heart' so as to 'discern between good and evil' (1 Kgs 3:9), and his 'wisdom' was celebrated at home and abroad (3:28; 4:29–34 [Heb. 5:9–14]; 5:12 [Heb. 5:26]; 10:4,6,7,8). The bulk of the account in Kings of Solomon's reign is devoted to the preparations for, and building of, the palace complex and its royal chapel, the temple in Jerusalem, along with all their relevant furnishings (1 Kgs 5–7). The construction program marked the terminus of the exodus from Egypt, the expectation of the promised 'rest' (6:1; 8:56).

But a clearly negative note is sounded in 1 Kings 11. Solomon's many foreign wives and concubines with their idolatrous influence is often seen as a sad aberration in the latter stages of Solomon's reign from what is an otherwise commendatory account. Raymond Dillard, for example, sees two distinct periods in the Kings account of Solomon's reign, 'a time of blessing and obedience (1 Kgs 1–10) followed by apostasy and judgment in the form of the schism (1 Kgs 11–12)'.[2] Even if, with Martin Noth, we extend the negative tone back into chapter 9, there would still be a perception that Solomon gets a substantially positive press in Kings.[3] The depiction of Solomon in Sirach is along these lines—a wise king whose reign was marked by peace, affluence, and international prestige in his youth, but who later brought ruin to the kingdom through subjecting himself to women (Sir. 47:12–23). Yet such a reading, a Solomon who is largely remembered for his positive attributes and accomplishments, would be at odds with the general biblical criterion for the evaluation of kings—their unswerving loyalty to Yhwh and suppression of idolatrous worship. It is also counter to a general biblical principle that one's standing with God is not determined on some balance of good and bad behaviour over one's lifetime. As Ezekiel 18 makes clear, past sinful behaviour is not taken into account when one repents and returns to God in obedience (Ezek. 18:21–22) and, equally, past righteousness counts for nothing when one turns away from Yhwh (Ezek. 18:24). What matters is the orientation of one's heart at the moment of God's assessment, and the narrator's assessment of Solomon is that 'his heart was not true to the Lord his God, as was the heart of his father David' (1 Kgs 11:4).

This prompts us to engage in a careful rereading of 1 Kings 1–10. This would suggest that the writer is nowhere near as positive about Solomon and his enterprises as is often imagined, and there are now a number of scholars who note the more nuanced stance towards Solomon's reign by the historian of Kings.[4] While it is possible that the historian of Kings was using a source, perhaps an official royal archive or a work based on this (see e.g. the 'Book of the Acts of Solomon', 1 Kgs 11:41), which was consistently congratulatory of Solomon's achievements, we should be open

---

2   Dillard, 'The Chronicler's Solomon'.
3   Noth, *Deuteronomistic History*, 60. There are intermediate positions: Kenik, *Design*; Frisch, 'Structure'; Parker, 'Solomon'; Knoppers, *Two Nations* 1: 57–134.
4   See Walsh, 'Characterization'; Sweeney, 'Critique'; Hays, 'Has the Narrator Come to Praise Solomon?'; Avioz, 'Characterization'; Davies, 'Discerning'.

to the historian making use of this source within his own agenda which was, at least in part, to provide a theological rationale for the breakup of the kingdom and the slide into exile (1 Kgs 9:1–9; 11:26–40; 2 Kgs 17:7–20), as well as to offer hope for a life for the nation beyond exile (1 Kgs 8:34; 2 Kgs 25:27–30).[5] The impetus that led to exile has its origin in Solomon's unfaithful behaviour. The account seems to be structured so as to draw attention to Solomon's flagrant breaches of the very things kings are explicitly forbidden to do, or the people are warned to look out for in their future kings—acquiring horses, with specific mention of Egypt as the source, taking many wives, amassing silver and gold, and the imposition of forced labour (Deut. 17:14–20; 1 Sam. 8:11–18; cf. 1 Kgs 4:26; 10:25–29). The requirement of the king to have close to hand a copy of the torah and to obey it, 'neither exalting himself above other members of the community nor turning aside from the commandment, either to the right or to the left' (Deut. 17:20) is clearly honoured in the breach in Solomon's case. The marriages Solomon contracts involve forbidden alliances with foreign nations with resulting idolatrous practices. Pharaoh's daughter is singled out from the outset and her presence is felt throughout the narrative (1 Kgs 3:1; 7:8; 9:16,24; 11:1), and while from one perspective this represents a diplomatic coup, it introduces a theme which is never far from the surface—Israel's bondage in Egypt—and Solomon's behaviour is at times closer to that of a despotic Pharaoh than an ideal king over God's people. The 'high places' which feature in the assessment of subsequent Judean kings make their appearance at the outset of the Solomon account. While prior to the building of the temple one might expect these traditional cult sites to have a place in the worship of Yhwh (witness the practice of Samuel, 1 Sam. 9:12), the way they are introduced in 1 Kings 3:2 (*raq* 'however'), before the account of Solomon's visit to the high place at Gibeon (v.4), indicates disapproval, and by 11:7 the high places are explicitly said to be for the worship of foreign gods.

The final assessment of Solomon in 1 Kings 11:6 that he 'did what was evil in the sight of the Lord' is damning. But this is not the first time that a characterisation of Solomon as an 'offender' has been made. Even before Solomon's accession, his mother's words, 'It will come to pass, when my lord the king sleeps with his ancestors, that my son Solomon and I will be offenders' (1 Kgs 1:21), will prove to be prophetic. Though in context the words, addressed to David, mean that Solomon, together with his mother, would be treated as a political 'offender' should Solomon's brother become king, in retrospect the word carries the force of an 'offender' (*ḥaṭṭa*, normally translated 'sinner') against God. When Solomon does become king, he is the one to 'offend' through his brutal treatment of his political rivals (1 Kgs 2:13–46). The words for 'sinner' and 'evil' thus bracket Solomon's reign. With the writer's final assessment of Solomon in mind, we go back and revisit even the apparently glowing descriptions in earlier chapters. Are his wealth, prestige, and even wisdom deliberately highlighted for a rhetorical purpose? There are echoes of the Garden of Eden in much of the account, such that Solomon is cast as a new Adam figure. We note his acclamation as king at Gihon, one of the primeval rivers of Genesis (Gen. 2:13), and the garden imagery which pervades the account of his reign.[6]

If Solomon is a new Adam, like the first Adam he fails the obedience test. When, in the context of a catalogue of Solomon's construction works, we read of 'whatever Solomon desired to build in Jerusalem, in Lebanon, and in all the land of his dominion' (1 Kgs 9:19), our sense of a man out of control is confirmed. This pejorative tone is perpetuated in Ecclesiastes. Here the fictive Solomon (who else could we be intended to picture as 'the son of David, king in Jerusalem', Eccl. 1:1?) speaks of his building and landscaping achievements:

---

5   Lovell, *Kings*.
6   Davies, 'Discerning', 48–49.

> I made great works; I built houses and planted vineyards for myself; I made myself gardens and parks, and planted in them all kinds of fruit trees. I made myself pools from which to water the forest of growing trees (Eccl. 2:4–6).[7]

The word 'houses' (*bottim*) includes the sort of royal buildings mentioned in 1 Kings 7:1–12. This 'Solomon' echoes the description (1 Kgs 9:19) of the king's unrestrained appetite: 'Whatever my eyes desired I did not keep from them; I kept my heart from no pleasure' (Eccl. 2:10). All of this is, on reflection, evaluated as 'vanity and a chasing after wind' (v.11).

The book of Chronicles gives an account from one perspective of the Davidic dynasty, with a focus on the establishment and maintenance of legitimate worship centred on the temple. In this, Solomon of course plays a vital role. In his portrayal of Solomon (2 Chr. 1–9) the Chronicler has expunged practically all of the negative notes from his source in Kings and added some positive ones of his own. Even those aspects of the Kings account that, because of their framing, might be considered negative (such as the acquisition of horses, or the amassing of silver and gold), the Chronicler would seem to view positively as signs of divine blessing (2 Chr. 9:13–28). Whereas the Solomon of Kings had come to power through bitter rivalry and connivance before a bed-ridden David (1 Kgs 1–2), the Chronicler's Solomon has no rival, is publicly endorsed by David, enthusiastically acclaimed by all the people, and, above all, divinely approved (1 Chr. 22:7–10; 28:6; 29:22–25). Where possible, the reigns of David and Solomon are closely associated, particularly in their intergenerational venture of temple building (e.g. 1 Chr. 22:5,7,17; 23:1; 28:11; 29:1,23; 2 Chr. 1:1; 3:1; 5:1; 7:10; 11:17; 30:26; 33:7; 35:3). No mention is made of Solomon's multitudinous foreign wives and their idolatrous influence. It is Rehoboam, not Solomon, who is given the blame for the division of the kingdom (2 Chr. 10).

In contrast with Kings, Chronicles makes the barest mention of Solomon's palace and other buildings (2 Chr. 7:11; 8:1,11; 9:16–20), but gives prominence to the temple, its attendants, and services (2 Chr. 3–5), not just in the account of Solomon's reign (where the temple and its dedication looms large, as it does in Kings), but beyond. There is a build-up to it before Solomon's reign (from 1 Chr. 6:10), with repeated references after Solomon has departed the scene (to 2 Chr. 35:3) to the temple and Solomon's role.

The groundplan of the Chronicler's temple may approximate the reality of the first temple (though it is four times the height of the one in Kings!: 1 Kgs 6:2; 2 Chr. 3:4), but the resources allocated for its construction far exceed anything feasible. The value of the silver alone would be in excess of 35 billion US dollars, with a further billion dollars' worth of gold (1 Chr. 22:14). Hyperbole can be an effective literary device.[8] An ancient reader would be expected to realise that something other than sober history writing is involved here. We have in Chronicles an account of an idealised temple, written against the background of a far more modest restoration temple, set in the era of a united Israel, and with some echoes of the Mosaic tabernacle, intended to inspire confidence in and foster commitment to upholding the legitimate cult as the hope for Israel's future.[9] Chronicles emphasises the era of Solomon's reign as one of rest for the people and a time when Yʜᴡʜ comes to dwell among them (1 Chr. 22:9, 18; 28:2; 2 Chr. 6:41).[10] The account has the

---

7   Unless otherwise stated, biblical citations are from the NRSV.
8   For another obvious example of hyperbole in the Solomon account, see 2 Chr. 1:9 where the population of Solomon's kingdom is said to be 'as numerous as the dust of the earth'. For the Chronicler's use of hyperbole, see Klein, 'How Many in a Thousand?'
9   Van Seters establishes the concern of the Chronicler for demonstrating continuity of the temple institutions from the past, through the present, into the future: Van Seters, 'The Chronicler's Account'.
10 See Braun, 'Solomon', 582–86.

characteristics of eschatology, somewhat on the trajectory on which also lie Ezekiel's visionary temple and city (Ezek. 40–48), those of the Qumran *Temple Scroll* (11Q19 and 11Q20), and the New Jerusalem of Revelation 21.[11]

Like Solomon's temple, its builder is projected as an eschatological figure. The Solomonic age, with its national unity and temple focus, is held up as an ideal to be aspired to by the returned Yehud community because it is envisaged as an age when God was truly worshipped as he ought to be.[12] Chronicles gives us the Solomon we would like to remember, and one for whom we may yet hope. While Kings focuses on the unfolding tragedy of a 'Paradise Lost', Chronicles suggests the prospect for a 'Paradise Regained'.

It should not be a problem that a character who lived hundreds of years earlier should be remembered differently at different times and in different contexts. The tendency among some scholars to downplay the negatives of the Kings account and focus on Solomon's achievements could be motivated (at least subconsciously) by the desire to harmonise the Solomon of Kings with the Chronicler's Solomon. But just as we must do in Gospels scholarship, we should allow each synoptic account of Solomon's reign its own voice. Another factor may be the attribution to, or association with, Solomon of several Old Testament books. The book of Proverbs may well contain some of the thousands of proverbs Solomon is said to have composed (1 Kgs 4:32; Prov. 1:1; 10:1; 25:1). But Solomon's association with Ecclesiastes and the Song that bears his name is surely intended to be fictive (Eccl. 1:1; Song 1:1,5; 3:7,9,11; 8:11,12). We also have the apocryphal and pseudepigraphical works associated with his name, the Wisdom of Solomon (late first century BCE to early first century CE), the *Psalms of Solomon* (first century BCE), the *Odes of Solomon* (first to second centuries CE) and the *Testament of Solomon* (first to third centuries CE).

Solomon in the New Testament

So which Solomon do we have in the New Testament? The Solomon of the Primary History, with his tarnished image, or the Chronicler's more saintly Solomon? Or some other Solomon, perhaps a composite figure, or one influenced by popular folklore in Second Temple Judaism?

Solomon in and out of the Genealogies

Both Matthew and Luke give a genealogy of Jesus which traces his ancestry through king David. However, while Matthew traces Jesus' line through David's son Solomon and the line of succession of Judean kings (Matt. 1:6–11), Luke offers an alternative lineage through another of David's sons, Nathan (Luke 3:31). It may be that Matthew gives the legal line of descent through Solomon, legitimising Jesus' messianic claims, while Luke gives a more realistic lineage.[13] Or Luke may be deliberately avoiding mention at this point of Solomon, the king responsible for the breakup of the kingdom, perhaps espousing the 'Branch Christology' that emerges from some Old Testament prophetic expectation—that the messiah would come from a 'branch' or 'shoot' that comes from David but not from the anticipated messianic line through Solomon (Isa. 11:1; Mic. 5:2 [Heb. 5:1];

---

11 See Stinespring, 'Eschatology'; Williamson, 'Eschatology'. For the depiction of the future temple in the *Temple Scroll*, see Davies, 'The *Temple Scroll* and the Missing Temple'; Davies, 'The *Temple Scroll* from Qumran'.
12 Mosis, *Untersuchungen*, 164–69.
13 See Bruce, 'Genealogy'; Marshall, *Luke*, 158.

Jer. 23:5–6; 33:15–16).[14] Luke makes no reference to the Messiah in his genealogy, whereas Matthew has three (Matt. 1:1,16,17).

Matthew's reference to Solomon's parentage is as follows: 'And David was the father of Solomon by the wife of Uriah' (Matt. 1:6). Given that this is a departure from Matthew's standard pattern (listing only the father), we look for an explanation. The only other such deviations are the references to Tamar (v.3) and Rahab and Ruth (v.5). Various explanations for these are offered, including the presumed Gentile origin of each of the women (though we do not know this in the case of Bathsheba, Solomon's mother). Whatever else may be intended, the reference to Solomon's parentage in this way (naming Uriah but not Bathsheba) calls attention to David's adultery and murder (2 Sam. 11), an inauspicious start to Matthew's treatment of Solomon. We also note that the section of fourteen generations that begins in this way with David ends in the judgement of exile (Matt. 1:11). Both Gospel writers, then, in their different ways, hint at a less than fulsome appraisal of Solomon.

Solomon and the Lilies

The name Solomon occurs twice in the teaching of Jesus: in the pericope which contrasts Solomon's glory with the beauty of 'lilies' (Matt. 6:25–34 // Luke 12:22–31) and in the allusion to the queen of Sheba's experience of Solomon's wisdom (Matt. 12:42 // Luke 11:31). These are generally assumed to have their source in the 'Q' material.[15]

Matthew 6:28–29 reads: 'And why do you worry about clothing? Consider the lilies of the field, how they grow; they neither toil nor spin, yet I tell you, even Solomon in all his glory was not clothed like one of these' (cf. Luke 12:27–28). These verses are set in a context dealing with 'worry' (Matt. 6:25–34). The verb μεριμνᾶν, 'worry', or 'be overly preoccupied with', occurs in vv.25,27,28,31,34 where Jesus counsels against being overly concerned with the affairs of daily life—food and drink, clothing, as well as one's lifespan (or height).[16] Such concern is not restricted to the poor, which may be implied by the English word 'worry'. The wealthy may exhibit such a preoccupation (μεριμνᾶν) with their possessions (Sir. 31:1), a fact which is relevant to the mention of Solomon.

Concern with clothing is clearly in view in vv.25,28 which use the verb ἐνδύειν for 'wear (clothes)' and Luke uses ἀμφιέζειν 'clothe' (Luke 12:28), while both Matthew and Luke use the noun ἔνδυμα 'clothing' (Matt. 6:25,28; Luke 12:23) within the pericope. Further, the word 'spin' (νήθειν, Matt. 6:28; Luke 12:27) reinforces the notion of garment manufacture.[17] What the reader of the English Bible will not pick up is that the word used to describe Solomon being 'clothed' is not one of these words, but the verb περιβάλλειν (Matt. 6:27, cf. v.31; Luke 12:27). In the central comparison between Solomon's glory and the 'lilies', translations will almost invariably have something like NRSV's 'even Solomon in all his glory was not clothed like one of these'. However, while the verb περιβάλλειν in the middle voice can be translated 'wear, be clothed' (e.g. Rev. 19:8), its primary meaning as given by BDAG is 'to encompass by erecting something around'. It

---

14 For the significance of the Lukan genealogy, see Fitzmyer, *Luke I–IX*, 490–505; Doble, 'Something Greater', 182–86; Bauckham, *Jude*, 315–73; Bolt, 'Breathing In Enoch', 166–68.
15 For comparison of the differences and textual variants of Matt. 6:25–33 and Luke 12:22–31 and their Q source see Skeat, 'Lilies'; Dillon, 'Ravens'; Naveros Córdova, 'Q [Luke] 12:27'; Gundry, 'Spinning the Lilies'; Olsthoorn, *Jewish Background*, 7–18.
16 For this pejorative sense of μεριμνᾶν, as well as its proper exercise, cf. 1 Cor. 7:32–34.
17 The Western text of Luke 12:27 has οὔτε νήθει οὔτε ὑφαίνει 'neither spin nor weave'.

can be used, for example, of the erection of an encompassing wall.[18] It is also the word used for 'surrounding' oneself with wealth and opulence.[19]

There is no mention in the Old Testament of Solomon's attire, though we are told of the splendour of the clothing of his attendants (1 Kgs 10:5; 2 Chr. 9:4), and one might assume, as does later tradition, that his own royal vestments were truly resplendent.[20] While Solomon's royal attire is doubtless part of the picture Jesus intends his listeners to contemplate, the verb περιβάλλειν encourages the reader to think more broadly of that with which Solomon surrounded himself, notably his luxurious palace and the other royal buildings in Jerusalem, and their magnificent contents (1 Kgs 5–7). These buildings included the House of the Forest of the Lebanon, the Hall of Pillars, the Hall of the Throne, the Hall of Justice, and the 'house for Pharaoh's daughter' and presumably also for his other wives and concubines (7:1–12). Moreover, Solomon's building projects extended throughout the land (9:19). Further, we note Jesus' use of the word 'glory' (δόξα) to describe that which surrounds Solomon. Matthew's previous use of the word was in 4:8 where it characterises 'all the kingdoms of the world' with which the devil tried to tempt Jesus. We might then detect a negative edge to the word when applied to Solomon, something the English words 'pomp' or 'aggrandisement' might capture.

Various efforts have been made to identify the precise flowers intended by τὰ κρίνα, traditionally rendered 'lilies'.[21] However, these discussions are beside the point for our purposes. The term could well apply to wildflowers in general (note the change to 'grass' in v.30 and cf. Isa. 40:6–8). More to the point (and generally overlooked) is the fact that representations of 'lilies' (LXX κρίνα) adorn various aspects of Solomon's temple, notably the capitals on top of the pillars in the vestibule, and the lily-shaped brim of the enormous 'sea' (1 Kgs 7:8,12; 2 Chr. 4:5) and these in turn echo the floral motifs that were to adorn the lampstands of the tabernacle (Exod. 25:31,33,34; Num. 8:4). There is thus a direct verbal link between the 'lilies' of Jesus' saying and Solomon's temple. Solomon's lilies, for all the artistry and craftsmanship that went into them, were 'made with human hands' like the rest of the temple (cf. Acts 7:48 below) and thus no match for God's handiwork. We have noted the negative frame in which the writers of Kings and Ecclesiastes present Solomon's public works (the extravagant and vain enterprises of a self-aggrandising megalomaniac). When Jesus speaks of Solomon's 'glory' with which he surrounded and adorned himself, then, we may discern more than a simple contrast of degree. There would seem to be more than a hint of a pejorative undertone.[22]

Further, Jesus observes that lilies do not 'toil' (κοπιᾶν, Matt. 6:28; Luke 12:27) and thus, by contrast, draws attention to the labour involved in Solomon's construction enterprises, labour that was conscripted, placing a heavy burden on the people (1 Kgs 5:13,14; 11:28; 12:10).[23] Ecclesiastes, speaking with Solomon's voice, reflects negatively on all his 'toil' (Eccl. 2).[24] Solomon exhibits the forbidden attitude of being overly preoccupied with his glory.[25] Jesus' followers are to seek the values of a different kingdom and the 'righteousness' Solomon failed to exhibit (Matt. 6:33; cf. Isa. 9:7).

---

18 Herodotus, *Hist.*, 6.46.2; Polybius, *Hist.*, 4.65.11.
19 Herodotus, *Hist.*, 3.71.4; Polybius, *Hist.*, 7.1.1.
20 Betz, *Sermon on the Mount*, 477.
21 Olsthoorn, *Jewish Background*, 45–49; Fitzmyer, *Luke X–XXIV*, 979; Instone-Brewer, *Prayer and Agriculture*, 236–38.
22 Davies and Allison rightly ask, 'Does the text imply a slight disparagement of Solomon?': *Matthew* 1: 655.
23 For Solomon's exploitative practices, rather than trust in God, see Soggin, 'Compulsory Labor'; Carter, 'Solomon'.
24 Similar sentiments are found in Prov. 23:4 and Psa. 127:1, both associated with Solomon.
25 The rabbis of the first and second centuries ce were highly critical of Solomon for his obsession with his own glory (*Sanh.* 104b). See Olsthoorn, *Jewish Background*, 49.

Solomon and the Queen of Sheba

The second overt reference to Solomon in Jesus' teaching is found in Matthew 12:42 and Luke 11:31 in substantially the same form. 'The queen of the South will rise up at the judgment with this generation and condemn it, because she came from the ends of the earth to listen to the wisdom of Solomon, and see, something greater than Solomon is here!' (Matt. 12:42). These words are part of a discussion Jesus has with the scribes and Pharisees, prompted by their sceptical attitude to Jesus and their request for a 'sign' (v.38). Jesus responds by referring to Jonah and his experience in the belly of the sea monster.[26] The reference to Jonah and the immediately following reference to the visit of 'queen of the South' to Solomon are to be taken closely together (Luke reverses the order of Solomon and Jonah but still keeps them together). They are bound by the fact that both the Ninevites and the queen are Gentiles, as well as by the common formula, 'see, something greater than Jonah / Solomon is here!' (Matt. 12:41,42). While the formula is not identical, we might also compare these with 12:6, 'I tell you, something greater than the temple is here'.

The visit of the queen of the South, that is, the trade and diplomatic mission of the queen of Sheba (probably situated in southern Arabia) to Solomon's court, is recorded in 1 Kings 10:1–13 and 2 Chronicles 9:1–12. The queen's visit serves as a foil for the display of Solomon's wealth and 'wisdom'. If, as noted above, his wealth has a negative connotation in Kings, what about his 'wisdom'? In 1 Kings 3:3–15 Solomon is commended for seeking wisdom, and is granted by God 'a wise and discerning mind' (v.12), but what we are told this 'wisdom' consisted of is all manner of general knowledge and, on the international stage envisaged in 4:29–34 and 10:1–13, may not have 'the fear of the LORD' as its uppermost concern. When the queen says to Solomon that YHWH 'has made you king to execute justice and righteousness' (10:9), because of the subtle critique of Solomon throughout, the reader of Kings is entitled to see this as a veiled rebuke by the author, for these qualities have not been foremost in his portrait of Solomon. However, the Chronicles account of the visit of the queen is closely parallel, and, with its different framing, is to be read as a celebration of that with which Solomon has been endowed. So when Jesus compares his mission and message ('greater' is neuter) with Solomon's reign, it may be simply a matter of degree, though, more likely, there is a stronger contrast implied (and likewise with Jonah—hardly an exemplary prophet). It is Jesus, through the 'sign' he has just given—the Jonah-like interment of the Son of Man for three days and three nights in the heart of the earth (12:40)—who will exhibit 'justice and righteousness'. Herein lies true wisdom.[27] Jesus transcends the priestly (v.6), prophetic (v.41), and royal (v.42) institutions of the Old Testament.

The Feast of Dedication

One of the Gospel references to Solomon, with a further two in Acts, is to the portico of Solomon (John 10:23; Acts 3:11; 5:12).[28] John tells us that Jesus was walking in this impressive colonnade, situated on the eastern side of the temple complex. This served as a meeting space, a place for discussion of Scripture. While this is of course part of Herod's redevelopment, the name of Solomon that is attached to this wing of the temple precincts is a reminder of the first temple's builder. While Herod's grand extension of the modest Second Temple was a sight to behold, one of the architectural wonders of the ancient world (Mark 13:1; Josephus, *Ant.* 15:11), in any reference to the temple in the first century CE the name of Solomon will not be too far from the minds of speaker or listeners.

---

26 For the 'sign of Jonah' see particularly Moscicke, 'Jesus' Three-day Journey'.
27 It is also possible that Jesus' 'wisdom' has a particular focus here in terms of his control over evil spirits. See Perkins, 'Greater than Solomon'; see also the discussion under 'Son of David' below.
28 Barrett, *Acts*, 44.

The Gospel of John records Jesus' activity and teaching in association with the Jewish festivals—Passover, Tabernacles, Dedication, and an unnamed feast.[29] There is a close association of these with the temple, the centre of religious life for Palestinian Jews and those in the diaspora. At each festival he attends Jesus takes the opportunity to speak of the fulfilment in himself and his mission of what the festival with its temple focus stood for (John 2:13–25; 5:1—6:71; 7:2–52; 11:55—19:42). So the detail that John records, that the discussion in 10:24–30 took place on the feast of Dedication and in Solomon's portico, is likely to be significant.[30] John does not waste words. This festival (Hanukkah) commemorates the rededication of the temple by Judas Maccabeus after its desecration by the Seleucid ruler Antiochus IV Epiphanes (1 Macc. 4:36–59). Its designation in Greek is 'the Renewal' (τὰ ἐγκαίνια). The Jewish authorities (οἱ Ἰουδαῖοι) ask Jesus how long he is going to keep them in suspense as to whether he is the Messiah. The idiomatic expression they use is literally, 'How long will you take away our life?' The irony is that it is they who will take away Jesus' life, for this encounter, with its threat of stoning (v.31), is the climactic one before the resolve to have Jesus put to death (11:53). As is often the case, Jesus' answer is indirect:

> I have told you, and you do not believe. The works that I do in my Father's name testify to me; but you do not believe, because you do not belong to my sheep. My sheep hear my voice. I know them, and they follow me. I give them eternal life, and they will never perish. No one will snatch them out of my hand. What my Father has given me is greater than all else, and no one can snatch it out of the Father's hand. The Father and I are one (John 10:24–30).

Here again is 'something greater than Solomon' or his temple. The real 'dedication' or 'consecration' (ἁγιάζειν, v.36) is not that performed by the Maccabees (1 Macc. 4:48), or before them by Solomon (1 Kgs 8:64; 2 Chr. 2:4; 7:7), but that of Jesus by the Father, a prelude to his impending sacrifice. Jesus' 'works' (ἔργα, vv.25,32,33,37,38) surpass those of Solomon. In the LXX ἔργον (in both singular and plural) is a theme word for Solomon's achievements, notably the temple (3 Kgdms 5:30[X2]; 7:2[X2],6[X2],8,12,15,16,19[X2],26,31,32,37,45; = 1 Kgs 5:16[X2]; 7:14[X2],18[X2],19,28,29,33[X2],40,45,47,51,8[sic]). If Jesus' interlocutors had Solomon and his 'works' in mind as a model for the Messiah and his activity, Jesus' 'works', in contrast to Solomon's, have eternal value. Jesus' life-giving 'works' have been evidenced in preceding chapters (John 4:34; 5:36; 7:3,21; 9:3,4). It is Jesus who brings true 'renewal', transformed lives as people respond to his summons. In fellowship with him his sheep are the new temple community, a theme evident elsewhere in John (2:19–22; 14).[31] Far from the blasphemer 'the Judeans' accuse Jesus of being (do they have Antiochus' blasphemy in mind?), Jesus has adduced evidence that it is God's work he has been doing, for he is one with God and therefore worthy of their worship.[32]

Solomon's Temple in Stephen's Speech

The early church had a range of attitudes to the temple.[33] On the one hand they continued to respect it and its institutions while it remained standing. Solomon's portico served as a meeting place (Acts 3:11; 5:12). But they were well aware of its transitory nature and of the fact that Jesus fulfilled what the temple was designed to represent, God dwelling among his people (Matt. 12:6;

---

29 See Yee, *Jewish Feasts*; Attridge, 'Temple'; Wheaton, *Role*; Daise, *Feasts*.
30 While some see the setting as incidental, Wheaton is one who appreciates the significance John gives to the occasion: *Role*, 159–82.
31 See Davies, 'Mansions'.
32 The theme of worship is developed by Wheaton, *Role*, 179–82.
33 See Attridge, 'Temple'.

24:2; 28:20; John 2:19-21). The speech of Stephen in Acts 7 is one of the important speeches of the book of Acts. In it Stephen recounts the successive leaders God sent to deliver Israel, each one of whom suffered some form of rejection. No doubt aware of Jesus' teaching about the fulfilment of the temple in himself, and his prophecy of the destruction of the temple, Stephen spoke in these terms just before his stoning:

> But (δέ) it was Solomon who built a house for him. Yet the Most High does not dwell in houses made with human hands; as the prophet says, 'Heaven is my throne, and the earth is my footstool. What kind of house will you build for me', says the Lord, 'or what is the place of my rest? Did not my hand make all these things?' (Acts 7:47–50).

It is not clear that the δέ of v.47 should be read as adversative, which would imply a contrast between Solomon's temple and the 'dwelling place' (σκήνωμα) David had sought to build (v.46). The Scriptural background to this reference would seem to be Psalm 132:5 (LXX 131:5) which (as often the case with citations of Scripture) is to be read against the background of the whole psalm, with its several references to the temple and God's commitment to it (vv.7,8,13,14), coupled with God's dynastic promise to David and his 'anointed' heir (χριστός, vv.10,11,12,17). As this promise is explicitly conditional on covenant faithfulness, which Solomon fell short of, it must refer to another, and Luke has been demonstrating who this 'Messiah' is (Acts 2:31,36; 3:20).

The other Scripture citation ('the prophet') is from Isaiah 66:1–2, which includes words not explicitly cited by Stephen, but which are relevant to its significance:

> Thus says the Lord: 'Heaven is my throne and the earth is my footstool; what is the house that you would build for me, and what is my resting place? All these things my hand has made, and so all these things are mine', says the Lord. 'But this is the one to whom I will look, to the humble and contrite in spirit, who trembles at my word' (Isa. 66:1–3).

In his prayer of dedication, Solomon had said something similar (2 Chr. 6:18), and had just prior to this echoed the conditional nature of God's dynastic commitment (vv.16–17). While the reference to Solomon's temple as 'made with human hands' (χειροποιήτοις) is often taken as a denunciation of the temple (for χειροποίητα is the LXX word for idols, Lev. 26:1; Isa. 2:18), it is more, in context, a rejection of Solomon, for his association with idolatry. It is to another χριστός 'Messiah' that Stephen points his listeners, one who is humble and righteous.[34]

Jesus as 'Son of David'

Finally, we should consider whether behind the references to Jesus as 'son of David', we are to discern specifically the figure of Solomon. One pericope where Solomon would seem to be in view is that of Jesus' entry to Jerusalem on a donkey to the shout 'Hosanna to the Son of David!' (Matt. 21:9). Whatever the crowds may have understood, the scene evokes the proclamation of Solomon as king (1 Kgs 1:32–40). Jesus' route into Jerusalem from Bethphage would have taken him past the Gihon spring, the site of Solomon's acclamation. Not only is Solomon the only king of David's line said, like Jesus, to ride on an equid at his acclamation as king on the outskirts of Jerusalem, but, strikingly, on both occasions we read of the earth shaking (1 Kgs 1:40; Matt. 21:10). The parallels serve to bring into focus the contrasts. Solomon rides on the royal mule (1 Kgs 1:33,38,44), Jesus on a lowly borrowed donkey (Matt. 21:5; cf. Zech. 8:9). Solomon's acclamation is accompanied by fanfare and his retinue is arranged (1 Kgs 1:38,39). Jesus' entry to the seat of his kingdom is

---

34 Dobie, 'Something Greater'.

without fanfare, but accompanied by the spontaneous shouts of the crowd (Matt. 21:8–9).

Of the sixteen times the appellation 'son of David' is used in the Gospels, no fewer than ten are addressed to Jesus in the context of appeals for or celebration of healings or exorcisms (Matt. 9:27; 12:23; 15:22; 20:30,31; 21:15; Mark 10:47,48; Luke 18:38,39).[35] While 'son of David' was adopted by Christians as a messianic designation, evidence for its use in this sense prior to the time of Jesus is minimal and there was not an unambiguous expectation during the ministry of Jesus that the Messiah, when he came, would be responsible for curing physical ailments. Nor were those seeking Jesus' attention likely to be aware of his royal ancestry.

While it is somewhat speculative, we should not dismiss the suggestion that behind the appeals to Jesus as 'son of David' we are to glimpse the Solomon of popular imagination. This has been argued, for example, by James Charlesworth with particular reference to Mark 10:47,48 which speaks of Bartimaeus' appeal to Jesus as son of David for his sight to be restored.[36] Within the Old Testament, 'son of David' particularly refers to Solomon (2 Chr. 1:1; 13:6; 35:3; Prov. 1:1; Eccl. 1:1; 1 Esd. 1:3).[37] Thus, while the Primary History (Kings) avoids the expression, the Chronicler, as noted above, wants to closely associate Solomon with his father David.

Within Hellenistic Judaism there developed a folkloric tradition of Solomon as a magician.[38] This was based on 1 Kings 4:29–34 (Heb. 5:9–14), the passage which outlines Solomon's proverbial 'wisdom'. This 'wisdom' extended to Solomon's encyclopaedic knowledge of plants, which presumably included their medicinal properties. The first century BCE Wisdom of Solomon (7:20) has Solomon rejoicing in the insight he has been given into 'the natures of animals and the tempers of wild animals, the powers of spirits and the thoughts of human beings, the varieties of plants and the virtues of roots'. Further, Solomon is given esoteric knowledge (κρυπτά, v.21). Josephus also knows of a tradition of Solomon as a healer (*Ant.* 8:44–46).[39]

Belief in and the practice of magic was widespread in Jewish circles of the first century CE (witness the magicians Simon in Acts 8:9 and Bar-Jesus in Acts 13:6). There was understood to be a close connection between illness, or disability, and demonic influence (e.g. Matt. 9:32; 12:22; Mark 1:34; 6:13). The demons responsible for physical ailments and all sorts of ills needed to be held in check or overcome. It is against this background that the figure of Solomon is portrayed as an exorcist in works such as the *Testament of Solomon* (perhaps a third century CE reworking of a first century CE Jewish work).[40] Chapter 18 depicts Solomon with extensive knowledge of which demon is responsible for which ailment, including eye conditions, and the measures needed to overcome them. Charlesworth proposes, then, that blind Bartimaeus may have invoked Jesus as a Solomon *redivivus* figure. For the superstitious belief that the departed might make a reappearance, compare Herod's fear that John the Baptist, whom he had beheaded, had come back (Matt. 14:2).

It would appear, then, that 'son of David' came to be associated with a royal healing figure and the popular image of Solomon may be the best fit as a model for such a healer. Whatever associations the appellation 'son of David' may have had for those who used it of Jesus, the Gospel

---

35 Of the remainder, one, as noted above, is shouted at Jesus' triumphal entry to Jerusalem (Matt. 21:9), two are in the discussion as to whether the Messiah is in fact David's son (Matt. 22:42; Mark 12:35; see below), and three are genealogical references (Matt. 1:1,20; Luke 3:31).
36 Charlesworth, 'Solomon'; cf. Duling, 'Solomon'; Evans, *Mark 8:27–16:20*, 132; Collins, *Mark*, 509–10. Lane rejects any messianic reference on the part of Bartimaeus, but less convincingly sees it as 'a respectful form of address colored by the vivid Davidic associations of Jerusalem but informed by the conviction that Jesus was the instrument of God for bringing healing and blessing to the land': Lane, *Mark*, 388.
37 The only other individual so styled is the otherwise unknown Jerimoth (2 Chr. 11:18).
38 See McCown, 'The Christian Tradition'.
39 Duling, 'The Eleazar Miracle'.
40 Duling, 'Testament', 940–43.

writers would want their readers to see its messianic significance, whether or not the figure of Solomon is particularly in mind.

The discussion as to whose son the Messiah is is instructive:

> Now while the Pharisees were gathered together, Jesus asked them this question: 'What do you think of the Messiah? Whose son is he?' They said to him, 'The son of David.' He said to them, 'How is it then that David by the Spirit calls him Lord, saying, "The Lord said to my Lord, 'Sit at my right hand, until I put your enemies under your feet'"? David thus calls him Lord, how can he be his son?' No one was able to give him an answer, nor from that day did anyone dare to ask him any more questions (Matt. 22:41–46).

It is Jesus' framing of the question that results in the Pharisees giving their answer 'the son of David'. It does not follow that they would independently have used 'son of David' as a messianic title. Jesus' response, while not absolutely negating Davidic ancestry for the Messiah, at least demonstrates the inadequacy of such a designation. Given the understanding that David is the speaker of Psalm 110:1, the 'Lord' who is invited to sit at God's right hand must be someone greater than simply David's offspring. So Jesus is not encouraging the understanding that 'son of David' should be used as a messianic title. If it were so understood when addressed to him, we would expect him to urge silence, as he does when he is recognised as Messiah (Mark 8:29–30; 9:9; Luke 4:41). He does not do this with Bartimaeus (Mark 10:46–52) or anyone else who addresses him as son of David.

While the discussion of Charlesworth reflected above has sharply distinguished a messiah from Solomon *redivivus* as an exorcist and healer, perhaps a sharp distinction cannot be maintained. In time, at least, we might expect the two anticipated figures to merge. A catalyst for this could be the portrayal of Solomon in Chronicles as an ideal eschatological model. The *Psalms of Solomon* (first century BCE) depicts a messiah figure, addressed as 'son of David' who looks rather like the Chronicler's Solomon—pre-eminent in wisdom and justice, adorning Jerusalem, upholding the worship of Yhwh, receiving tribute from foreign rulers who come to admire his glory (*PsSol.* 17:21–46), with the caveat that (unlike Solomon) he will not rely on horses or amass silver and gold.[41]

Conclusion

The Solomon we encounter in the New Testament draws on elements of both the flawed king of the Old Testament's Primary History and the eschatological ideal of Chronicles, along with Second Temple developments of this royal figure. There may be elements of the popular image of Solomon as an exorcist and healer in the minds of those who address Jesus as 'son of David', though the Gospel writers would want us to hear in these words a messianic title. Jesus both outshines and stands in marked contrast with these Solomons. He is David's true son and heir, whether his lineage be traced through the official royal line, or bypasses it. He is the ultimate Temple-builder of a Temple not made with human hands. Jesus' work surpasses that of Solomon and it is not for his own aggrandisement. He is the embodiment of wisdom, the humble King who is truly worthy of the tribute and worship of the nations.

John A. Davies
Sydney College of Divinity
john.a.davies@optusnet.com.au

---

41 So Wright, 'Psalms of Solomon', 641.

Bibliography

Attridge, H. W. — 'The Temple and Jesus the High Priest in the New Testament', in J. H. Charlesworth (ed.), *Jesus and Temple: Archaeological Explorations* (Minneapolis, MN: Fortress, 2014), 21–37.

Avioz, M. — 'The Characterization of Solomon in Solomon's Prayer (1 Kings 8)', *Biblische Notizen* 126 (2005), 18–28.

Barrett, C. K. — *The Acts of the Apostles: A Shorter Commentary* (London: T & T Clark, 2002).

Betz, H. D. — *The Sermon on the Mount* (Hermeneia; Minneapolis, MN: Fortress, 1995).

Bauckham, R. — *Jude and the Relatives of Jesus in the Early Church* (Edinburgh: T&T Clark, 1990).

Bolt, P. G. — 'Breathing In Enoch to Breathe Out Jesus: Two Examples of Luke's Apocalypticism', in P. G. Bolt (ed.), *The Future of Gospels and Acts Research* (Sydney: SCD, 2021), 153–88.

Braun, R. — 'Solomon, the Chosen Temple Builder: The Significance of 1 Chronicles 22, 28, and 29 for the Theology of Chronicles', *JBL* 95 (1976), 581–90.

Bruce, F. F. — 'Genealogy of Jesus Christ', in J. D. Douglas (ed.), *The New Bible Dictionary* (London: Inter-Varsity, 1962), 458–59.

Brueggemann, W. — *Solomon: Israel's Ironic Icon of Human Achievement* (Columbia, OH: University of South Carolina Press, 2005).

Carter, W. — 'Solomon in All His Glory: Intertextuality and Matthew 6.29', *JSNT* 65 (1997), 3–25.

Charlesworth, J. H. — 'Solomon and Jesus: The Son of David in Ante-Markan Traditions (Mk 10:47)', in L. B. Elder, D. L. Barr, and E. S. Malbon (eds.), *Biblical and Humane: A Festschrift for John H. Priest* (Atlanta, GA: Scholars, 1996), 125–51.

Collins, A. Y. — *Mark: A Commentary* (Hermeneia; Minneapolis, MN: Fortress, 2007).

Daise, M. A. — *Feasts in John: Jewish Festivals and Jesus' 'Hour' in the Fourth Gospel* (Tübingen: Mohr Siebeck, 2007).

Davies, J. A. — 'Mansions in the Sky or the Indwelling of the Spirit (John 14:1–4)?', *JGAR* 3 (2019), 87–111.

Davies, J. A. — '"Discerning between Good and Evil": Solomon as a New Adam in 1 Kings', *Westminster Theological Journal* 73 (2011), 39–58.

Davies, J. A. — 'The *Temple Scroll* and the Missing Temple of the New Covenant', *RTR* 57 (1998), 1–21.

Davies, J. A. — 'The *Temple Scroll* from Qumran and the Ultimate Temple', *RTR* 57 (1998), 70–79.

Davies, W. D. and D. C. Allison Jr. *A Critical and Exegetical Commentary on the Gospel according to Saint Matthew. Vol. 1. Matthew 1–8* (Edinburgh: T&T Clark, 1988).

Dillard, R. B. 'The Chronicler's Solomon', *Westminster Theological Journal* 43 (1981), 289–300.

Dillon, R. J. 'Ravens, Lilies, and the Kingdom of God (Matthew 6:25–33 / Luke 12:22–31)', *CBQ* 53 (1991), 605–27.

Dobie, P. 'Something Greater than Solomon: An Approach to Stephen's Speech', in S. Moyise (ed.), *The Old Testament in the New Testament: Essays in Honour of J. L. North* (JSNTSup; Sheffield: Sheffield Academic, 2000), 181–207.

Duling, D. C. 'The Eleazar Miracle and Solomon's Magical Wisdom in Flavius Josephus's *Antiquitates Judaicae* 8:42–49', *HTR* 78 (1985), 1–25.

Duling, D. C. 'Testament of Solomon', in J. H. Charlesworth (ed.), *The Old Testament Pseudepigrapha*. 2 vols. (New York, NY: Doubleday, 1983), 1: 935–87.

Duling, D. C. 'Solomon, Exorcism, and Son of David', *HTR* 68 (1973), 235–52.

Evans, C. A. *Mark 8:27–16:20* (WBC; Grand Rapids, MI: Zondervan, 1988).

Fitzmyer, J. A. *The Gospel according to Luke I–IX* (AB; New York, NY: Doubleday, 1981).

Fitzmyer, J. A. *The Gospel according to Luke X–XXIV* (New York, NY: Doubleday, 1985).

Frisch, A. 'Structure and Significance: The Narrative of Solomon's Reign (1 Kings 1–12:24)', *JSOT* 51 (1991), 3–14.

Gundry, R. H. 'Spinning the Lilies and Unravelling the Ravens', in *The Old Is Better: New Testament Essays in Support of Traditional Interpretations* (WUNT; Tübingen: Mohr Siebeck, 2005), 149–70.

Handy, L. K. 'Solomon', in B. T. Arnold and H. G. M. Williamson (eds.), *Dictionary of the Old Testament: Historical Books* (Downers Grove, IL: InterVarsity, 2005), 921–29.

Hays, J. D. 'Has the Narrator Come to Praise Solomon or to Bury Him? Narrative Subtlety in 1 Kings 1–11', *JSOT* 28 (2003), 149–74.

Herbst, J. W. *Development of an Icon: Solomon before and after King David* (Eugene, OR: Pickwick, 2017).

Instone-Brewer, D. *Prayer and Agriculture* (Traditions of the Rabbis from the Era of the New Testament, 1; Grand Rapids, MI: Eerdmans, 2010).

Kenik, H. A. *Design for Kingship: The Deuteronomistic Narrative Technique in 1 Kings 3:4–15* (SBLDS; Missoula, MT: Scholars, 1983).

Klein, R. W. 'How Many in a Thousand?' in M. P. Graham, K. G. Hoglund, and S. L. McKenzie (eds.), *The Chronicler as Historian* (JSOTS; Sheffield: Sheffield Academic, 1997), 270–82.

Knoppers, G. N.	*Two Nations under God: The Deuteronomistic History of Solomon and the Dual Monarchies.* 2 vols. (Atlanta, GA: Scholars, 1993, 1994).
Lane, W. L.	*The Gospel according to Mark* (Grand Rapids, MI: Eerdmans, 1974).
Lovell, N.	*The Book of Kings and Exilic Identity: 1 and 2 Kings as a Work of Political Historiography* (LHB/OTS; London: T&T Clark, 2021).
Marshall, I. H.	*The Gospel of Luke: A Commentary on the Greek Text* (Exeter: Paternoster, 1978).
McCown, C. C.	'The Christian Tradition as to the Magical Wisdom of Solomon', *Journal of the Palestinian Oriental Society* 2 (1922), 1–24.
Moscicke, H. M.	'Jesus' Three-day Journey in the Belly of the Sea Monster: Jonah Typologies and Traditions in Matthew's Passion Narrative', *JGAR* 7 (2023), 21–38.
Mosis, R.	*Untersuchungen zur Theologie des chronistischen Geschichtswerkes* (Freiburg: Herder, 1973).
Naveros Córdova, N.	'Q [Luke] 12:27: The Lilies of the Field and the Kingdom of God', *CBQ* 82 (2020), 48–63.
Noth, M.	*The Deuteronomistic History* (JSOTS; Sheffield: JSOT Press, 1981 [1957]).
Olsthoorn, M.	*The Jewish Background and the Synoptic Setting of Mt 6,25–33 and Lk 12, 22–31* (Jerusalem: Franciscan, 1975).
Parker, K.	'Solomon as Philosopher King? The Nexus of Law and Wisdom in 1 Kings 1–11', *JSOT* 53 (1992), 75–91.
Perkins, L.	'"Greater than Solomon" (Matt 12:42)', *TrinJ* ns. 19 (1998), 207–17.
Skeat, T. C.	'The Lilies of the Field', *ZNW* 37 (1938), 211–14.
Soggin, J.	'Compulsory Labor under David and Solomon', in T. Ishida (ed.), *Studies in the Period of David and Solomon and Other Essays* (Winona Lake, IN: Eisenbrauns, 1982), 239–57.
Stinespring, W. F.	'Eschatology in Chronicles', *JBL* 80 (1961), 209–19.
Sweeney, M. A.	'The Critique of Solomon in the Josianic Edition of the Deuteronomistic History', *JBL* 114 (1995), 607–22.
Van Seters, J.	'The Chronicler's Account of Solomon's Temple-building: A Continuity Theme', in M. P. Graham, K. G. Hoglund, and S. L. McKenzie (eds.), *The Chronicler as Historian* (JSOTS; Sheffield: Sheffield Academic, 1997), 283–300.
Verheyden, J. (ed.)	*The Figure of Solomon in Jewish, Christian and Islamic Tradition: King, Sage and Architect* (Themes in Biblical Narrative; Leiden: Brill, 2013).
Walsh, J. T.	'The Characterization of Solomon in 1 Kings 1–5', *CBQ* 57 (1995), 471–93.

Wheaton, G.	*The Role of Jewish Feasts in John's Gospel* (SNTS Monograph; Cambridge: Cambridge University Press, 2015).
Williamson, H. G. M.	'Eschatology in Chronicles', *TynBul* 28 (1977), 115–54.
Wright, R. B.	'Psalms of Solomon', in J. H. Charlesworth (ed.), *The Old Testament Pseudepigrapha*. 2 vols. (New York, NY: Doubleday, 1985), 2: 639–70.
Yee, G. A.	*Jewish Feasts and the Gospel of John* (Zacchaeus Studies. New Testament; Wilmington, DE.; Michael Glazier

The mechanisms of unity
The social identity-forming power of the eucharist

NICKOLAS A. FOX

Abstract

One of the most iconic rituals in the Christian church throughout the millennia is the practice of the Lord's Supper. The practice is rooted in New Testament and the early Christian communities. As a shared ritual, it carries significant social identity-forming power. This article explores the social identity-forming force of the Lord's Supper in the first few centuries of practice. While its effectiveness in forming social identity comes from a number of intersecting aspects, this article explores the intersection of four key factors: (1) cultural memory sharing a story experienced as a (2) shared meal (3) practised as a ritual of a (4) dysphoric experience of both Christ and the participants. These elements combine to create a new social universe for the participant. This article examines three primary streams of early eucharistic literature: The Gospel of Mark, 1 Corinthians, and The *Didache*.

1. Introduction

λάβετε φάγετε, τοῦτό ἐστιν τὸ σῶμά μου. 'Take and eat. This is my body' (Matt. 26:26). πίετε ἐξ αὐτοῦ πάντες, τοῦτο γάρ ἐστιν τὸ αἷμά μου τῆς διαθήκης. 'Drink from it, all of you. This is my blood of the Covenant' (Matt. 26:27b–28a). These words of the Eucharist ritual are iconic and meaningful to Christians around the world.[1] This particular spiritual practice, with two thousand years of history, remains an area of fascination among scholars. We can rightly wonder about the origins of such a ubiquitous practice. Why did this ritual catch on in the early church? What are the social identity mechanisms that give a ritual like this its power? This article seeks to bring together the various elements present in the practise of the Lord's Supper[2] and explain why this particular ritual emerged from the first centuries of Christianity. In short, the Eucharist uses *cultural memory* to communicate the story of Jesus experienced as a *shared meal ritual* that recalls

---

1   I am indebted to Diane Holmquist who served as an early editor on this article and to Kylee Tollefsrud, who offered feedback on a near final draft.
2   There are multiple words employed for the ritual: Eucharist, Lord's Supper, Last Supper, communion. Some may see the Eucharist (or communion) as the ritual that gets developed later in the church, and the Lord's Supper or Last Supper as the specific event that occurred with Jesus and his disciples in the upper room. However, Paul talks of the Lord's Supper, κυριακὸν δεῖπνον, in 1 Cor. 11:20. Thus, I will use the terms Lord's Supper and Eucharist somewhat interchangeably, opting mostly for Eucharist, but always in reference to the ritual unless otherwise specified.

a *dysphoric experience* of both Christ and the participants. The result is that the Eucharist creates a new social universe for the Christian.[3] Each of the elements mentioned contains social identity forming power that should be examined individually in order to understand why the practice was so powerful for the early church and remains important today.

As an introductory note on the selection of texts, this study focuses primarily on three textual versions of the Lord's Supper: 1 Corinthians 10—11, The Gospel of Mark chapter 14, and the *Didache* 9. All of these are significant, early texts that can help us see the forming of a tradition.[4] While the dating for each of these texts may be debated, they are sufficiently early, and thus good enough for the purposes of examining the social identity-forming mechanisms of this ritual. These specific versions also come from three different textual streams: a Synoptic Gospel, a Pauline epistle, and a non-canonical catechistic text.[5] These three streams will help us flesh out the early traditions and insight into the purpose and practise of this ritual.[6]

2. Storytelling and Collective Memory

We must first establish a basic understanding of social identity and how rituals contribute to it. Social Identity Theory is a relatively new movement in the landscape of the social sciences.[7] The key figures in Social Identity Theory were Henri Tajfel and his student John Turner who said, 'Social groups [...] provide their members with an identification of themselves in social terms'.[8] The theory seeks to explain 'intergroup discrimination and conflict, on the basis that "individuals seek to differentiate their own groups positively from others to achieve a positive social identity"'.[9] As humans living in the world, we experience self-related uncertainty, which leads us to look for comfort and validation in others around us. Belonging to a well-defined group is one of the best ways to reduce self-related uncertainty.[10] Thus, we always see ourselves and others as members of groups and tend to understand identity in these terms. Furthermore, Turner helpfully describes the idea of salience, that is, when membership in a specific group 'becomes cognitively prepotent

---

3   Draper, 'The Role', 50–51. Draper relies on the study of Victor Turner's theory of ritual process.
4   Alikin, 'The Lord's Supper', 103, considers 1 Corinthians the earliest account of the practice, around 55 CE. Mark is often considered the earliest of the synoptic Gospels, with the scholarly majority tending toward a date in the late 60s or early 70s, likely making it, according to Alikin, the first after Paul to use the tradition. Finally, while the final form *Didache* likely dates to the first half of the Second Century, Draper suggests that the Jesus tradition comes from Q, and thus predates Matthew and Luke. See Draper, 'Ritual Process', 153. Not all agree that the *Didache* comes from Q, or that Q even exists. However, it does provide another interesting early stream to investigate regarding this practice. See Goodacre, *The Case*. It should also be noted that the dating of New Testament documents is a topic of intense debate among scholars. While an in-depth treatment of this issue goes beyond the scope of this article, an argument for early dates can be found in Robinson, *Redating*; for an argument for late dates, Sturdy, *Redrawing*; for the majority, typically occurring in the middle of the two other extremes, see von Harnack, *Die Chronologie*. A recent look at all these approaches, with an argument for early dates, is Bernier, *Rethinking*.
5   Alikin, 'The Lord's Supper', 113, suggests that the Eucharist practice in the *Didache* is older than the tradition in 1 Corinthians. Holmes, *Fathers*, 337, offers a brief summary of attempts to date the final form. For a much longer overview of the debate, see Draper, 'The Didache'.
6   Mark is serving as something of a stand-in for the other Synoptic Gospels, Matthew and Luke. The traditions are very similar in each, though at times they will be compared when it benefits the study.
7   For a fuller treatment of Social Identity Theory and the key players involved, see Fox, *Hermeneutics*, 13–52.
8   Tajfel and Turner, 'Integrative Theory', 40.
9   Esler, 'Outline'.
10 Hogg, 'Religion', 74; Fox, *Hermeneutics*, 16.

in self-perception to act as the immediate influence on perception and behavior'.[11]

Additionally, all groups have stories associated with them. The stories associated with groups—their preservation and transmission—can best be understood by Assmann's discussion of the different types of memory. Assmann defines two types of memory: first, communicative memory is from the recent past, usually experienced first-hand by participants;[12] cultural memory, on the other hand, is memory in which later group members can share. It takes the origin story or other key narratives of the group and preserves them to be shared with new members and new generations.[13] These stories become powerful culture-creating narratives for groups to use to form group identity and establish group norms. This helps us understand the Eucharist, then, since when the early church practises this ritual, it tells the story of the crucifixion of Christ through cultural memory. The mere telling of this story in a social setting would itself be a social identity-forming exercise. Indeed, Flannelly suggests that telling the Christian story 'offers images that not only confirm, but also critically challenge our experiences of ourselves'.[14] However, that this practice is the ritualised reenactment of the story causes a dramatic increase of the social identity-forming power. One's membership in the body of Christ becomes salient, to use Turner's word, in the practising of the ritual and retelling the story.

3. Examining the Mechanisms

With the tools of Social Identity Theory, cultural memory, and group salience in hand, we now turn to look more deeply into the mechanisms that collectively enhance the power of the Eucharistic practice. We will examine the social identity-forming power of shared meals, rituals, and dysphoric experiences. We will also integrate the texts we have identified throughout these discussions.

3.1 Shared Meals

Shared meals are a common feature of the Synoptic Gospels. Jesus regularly ate with people and those shared meals become the context for many of the teachings and miracles in Jesus' ministry. The night that he is betrayed by Judas, Jesus celebrates the Passover meal with the Twelve (Mark 14:17–26). This shared meal becomes one of the most important and iconic rituals in the Christian movement. The Gospel of Mark tells of Jesus' Last Supper with his disciples, when he connects the broken bread with his body and the wine with his blood. The Eucharist recalls and reenacts this time in Jesus' life.

It is significant that the Eucharist is a shared meal. The importance of shared meals in the ancient Graeco-Roman world is a matter of robust discussion among scholars. In addition, the

---

11 Turner, *Rediscovering*, 54. Social Identity Theory comes primarily from the work of Tajfel and focuses largely on intergroup conflict, such as prejudice, racism, and nationalism. This is because of Tajfel's experiences as a Jew during WWII. However, Turner's subsequent work, sometimes called Self-Categorization Theory, may be more helpful for our purposes since we are discussing intergroup cohesion and rituals, rather than conflict. Nonetheless, since the two theories and two scholars are so conversant and similar, I will not draw robust lines of distinction between them.
12 Assmann, *Das kulturelle Gedächtnis*.
13 Although it is outside of the scope of an article like this, Liu and László expound upon this process of how experiences form into public narratives to be shared by other group members. See Liu and László, 'Narrative Theory', 88. Also, see Fox, *Hermeneutics*, 14–27 for an interaction with these ideas.
14 Flannelly, 'Eucharist as Worship', 58–69, is primarily talking about personal identity as opposed to Social Identity; however, her addition to the effects of the Christian story remain valuable for our conversation.

Lord's Supper stems from a Jewish ritual meal, namely the Passover feast. Jewish and Graeco-Roman meal customs had similarities and differences. The most salient similarities come from the unity of the participants and the larger significance that shared meals communicate from a symbolic sense. We will discuss some of the scholarly work on shared meals in the ancient world and then demonstrate, from the primary sources, how this can be observed.

With regard to shared meals in a Graeco-Roman context, it should be noted, 'Meals are never just meals, they are always more than merely a way of taking in food'.[15] More specifically, meals in the ancient world were always about social boundaries. For example, on the walls of the ruins of the city of Pompeii there is a piece of ancient graffiti that says, 'the man with whom I do not dine is a barbarian to me'.[16] The Christian Scriptures record the scandal of early leaders including outsiders in shared meals to the chagrin of the religious leaders (Mark 2:13–17; Acts 10—11). In addition, Rouwhorst suggests, 'Every meal—especially when taken together by more than one person—encodes significant messages about social and hierarchical patterns prevailing in the group'.[17] He continues, suggesting that every meal has an element of inclusion—those who are a part of the meal—and exclusion—those who are not. Thus, to examine the early Christian practice of the Eucharist is to enter a world already rife with cultural assumptions.[18]

This use of symbols in a shared meal and the politics of inclusion and exclusion can be clearly observed commingled in the Corinthian account. Paul states in 1 Corinthians 10:17, 'Because there is one loaf, we, who are many, are one body, for we all share the one loaf'. He goes on to describe the abuses present in the community, including private suppers (11:21a), some going hungry and others getting drunk (11:21b), resulting in humiliation of certain members (11:22), as well as a failure to connect the ritual act to the body of Christ (11:29). Thus, the symbol of the bread—the one loaf, the one body of Christ—mirrors the necessary oneness of the community.[19] As they communally participate in the one loaf and one cup, they proclaim the social pattern of equality and oneness. Participation in the sacred shared meal tore down social barriers, where there was neither 'Jew nor Gentile, neither slave nor free, nor is there male and female, for you are all one in Christ Jesus' (οὐκ ἔνι Ἰουδαῖος οὐδὲ Ἕλλην, οὐκ ἔνι δοῦλος οὐδὲ ἐλεύθερος, οὐκ ἔνι ἄρσεν καὶ θῆλυ· πάντες γὰρ ὑμεῖς εἷς ἐστε ἐν Χριστῷ Ἰησοῦ, Gal. 3:28). With the challenges in Corinth, we could imagine Paul adding, 'neither rich nor poor'. Regardless of the specific social boundaries one has in mind, the Eucharist was a unifying practice that minimised differences and elevated the groups' commitment to the community and to Christ. Unity is so important to this shared meal that its absence prompts Paul to assert that the meal they are eating in Corinth does not qualify as the Lord's Supper (11:20).

The *Didache* also describes a shared meal. While modern Christians may only be aware of the ritual practice apart from a larger meal, 10:1 states, Μετὰ δὲ τὸ ἐμπλησθῆναι, 'And after you have had enough',[20] showing that the participants were eating to a state of fullness. This passage of the *Didache* offers Eucharistic prayers for early group members to participate in together as part of a shared meal. It is also a very clear statement of unity. The *Didache* sees God's hand in bringing

---

15   Ben-Smit and Al-Suadi, *Handbook*, 1.
16   Growers, *The Loaded Table*, 26. Also, see Dunne, 'Eucharist'. Pompei was destroyed by Mt Vesuvius in 79 CE.
17   Rouwhorst, 'Table Community', 69. Further, Douglas, in her important work 'Deciphering', 69, says, 'Each meal is a structured social event which structures others in its own image'.
18   Another interesting examination of this is Naranjo-Huebl, 'Food Imagery', which discusses food preparation and feeding in literature as a sacred ritual.
19   'Factions' were a particular breach of etiquette for a communal meal in the ancient world. See Smith, 'Meal Customs', 652.
20   Holmes, *Fathers*, 359.

together this group into this place as one. This strongly echoes the sentiment in Corinthians about unity being essential to the practice of Eucharist. In Mark, too, we see some measure of unity in the disciples and Jesus eating together and sharing a meal. However, Jesus predicts his impending betrayal at the hands of Judas in the meal, which shifts the focus from unity to disunity. However, this counter example seems to prove the point of the intended unity of the shared meal. Corinthians and the *Didache* seem to further prove the ultimate goal of unity in the practice of the *Didache*.

3.2 Rituals

Rituals are an obvious and natural outflow of the social identity experience, particularly as it relates to the Eucharist. As we examine the research on rituals, we must keep shared meals in mind. It is difficult to separate these discussions, since the practice of the Eucharist is both a shared meal and a ritual. The discussions, as well as the social identity effects, overlap. Is the Eucharist a unifying force in the early church because it is a shared meal or because it is a ritual? It is obviously both, and we need not delineate between those too finely.

Regarding rituals, Whitehouse and Lanman report:

> Ritualized behavior is rooted in our evolved psychology, closely linked to our natural propensity to imitate trusted others. Collective rituals have some striking affordances for group building, hijacking our kinship psychology by fusing us to fellow ritual participants or exploiting our coalitional psychology by enabling us to identify with potentially vast imagined communities.[21]

Thus, since belonging to a well-defined group is one of the best ways to eliminate self-related uncertainty, partaking in a community ritual is an effective way to reinforce group membership and social identity, giving the group member an identity payoff. Furthermore, Taussig, in studying the ritual of the Lord's Supper, suggests that it offers catharsis, community, friendship, and reduction of status inequality.[22] In practising this ritual, members of the early church would affirm and make salient their identity as members of this community. As with the trappings of a shared meal, a shared ritual brought about similar unifying imagery. Alikin says,

> [T]he purpose of [the Eucharist], among other aims, was to realise the communion (fellowship, solidarity and brotherhood [sic]) between the members of the congregation; a communion they sorely missed in the harsh, hierarchical class society of the outside world. The Lord's Supper was intended to unite the participants, whether they were 'Jews or Greeks, slaves or free'.[23]

As discussed, the ritualised shared meal makes plain the symbolic logic in 1 Corinthians with Paul connecting the one loaf with the community (1 Cor. 10:17). However, there are fewer ritual elements in Mark. While there is the sharing of the bread and cup, there is not the command to repeat the practice, and the words τοῦτο ποιεῖτε ... εἰς τὴν ἐμὴν ἀνάμνησιν, 'do this in remembrance of me' are missing.[24] The reader of Mark observes, however, that three times Jesus performs the fourfold sequence of *took, blessed, broke, and gave*: the feeding of the 5000 (6:41), the feeding of the

---

21 Whitehouse and Lanman, 'Ties', 683.
22 Taussig, *Beginning*, 63. Taussig's primary argument is that the early Christian communities formed around Graeco-Roman shared meals. A discussion of the finer points of shared meals and whether that was the start of early Christianity goes beyond the scope of this article. However, for more on shared meals in early Christianity, see Klauck, *Hausgemeinde*, and Smith, *Symposium*.
23 Alikin, 'The Lord's Supper', 105.
24 Those words are only present in Luke 22:19 about the bread and in 1 Cor. 11:24–25 where it is said about both elements.

4000 (8:6), and the Last Supper (14:22).[25] In addition to these scenes confirming Jesus' identity in Mark, the repetition serves to offer a repeatable ritual, demonstrated through the narrative.

Despite the strong emphasis on unity in these texts, rituals and shared meals do not always work so perfectly to unify a group. Taussig suggests that rituals can serve to preserve, rather than eliminate, social inequities.[26] Likewise, shared meals almost always had a hierarchical element to them, often with assigned seats relative to a person's honour and shame (as observable in Luke 14:7–11).[27] Contrary to this custom, though, the Eucharist is a radical counter-cultural force, pushing firmly against any hierarchical or divisive assumptions in rituals and shared meals. The same power that may be used by the outside world to divide is here used to unify.

Paul's corrective to the abuses and inequalities in Corinth helps make this point clear: the purpose is unity, removing any barriers between group members, and seeing all as one in Christ. As stated previously, his response is to deny that what the Corinthians are practising even constitutes the Eucharist: Συνερχομένων οὖν ὑμῶν ἐπὶ τὸ αὐτὸ οὐκ ἔστιν κυριακὸν δεῖπνον φαγεῖν, 'So then, when you come together, it is not the Lord's Supper you eat' (1 Cor. 11:20). Paul's reasoning is that since the Corinthian experience is individualised, some having their own private meal (τὸ ἴδιον δεῖπνον), rather than communal, and the practice is marked with inequity, with some getting drunk and others going hungry, rather than equality, what they are practising is not really the Lord's Supper. Paul asks, ἢ τῆς ἐκκλησίας τοῦ θεοῦ καταφρονεῖτε, καὶ καταισχύνετε τοὺς μὴ ἔχοντας; 'Do you despise the church of God and humiliate the ones who have nothing? (1 Cor. 11:22)'.[28] Because of the unifying purpose of the meal, the practices in Corinth are egregious abuses. Where some rituals and shared meals sought to maintain social inequities, the Lord's Supper was meant to abolish them.[29] While Graeco-Roman meals intended to mete out various levels of honour and shame, Paul 'rejects the old behaviours pervading the Mediterranean world and encourages new behaviours that reflect the social identity of a follower of Jesus'.[30]

We also see very clear elements of a ritual in the *Didache*.[31] Indeed, we might rightly call the *Didache* a ritual text.[32] There are prayers spoken over the cup and the bread, similar to but different from Corinthians. Like Corinthians, we see the prescriptive form that the *Didache* takes (not a narrative as in Mark). Unlike Corinthians, though, the *Didache* is not correcting abuses; it is less episodic in nature and reads more like a manual of how to practise the Eucharist in a local church community. Whereas Paul's is the tone of stern rebuke, the tone of the *Didache* is much less severe, with a specific focus on the words to pray. It also lacks the theological reasoning present in Paul, again because of the apparent difference in circumstance.

The *Didache* does contain a very clear statement that only the baptised are allowed to share in the Eucharist, quoting the line, Μὴ δῶτε τὸ ἅγιον τοῖς κυσί, 'Do not give what is holy to dogs'.[33] The early practice of the Eucharist was closed. This exclusion of outsiders serves to build social identity

---

25 Perrin, 'Last Supper', 493. Similarly, although Luke does not include the feeding of the 4000, he has this threefold repetition by adding in the meal scene with the travellers on the road to Emmaus.
26 Taussig, *Beginning*, 63.
27 Honour and shame may be another area to explore with regard to rituals and shared meals, specifically as it relates to the Eucharist. See McRae, 'Honor', 169.
28 Author's translation.
29 DeMaris, *New Testament*, 33.
30 McRae, 'Honor', 181.
31 Other rituals are included in the *Didache*, including baptism (7:1–4) and praying the Lord's Prayer three times a day (8:2–3).
32 Draper, 'Ritual Process', 121.
33 *Didache* 9.5. Holmes, *Fathers*, 359.

among the in-group. Indeed, the Eucharist is merely one part of the vast and transformative changes a convert to Christianity experiences in the world projected by the text of the *Didache*.[34] Their entire life changes, with numerous steps taken to separate from the world and to join into their new and eternal family.[35] For example, 7:1—10:7 serves as something of a progression of the catechistic process for the new convert. It follows baptism (7:1–4), fasting (8:1), prayer (8:2–3), the Eucharist (9:1–5), and prayers following the gathering (10:1–7). The ritual of the Eucharist stands as the climax of both the conversion process and the weekly gathering. It is the climax of the conversion experience, culminating this catechistic progression, and the weekly gathering, as all participants come together to share in this meaningful ritual.[36] The estrangement from the culture around them serves to form strong bonds within the church, built through the regular communal practice of rituals like the Eucharist.

3.3 Dysphoric Experiences

In addition to being a shared meal and a ritual, the Lord's Supper in the early church is rooted in suffering. More specifically, the language social scientists use here is a *collective dysphoric ritual*, that is, remembering and ritualising a difficult or painful episode from one's past. The study of dysphoric rituals relates to the Eucharist in two ways: (1) the Eucharist is a dysphoric ritual as it remembers the crucifixion of Christ and (2) members of the early church share in Christ's suffering as they suffer themselves. We will examine each of these relationships, after we look at the scholarship on dysphoric rituals.

Social scientists attest to the power of a collective dysphoric ritual. Whitehouse and Lanman suggest,

> Participation in collective dysphoric rituals has been linked to fusion with the group and parochial altruism. Dysphoric rituals are remembered as distinctive episodes in a person's life experience. When people recall such experiences, they reflect on their significance, over time developing highly elaborated webs of interpretation that they assume resemble the thoughts and feelings of others who have undergone the same experiences. The result is a fusion of self and other. Personal and group interests and destinies are aligned, and threats to the group are experienced as threats to self.[37]

These authors go on to say, 'While a variety of experiences can become essential elements of one's autobiographical self-concept, a significant body of evidence suggests that highly dysphoric experiences [...] are especially powerful'.[38] There are numerous examples of this phenomenon. Consider soldiers in basic training or in battle. Sources found that the degree of shared dysphoria in battle predicted the strength of connection with fellow soldiers and loyalty to country.[39] Or

---

34 The first third of the text, 1:1–5:2, largely deals with Ὁδοὶ δύο, 'The Two Ways', the way of life and the way of death, which both prescribes and prohibits specific behaviours.
35 Milavec, *Didache*, 107, shows this process in a visually profound way in the form of a flowchart.
36 Draper, 'Ritual Process', 127.
37 Whitehouse and Lanman, 'Ties', 683.
38 Whitehouse and Lanman, 'Ties', 677.
39 'For example, in a survey of fighters in the 2011 revolution in Libya, we found that degree of shared dysphoria in battle predicted strength of fusion with brigade (Whitehouse 2012); Matthews et al. (2014, in prep.) found that veterans of the Vietnam War who witnessed comrades being killed or wounded became more fused with the identity "Vietnam veterans" but not more identified; in a recent survey of over 450 Spaniards, Gómez et al. (2014, in prep.) found that thinking about shared dysphoric experiences with other Spaniards predicted greater willingness to fight and die for Spain', in Whitehouse and Lanman, 'Ties', 677.

consider how the unity, camaraderie, and willingness to help other community members increases when a natural disaster, like hurricane Katrina, or a terrorist attack, like 9/11, occurs. These dysphoric experiences are so effective at forming our social identity in a group that even when other group members, namely leaders, inflict new recruits with dysphoric experiences (in a hazing ritual, for example), it still works to form social identity and group cohesion.[40]

While none of these examples corresponds exactly with the early church's experience of the crucifixion of Jesus, it certainly helps us understand the potential power that dysphoric experiences can have in shaping a group, as well as the formative nature of a ritual that remembers that dysphoric experience for the early Christians. The Eucharist ritual remembers the public execution of Jesus Christ and reenacts his final meal with his followers. All four canonical Gospels tell the story of Jesus' crucifixion by the Romans, followed by his surprise resurrection, as climactic events in their narratives.[41] Additionally, Paul and the other early Christian writings regularly refer to Jesus' crucifixion and resurrection.[42] First Corinthians and Mark both specifically connect the elements to Jesus' death through his body and blood, Mark through a narrative rendition of Jesus sharing the Last Supper with his disciples and Paul prescribing the words of institution over the communal meal (Mark 14:12–26; 1 Cor. 11:23–34).[43] Paul specifically mentions receiving an earlier tradition ἀπὸ τοῦ κυρίου, 'from the Lord' and passing it on to the Corinthians (11:23). These early traditions seem to suggest that connection of the meal with Jesus' death was a part of the ritual from the earliest days.[44]

The experience of remembering the leader of the group—more, the Christ—killed by the Romans, and reenacting his final meal before his arrest through a ritual produces a powerful social identity-forming force. However, unlike soldiers, firefighters, or fraternity brothers, the early Christians are not remembering a dysphoric experience they experienced themselves, but rather one that their leader experienced. Through cultural memory, as discussed above, group members are able to share in the memory despite not experiencing it themselves. Remembering the event through practising the ritual builds social identity in the participants.

However, it must be noted that the resurrection of Jesus significantly colours the experience of the Eucharist for participants. While group members do actively remember Jesus' tragic death, even suggesting that in practising the ritual τὸν θάνατον τοῦ κυρίου καταγγέλλετε, 'you proclaim the Lord's death', the triumph of the resurrection is never fully out of mind.[45] Moving from the tragedy of the crucifixion to the triumph of the resurrection might be best understood by Tolkien's term *eucatastrophe*, that is, 'a sudden, joyous turn' in a story.[46] Indeed, it is in the process of remembering the tragedy of the dysphoric experience that the triumph of the resurrection can be fully appreciated.

---

40 See Cimino, 'Evolution'.
41 Indeed, over a hundred years ago, Kähler suggested that the Gospels are passion narratives with extended introductions. See Kähler, *Historical Jesus*, 80 n.11.
42 Rom. 4:25, 5:6,8; 8:32; 1 Cor. 15:3; 2 Cor. 5:14,15; Gal. 1:4; 2:20; Eph. 5:2,25; 1 Thess. 5:10; 1 Tim. 2:6; Titus 2:14.
43 Alikin, 'The Lord's Supper', 111.
44 Alikin, 'The Lord's Supper', 111–20, argues that the *Didache* is representative of an older tradition than that of Mark or 1 Corinthians and that the earliest community meals were not associated with the death of Jesus, seeing the accounts of the Lord's Supper in the Gospels as etiologies. While there may be good reasons to argue for the early tradition being associated with Jesus' death, even if Alikin's point is correct, we still have a Eucharistic practice associated with the death of Jesus by the early 60's, which would allow for the dysphoric social identity experience. Another helpful perspective on this is Duling, 'Social Memory', 289–306, who argues that the Lord's Supper was 'keyed' to Jesus' traumatic death.
45 As evidenced by the numerous references to the resurrection of Jesus in early Christian literature. Matt. 28:5–6; Mark 16:6; Acts 2:24, 26:23; Rom. 6:5; 1 Cor. 15; 2 Cor. 5:14–15; Gal. 1:1; Phil. 3:10; 1 Thess. 4:14; Heb. 13:20; 1 Pet. 1:3.
46 Tolkien, 'Fairy-Stories', 153.

A second way dysphoric rituals are important in this discussion is more direct: the suffering the early Christians experienced in their lives. Paul regularly reminds his readers that as they experience suffering, they share in and participate in Christ's suffering (Rom. 8:17; 2 Cor. 1:5; Phil. 3:10). The early Christians experienced suffering in their lives—either from normal life situations, such as sickness and loss, or as a direct consequence of their Christian faith, namely, rejection and persecution[47]—and looked to the death of Christ as a comfort. The ritualised shared meal of the Eucharist helps the participants embody that connection with Christ and his sufferings. Indeed, the remembering plays an important role. Paul records Jesus as saying, 'Do this in remembrance of me' (1 Cor. 11:25).

The *Didache*, interestingly, does not specifically connect the meal to Jesus' death. There is no explicit reference to the body and blood of Jesus with regard to the elements and indeed some have even openly questioned whether this constitutes a Eucharistic practice at all.[48] However, the majority of scholars rightly recognise the elements of the single cup and the shared, broken loaf, the ritual and shared meal components, the goal of building unity, and the use of εὐχαριστῶ all pointing to this being a Eucharistic meal.[49] Rather than an explicit connection to the suffering of Jesus—which still may be implicit—the *Didache* compares the broken, scattered ingredients that are gathered together to become bread in connection with the community and the hope of an eschatological coming together in the kingdom. While this does not mention the suffering of Christ, the image of being scattered applied to the community seems to represent some sort of isolation or perceived estrangement. *Didache* 9:4 says, 'Just as this broken bread was scattered upon the mountains and then was gathered together and became one, so may your church be gathered together from the ends of the earth into your kingdom'. Here we see the hope and joy that the practice of the Eucharist can bring. Despite the sufferings that may be present in their lives, they look forward to a *eucatastrophe*, the sudden joyous turn of Christ's eschatological kingdom. The ritual helps them focus on the presence of Christ and the unity he brings.

4. Conclusion: Creating a New Social Universe

The result of these mechanisms of identity coming together in the practice of the Eucharist is to create a new social universe—to use Draper's term—for the participants.[50] The early Christians are unified around the practice of a shared meal. They experience community and gain respite from the 'harsh, hierarchical' world outside. The ritual creates social equity in the group, tearing down the different divisions of class, wealth, race, and social standing, making participation in Christ's church salient. It allows them the ability to understand their sufferings in this world in light of the sufferings of Christ. And it allows them to hope in a future eschatological kingdom, when God will gather the church together from the ends of the earth. Indeed, this is a new social reality created for these participants, one that is 'above all pointing to unity and union. To share the cup and loaf

---

47 There is a long and complex debate among scholars regarding the nature and degree of the opposition to early Christianity. For a good summary of this debate, see chapters 2 and 3 in Engberg, *Impulsore Chresto*.
48 Milavec, 'Kingdom Expectations', 379–80. Also, see O'Loughlin, *Didache*, 8–9, who offers a short history and a critique on this view.
49 Interestingly, Draper connects this to the *Didache* community taking its Jesus tradition from Q, which lacks a passion narrative. See Draper, 'Ritual Process'; O'Loughlin, *Didache*, 8–9, 93–97.
50 Draper, 'Social Universe', 50–51.

means that the community are one body; they are united by this eating and drinking'.[51] Sitting at the intersection of multiple social identity-forming powers—cultural memory, a shared meal, a ritual, a dysphoric experience—all contributing in different ways and to different degrees, the Eucharist remains an area of distinct interest to readers of the early church documents.

Nickolas A. Fox
Crown College
foxn@crown.edu

---

[51] O'Loughlin, *Didache*, 97.

Bibliography

Alikin, V. A. — 'The Lord's Supper in the Early Church', in V. A. Alikin, *The Earliest History of the Christian Gathering: Origin, Development, and Content of the Christian Gathering in the First to Third Centuries* (Leiden: Brill, 2010), 103–46.

Assmann, J. — *Das kulturelle Gedächtnis: Schrift, Erinnerung und politische Identität in frühen Hochkulturen* (München: Beck, 1992).

Ben-Smit P. and S. Al-Suadi — *T&T Clark Handbook to Early Christian Meals in the Greco-Roman World* (London: Bloomsbury, 2019).

Bernier, J. — *Rethinking the Dates of the New Testament: The Evidence for Early Composition* (Grand Rapids, MI: Baker Academic, 2022).

Cimino, A. — 'The Evolution of Hazing: Motivational Mechanisms and the Abuse of Newcomers', *Journal of Cognition and Culture* 11 (2011), 241–67.

DeMaris, R. E. — *The New Testament in its Ritual World* (New York, NY: Routledge, 2008).

Douglas, M. — 'Deciphering a Meal', *Daedalus* 101:1 (1972), 61–81.

Draper, J. A. — 'The Didache in Modern Research: An Overview', in *The Didache in Modern Research* (Leiden: Brill, 1996), 1–42.

Draper, J. A. — 'Ritual Process and Ritual Symbol in Didache, 7—10', *Vigiliae Christianae* 54:2 (2000), 121–58.

Draper, J. A. — 'The Role of Ritual in the Alternation of Social Universe: Jewish-Christian Initiation of Gentiles in the Didache', *Listening* 32 (1997), 50–51.

Duling, D. C. — 'Social Memory and Commemoration of the Death of "The Lord": Paul's Response to the Lord's Supper Factions at Corinth', in T. Thatcher (ed.), *Memory and Identity in Ancient Judaism and Early Christianity* (Atlanta, GA: SBL Press, 2014), 289–306.

Dunne, J. — 'Eucharist and Early Christian Meals', in *The Mountains Shall Drip with Wine* (Grand Rapids, MI: Zondervan, forthcoming).

Engberg, J. — *Impulsore Chresto: Opposition to Christianity in the Roman Empire cc.50–250AD* (Early Christianity in the Context of Antiquity 2; Frankfurt am Main: Peter Lang, 2007).

Esler, P. — 'An Outline of Social Identity Theory', in J. A. Tucker and C. A. Baker (eds.), *T&T Clark Handbook to Social Identity in the New Testament* (London: Bloomsbury, 2014), 13–40.

Flannelly, J. — 'Eucharist as Worship: Journey to Identity', *New Theology Review* 10:1 (1997), 58–69.

Fox, N. A. — *The Hermeneutics of Social Identity in Luke-Acts* (Eugene, OR: Pickwick, 2021).

Goodacre, M.	*The Case Against Q: Studies in Markan Priority and the Synoptic Problem* (Harrisburg, PA: Trinity, 2002).
Growers, E.	*The Loaded Table: Representations of Food in Roman Literature* (Oxford: Oxford University Press, 1993).
Hogg, M. A., J. A. Adelman, and R. D. Blagg	'Religion in the Face of Uncertainty: An Uncertainty-Identity Theory Account of Religiousness', *Personality and Social Psychology Review* 14.1 (2010), 72–83.
Holmes, M. W. (ed., trans.)	*The Apostolic Fathers: Greek Texts and English Translations* (3rd edn; Grand Rapids, MI : Baker, 2007).
Kähler, M.	*The So-called Historical Jesus and the Historic, Biblical Christ* (Reprint Edition; Minneapolis, MN: Fortress, 1988).
Klauck, H.	*Hausgemeinde und Hauskirche im frühen Christentum* (Stuttgart: Katholisches Bibelwerk, 1981).
Liu, J. H. and J. László	'A Narrative Theory of History and Identity', in Gail Moloney and Iain Walker (eds.), *Social Representations and Identity: Content, Process, and Power* (New York, NY: Palgrave McMillan, 2007), 85–107.
McRae, R. M.	'Eating with Honor: The Corinthian Lord's Supper in Light of Voluntary Association Meal Practices', *JBL* 130.1 (2011), 165–81.
Milavec, A.	*The Didache: Faith, Hope, and Life of the Earliest Christian Communities, 50–70* c.e. (Mahwah, NJ: Newman Press, 2003).
Milavec, A.	*The Didache: Text, Translation, Analysis, and Commentary* (Collegeville, MN: Liturgical, 2003).
Naranjo-Huebl, L.	'"Take, Eat": Food Imagery, the Nurturing Ethic, and Christian Identity in The Wide, Wide World, Uncle Tom's Cabin, and Incidents in the Life of a Slave Girl', *Christianity and Literature* 56.4 (2007), 597–631.
O'Loughlin, T.	*The Didache: A Window on the Earliest Christians* (Grand Rapids, MI: Baker Academic, 2010).
Perrin, N.	'Last Supper', in Joel B. Green (ed.), *The Dictionary of Jesus and the Gospels* (Downers Grove, IL: Inter-Varsity, 2013), 492–501.
Robinson, J. A. T.	*Redating the New Testament* (Reprint; Eugene, OR: Wipf & Stock, 2012).
Rouwhorst, G.	'Table Community in Early Christianity', in Marcel Poorthuis and Joshua J. Schwartz (eds.), *A Holy People: Jewish and Christian Perspectives on Religious Communal Identity* (Leiden: Brill, 2006), 69–84.
Smith, D. E.	*From Symposium to Eucharist: The Banquet in the Early Christian World* (Minneapolis, MN: Fortress, 2003).
Smith, D. E.	'Greco-Roman Meal Customs', in David Noel Freedman, et. al. (eds.), *The Anchor Bible Dictionary* (New York, NY: Doubleday, 1992), 4.648–55.

Sturdy, J. V. M. and J. Knight (eds.) *Redrawing the Boundaries: The Date of Early Christian Literature* (London: Routledge, 2007).

Tajfel H. and John C. Turner 'An Integrative Theory of Intergroup Conflict', in William G. Austin and Stephen Worchel (eds.), *The Social Psychology of Intergroup Relations* (Monterey, CA: Brooks/Cole, 1979), 33–47.

Taussig, H. *In the Beginning was the Meal: Social Experimentation and Early Christian Identity* (Minneapolis, MN: Fortress, 2009).

Tolkien, J. R. R. 'On Fairy-Stories', in Christopher Tolkien (ed.), *The Monsters and the Critics and Other Essays* (Grand Rapids, MI: Harper Collins, 2006), 109–61.

Turner, J. C. *Rediscovering the Social Group: Self-Categorization Theory* (New York, NY: Blackwell, 1987).

von Harnack, A. *Die Chronologie der Litteratur von Eusebius bis Irenaeus* (Vol. 2, part 1 of Geschichte der Altchristlichen Litteratur bis Eusebius; Leipzig: Hinrichs, 1897).

Whitehouse H. and J. A. Lanman 'The Ties That Bind Us: Ritual, Fusion, and Identification', *Current Anthropology* 55.6 (December, 2014), 674–95.

The Holy Spirit and Luke's infancy narrative
Reading a legitimatory role

FRANCIS OTOBO

Abstract

The Holy Spirit is a strong theme in Luke-Acts, actively present from the infancy narrative right through to the end of Acts. In the infancy narrative Luke shows that the main human characters are filled with the Holy Spirit before they carry out specific tasks. This becomes programmatic for the rest of Luke-Acts. Focusing on the infancy narrative, this article argues that, much more than inspiring utterances, Luke employs the Holy Spirit to assert the authenticity and legitimation of the various human characters and their participation in the divine purpose.

Key words: Luke-Acts, Holy Spirit, infancy narrative, legitimation, Luke's purpose, virgin birth, prophecy.

1. Introduction

The author of Luke-Acts begins the infancy narrative with the accounts of two conceptions—John (1:5–25), and Jesus (1:26–38). As prelude to the Gospel, the infancy narrative introduces some of the main themes that Luke will develop throughout his account of the Jesus story.[1] One such theme is the roles played by the Holy Spirit in Luke's narrative.[2] In comparison to Matthew's account the infancy narrative in Luke's Gospel accords the Holy Spirit greater prominence. Whereas Matthew passively refers to the Holy Spirit twice (Matt. 1:18,20), Luke actively engages the Holy Spirit as working with certain individuals who are filled with the Holy Spirit (Luke 1:15,35,41,67; 2:25–27). Luke also shows the Holy Spirit inspiring four prophetic utterances in this early stage of the narrative (Luke 1:42–45;68–79; 2:29–32,38). From this beginning, Luke shows that the key characters who serve God's purpose are 'filled with' the Holy Spirit before they carry

---

1 Turner, *Power from on High*, 140; Brown, *The Birth of the Messiah*, 242; Bock, *Luke*, 33; Minear, 'Luke's Use of the Birth Stories', 116; Stronstad, *Charismatic Theology*, 43; Johnson, *The Gospel of Luke*, 35.
2 Robert Tannehill identifies four other such themes in the infancy narrative: (1) reviews and previews, (2) use of scriptural quotations revealing God's purposes, (3) revelation of that purpose through dialogue from God's commissioned agents, and (4) testimony through reliable characters within the account. See Tannehill, *Narrative Unity*, vol. 1, 21.

out their tasks.³ Herod, the first human character mentioned (Luke 1:5) is not filled with the Holy Spirit because he does not advance the divine purpose.

Much has been written about the Holy Spirit in Luke-Acts. For instance, Craig Keener echoes the view of many Lukan scholars on the Spirit's role as empowerment for mission—a theme central to the narrative of Acts.[4] John Carroll reiterates earlier assertions that the Spirit inspires prophecy / witness, a theme observable in the infancy narrative and throughout Luke-Acts.[5] This article will focus on Luke's infancy narrative with the aim to explore the argument that Luke may have employed the Holy Spirit here to assert the authenticity and legitimation of the various human characters and their roles in the divine purpose. In other words, as will be argued, the infilling 'with the Holy Spirit' serves to authenticate these characters and their roles in the unfolding story of Jesus. This role of the Spirit has not been adequately explored (or has been largely overlooked) by earlier scholars.[6] In this way Luke provides a solid foundation for the unfolding story of Jesus and the mission of the followers of Jesus in Acts. This technique which Luke firmly establishes in the infancy narrative becomes programmatic for the rest of the Gospel and for Acts (cf. Luke 3:22; Acts 2:1–4; 8:17; 10:44; 19:6). Contrary to the Talmud (*Sanhedrin* 11a, p.72) which suggests that with the death of the last prophets, the Spirit departed from Israel, Luke emphasises the reception of the Spirit, not just by Jesus (the Messiah, Luke 3:22), but also by those who believe in Jesus (Acts 2:38–39).[7]

But why would Luke argue for the authentication / legitimation of these characters and their roles? This question forms the nucleus around which this article revolves. It will examine the various characters in the infancy narrative who are endowed with the Holy Spirit with the aim of determining how the Holy Spirit provides legitimation for their respective tasks. It may be profitable to begin from the question of legitimation and Luke's purpose.

2. Legitimation and Luke's Purpose

Philip Esler, in his book *Community and Gospel in Luke-Acts*, discusses the topic of legitimation in relation to Luke-Acts.[8] Defining legitimation as 'the collection of ways in which an institution is explained and justified to its members',[9] Esler asserts that much of what is unique to Luke-Acts 'should be attributed to Luke's desire to explain and justify, to 'legitimate', Christianity to his Christian contemporaries'.[10] Esler argues strongly that Luke's main objective is one of legitimation, and contends that 'Luke wrote in a context where the members of his community ... who had been

---

3   With the exception that Anna is not overtly mentioned as being filled with the Spirit. However, the fact that she is introduced as a prophetess suggests that she shares in the prophetic Spirit which leads Simeon into the Temple. In the case of Mary, 'the Holy Spirit will come upon' her, and the 'power of the Most High will overshadow' her (Luke 1:35).
4   Keener, 'Spirit and the Mission', 25, 27, 28. See also Keener, 'Power of Pentecost', 47–73; Miller, *Empowered for Global Mission*, 62, 69; Talbert, *Reading Luke-Acts*, 161–73.
5   Carroll, *The Holy Spirit in the New Testament*, 52–68. See also Menzies, *Empowered*, 44, 227; Penney, *Missionary Emphasis*, 111; Turner, *Power from on High*, 86–138.
6   Cf. Turner, 'The Work of the Holy Spirit', 147; and Bonnah, *Narrative Factor*, 266, 402; who sparingly refer to the legitimating role of the Holy Spirit, but fail to attend to the question in the body of the work.
7   Cf. Kuhn, *The Kingdom According to Luke and Acts*, 319, on the unity of Luke-Acts.
8   Esler, *Community and Gospel in Luke-Acts*, 16–23.
9   Esler, *Community and Gospel in Luke-Acts*, 16–17.
10 Esler, *Community and Gospel in Luke-Acts*, 16.

associated with synagogues before becoming Christians … needed strong assurance that their decision to convert and to adopt a different life-style had been the correct one'.[11] Interestingly, as one reads Luke's infancy narratives in comparison with Matthew's, it becomes obvious how Luke particularly appeals to the Holy Spirit to provide justification for the unfolding narrative. Much of the stories and references to the Holy Spirit here are unique to Luke. This then affirms the argument of this essay which confirms a legitimating role in Luke's infancy narratives with respect to the role of the Spirit.

Legitimation, as employed in this article, thus refers to an attempt at convincing someone or a group of people about something that is claimed to be true by the one who wants to convince them. The preface to the Gospel makes it clear that Luke aims to provide the reader with certainties of what the reader already knows (Luke 1:4). This suggests that what follows after Luke 1:4 is Luke's attempt to convince the reader about some elements of which the reader is already informed. In doing this Luke seeks to explain and justify the 'social order' in the community. This is what legitimation does—seeking to provide answers to questions about community arrangements.[12] As Berger and Luckmann observe, 'the problem of legitimation inevitably arises when the objectivations of the (now historic) institutional order are to be transmitted to a new generation'.[13] At this point, 'there must be "explanations" and justification of the salient elements of the institutional tradition'.[14] Since the composition of Luke's Gospel is widely thought to be around 80 CE (nearly fifty years after Jesus' death), it may well be the case that a new generation in the community is asking questions about certain things handed on in the community (Luke 1:2). For instance, Luke shows in Acts that as the mission moves from the predominantly Hebrew / Aramaic-speaking congregation (Acts 6:1) to other ethnic groups, tensions erupt.[15] The cultural and ethnic composition of the Lukan communities is affected, prompting questions that need answers: should the Jewish followers of Jesus fellowship with believers of non-Jewish background? (cf. Acts 11:1–3); should Gentile believers be circumcised? (cf. Acts 15:1–5); is mission to the Gentiles (which follows Jesus' injunctions, Acts 1:8) in conformity with the plans of God? (cf. Luke 2:29–32; Acts 1:8).[16] This explains why, though Luke is aware of many earlier accounts of the story of Jesus, he yet feels obliged to write another (Luke 1:3).[17] Luke's offer of 'the certainty concerning the things about which you have been instructed' (Luke 1:4) thus becomes clearer when read against this backdrop.

3. The Spirit of the Lord as Legitimating Authority

One technique of legitimation involves an appeal to an authority that gives credence leading to trust in what is claimed. For instance, in the ancient Near East, kings who conducted cultic reforms obtained legitimation first and foremost by receiving divine approval from the gods by way of an oracle, even if the power-brokers organised the very oracle that gave legitimation for

11 Esler, *Community and Gospel in Luke-Acts*, 16.
12 Berger, *Social Reality of Religion*, 38. See also, Berger and Luckmann, *Social Construction*, 110–146.
13 Berger and Luckmann, *Social Construction*, 111.
14 Berger and Luckmann, *Social Construction*, 111.
15 Commentators suggest that Aramaic was the language of Palestinian Jews spoken in Jerusalem in the First Century but that the distinction between the two languages (Hebrew and Aramaic, which use the same alphabet) may not have been made by Luke. See Johnson, *Acts*, 105; Dunn, *Acts*, 81; Mullins, *Acts*, 90.
16 See, Neyrey, 'The Symbolic Universe of Luke-Acts', 271–304, who provides some explanation on the purity system of ancient Jewish society. Detail discussion on these questions is beyond the scope of this article.
17 Shelton, *Mighty in Word and Deed*, 4.

their program.[18] In the OT, Josiah presented the discovered scroll before the community and this supplied the required legitimation for the reform (2 Kgs 22—23). Reference to the discovered scroll 'demonstrated that the reform was not an innovative step but rather served as the restoration of ancient divine laws'.[19]

In the OT, the Spirit of God on individuals was the principal determinant of the legitimacy of their authority or mission. In Numbers 11, seventy elders were chosen to help Moses bear the burden of leadership. Moses is already privileged as possessing the Spirit of God and so has authority to lead Israel (Num. 11:17). But the seventy elders could not fit into this office until the Spirit rested upon them. As the narrative pointed out, it was only after the Spirit rested upon them that they prophesied and so could share in Moses' burden (Num. 11:25,26,29). The narrative of the Spirit resting upon them and provoking prophecy provides legitimation for their ministry. Similarly, Joseph, who is presented as having the Spirit of God, interpreted Pharaoh's dreams (Gen. 41:38; cf. Dan. 5:5–30). For Joshua to be commissioned as leader of Israel he had to have the Spirit of God (Num. 27:18; Deut. 34:9). Elijah and Elisha were portrayed as people of the Spirit (1 Kgs 18:12; 2 Kgs 2:9). The prophet, in Isaiah 61:1, was anointed and sent because the Spirit of the LORD was upon him. Joel prophesied an eventual outpouring of the Spirit upon all flesh (Joel 2:28–29), which Luke appealed to in Peter's Pentecost sermon.[20]

To be shown to be Spirit-filled becomes a declaration of divine approval of the bearer of the Spirit through whom God accomplishes God's divine purposes.[21] The Spirit's presence is God's endorsement and commission of a person (1 Sam. 9:6, 13); and the departure of the Spirit is God's rejection of the individual (1 Sam. 16:14; 1 Kgs 22:24; 2 Chr. 18:23). When God calls and commissions, it is still the presence of the Spirit of God that activates the commission.[22] This strategy is actively employed in Luke's narrative. Even where Luke refers to other legitimating authorities, the Holy Spirit plays a major role in complementing such an authority.[23]

Given the above background, let us now explore Luke's use of the Holy Spirit in the infancy narrative.

4. The Holy Spirit in the Infancy Narrative

The argument will now focus on how the Holy Spirit plays a legitimating role at this early stage of the narrative, laying the foundation for the rest of Luke-Acts. The starting point is the first reference to the Holy Spirit in the narrative—John the Baptist (1:15).

---

18   Na'Aman, 'The "Discovered Book"', 58.
19   Na'Aman, 'The "Discovered Book"', 58.
20   For other instances, see Balaam (Num. 24:2); Othniel (Judg. 3:10); Gideon (Judg. 6:34); Jephthah (Judg. 11:29); Samson (Judg. 13:25; 14:6,19; 15:14); Saul (1 Sam. 10:6,10; 11:6; 19:23); David (1 Sam. 16:13; 2 Sam. 23:2); Saul's messengers (1 Sam. 19:20); Amasai (1 Chr. 12:18); Azariah (2 Chr. 15:1); Jahaziel (2 Chr. 20:14); Zechariah son of Jehoiada (2 Chr. 24:20); Ezek. 2:2; 3:24; 11:5,24; Dan. 4:8,9,18; Mic. 3:8.
21   Hur, *Dynamic Reading*, 41.
22   Cf. for instance, Bezalel (Exod. 31:1); Othniel (Judg. 3:7–10); Gideon (Judg. 6:11–35).
23   Other legitimating authorities for instance, are Scripture (Luke 3:6; Acts 2:16–21; 10:19–20; 13:47; 15:15–17; 28:25); God / the Lord / angel of the Lord (Luke 2:10; Acts 10:15; 13:47); and the risen Jesus (Acts 1:8; 9:5; 22:8; 26:15–17). For instance, the Holy Spirit inspires Scripture (Acts 1:16; 28:25); the Holy Spirit is in agreement with a 'voice' that speaks to Peter (Acts 10:1ff), see especially vv.17–20; and while the risen Jesus calls Saul (Paul) to mission (Acts 9:5), Paul must receive the Spirit before he commences the mission (Acts 9:19); and in fact it is the Holy Spirit that calls Barnabas and Paul to mission (Acts 13:2).

4.1 John the Baptist: Forerunner of the Messiah (Luke 1:15)

It is already common knowledge in the community that John has a prophetic ministry (Luke 3:4–14; cf. Matt. 3:3; Mark 1:2–3). Luke particularly draws attention to John's role as the forerunner of the Messiah (cf. Mal. 4:5–6 // Luke 1:16–17,76; 3:4; 7:26–27). Therefore John must be shown to be inspired by the Spirit of God as Elijah was (and the prophets) in the OT (cf. 1 Kgs 18:12; 2 Kgs 2:15–16). Only by being inspired by the Holy Spirit will his words as prophet and his ministry as forerunner of the Messiah carry any weight. As it is, only Luke tells the reader that John is filled with the Holy Spirit, which gives credit to his careful research (1:3).[24]

The context for this first reference to the Holy Spirit in Luke's Gospel is the announcement of the angel Gabriel to Zechariah concerning the birth of a child whom Zechariah is to name John.[25] The angel announced that 'even before his birth', John 'will be filled with the Holy Spirit' (πνεύματος ἁγίου πλησθήσεται, Luke 1:15c).[26] For the reader familiar with the role of the Spirit of God upon individuals in the OT, this announcement already delineates John's future mission—a mission which Luke shows will be guided by the inspiration of the Holy Spirit.[27]

A reading of Luke 1:8–23 shows on the one hand that Luke places emphasis on the angelic message concerning John's birth and his role in salvation history (vv.13–17).[28] On the other hand, a careful unpacking and critical reading of the angelic announcement in verses 13–17 reveals that the weight of the message is on John's infilling with the Holy Spirit 'even from his mother's womb' (ἔτι ἐκ κοιλίας μητρὸς αὐτοῦ, v.15c).[29] The pointer to the infilling with the Holy Spirit accords the bearer (John) and his message divine approval. As with the OT pneumatics, this announcement of Spirit-endowment announces John's divine endorsement. By appealing to the Spirit of God in John's ministry, Luke keeps up with his objective of establishing the reliability (τὴν ἀσφάλειαν) of what the reader already knows (1:4).

The chiastic structure of Luke 1:13–17 can be set out as follows:

A John's birth announced: the angel announces the birth and name of John (v.13).

    B John's importance: to Zechariah, many, and in the sight of the Lord (vv.14–15a).

        C John's distinctiveness: must never drink wine or strong drink (v.15b).

            D even before his birth he will be filled with the Holy Spirit (v.15c).

        C' John's distinctiveness: He will have the spirit and power of Elijah (v.17a).

    B' John's importance: to Israel, he will effect reconciliation and righteousness (vv.16,17b).

A' John's task announced: to make ready a people prepared for the Lord (v.17c).

---

24 Cf. the corresponding passages in Matt. 3:1–12 and Mark 1:4–8 and John 1:19–28.

25 For other angelic appearances in the infancy narrative cf. 1:11,26; 2:9. For parallel angelic appearances in Acts see Acts 5:9; 8:26; 10:3; 12:7; 27:23. For angelic appearances in the OT, see for instance, Gen. 16:7–13; 21:17; 22:10–18; 31:11–13; Exod. 3:2–6; 14:19–24; Judg. 2:1–5; 13:3; Zech. 1:11–14.

26 The phrase 'filled with the Holy Spirit' occurs frequently in Luke-Acts (for instance, Luke 1:41,67; Acts 2:4; 4:8,31; 9:17; 13:9). It can refer to the continuous state of Spirit-empowerment or to a special Spirit in-filling for a particular task (Acts 4:8). In Luke 1:15, the continuous state of empowerment is in view, judging from the qualification, 'even before his birth'. 'Filled with the Holy Spirit', together with 'full of the Holy Spirit' is always accompanied by inspired speaking (cf. Luke 1:41,67; Acts 4:8; 7:55). However, Luke 1:15 is unique in that the inspired speaking is delayed to a later stage (cf. Luke 1:41).

27 Hur, *Dynamic Reading*, 198.

28 Green, *The Gospel of Luke*, 67. So also, Tannehill, *Narrative Unity*, Vol. 1, 20.

29 The angelic epiphany gives the primal authority to the message. The pointer to the infilling with the Holy Spirit accords the bearer and his message divine approval.

The chiastic structure indicates that the first three items (A, B, C) pertain to the person of John. The last three categories (C', B', A') concern his mission. At the centre of these two segments (D) is the infilling with the Holy Spirit: καὶ πνεύματος ἁγίου πλησθήσεται ἔτι ἐκ κοιλίας μητρὸς αὐτοῦ (literally: and of the Holy Spirit he will be filled even from the womb of his mother, v.15c).

Even from his mother's womb: According to Luke, John's birth is the result of divine intervention.[30] It is an answer to Zechariah's prayer (v.13a).[31] The announcement of John's name before his conception highlights John's greatness in the sight of the Lord (v.15a; cf. 7:28).[32] Verse 15b emphasises that John is to abstain from both wine and strong drink (οἶνον καὶ σίκερα; cf. Lev. 10:9; Num. 6:3; Deut. 29:6; Judg. 13:4,7,14; 1 Sam. 1:15; Prov. 20:1), which parallels John with Samson who will be empowered by the Spirit of the LORD (Judg. 13:3–6; 14:19).[33] Like Samson, Luke has crafted his narrative such that John is set apart by God before his conception; but over and unlike Samson, John is filled with the Spirit even while still in his mother's womb (cf. 1:41). This is one detail that is unique about John in Luke's narrative.

The expression 'even from his mother's womb' (ἔτι ἐκ κοιλίας μητρὸς αὐτοῦ) is grounded in the language of prophetic calling.[34] Thus, John being filled with the Holy Spirit resonates with the Spirit's presence among the OT prophets (cf. 1 Sam. 10:10; 2 Kgs 2:9–16; see Isa. 61:1; Ezek. 11:5; Joel 2:28).[35] However, Luke makes the claim that John is not just called before he is born (like Jeremiah; cf. Jer. 1:5), but John will experience the eschatological gift of the Spirit in a way and manner surpassing that of the prophets, 'even' from his mother's womb.[36] Thus, though John's

---

30 This recalls the birth stories in the OT: Isaac (Gen. 18:1-15), Samuel (1 Sam. 1—2) and Samson (Judg. 13:11-25). Both Zechariah and Elizabeth were advanced in age, and Elizabeth was barren (Luke 1:7). Neither Matthew nor Mark is concerned with how and from where John came. Only Luke tells the reader about John's beginning and parents.

31 This is reminiscent of Hannah's prayer for a child (1 Sam. 1:11). Zechariah's 'prayer' (ἡ δέησίς σου — your request) in the context of the narrative refers to his personal intercession. However, the answer to the personal prayer converges with the prayer (προσευχή) of the nation, which according to Luke awaits redemption (Luke 1:68). With the coming of John, the new age dawns for the entire nation on whose behalf Zechariah was in the temple. Cf. Bovon, *Gospel of Luke 1:1—9:50*, 35. See also Brown, *The Birth of the Messiah*, 260-261; Marshall, *Gospel of Luke*, 56; Evans, *Saint Luke*, 148; Fitzmyer, *Gospel According to Luke I-IX*, 325.

32 Pre-natal namings in the OT are generally retrospective interpretations. The task and accomplishment which are already known about a character are used to interpret the character's name. It tells the reader that God foresaw and ordained the role the individual was to play (cf. Gen. 16:11; 17:19; 1 Kgs 13:2; Isa. 7:14; 49:1). Cf. Brown, *The Birth of the Messiah*, 272, n.29.

33 Scholars argue whether John is called to be a Nazirite or just to an ascetic way of life. Bovon, *Luke 1: A Commentary*, 36-37, asserts that since the words about abstinence from wine are closer to Lev. 10:19 than they are to Num. 6:3, they are reminiscent of the regulations for priests (and their children) preparing for service than they are of the life of a Nazirite. See also Marshall, *Gospel of Luke*, 57. The ban on hair cutting does not appear in the Lukan text, and Samson is not directly excluded from alcohol consumption; only Samson's mother is instructed not to drink wine or strong drink (Judg. 13:4). As for Samuel, both the ban on haircut and the prohibition of alcohol are mentioned (1 Sam. 1:11). Marshall argues therefore that, considering Luke 7:33, John's is more of an ascetic lifestyle. Creed also argues that since there is no mention of allowing the hair to grow, John was not to be a Nazirite. Cf. Creed, *Gospel According to St Luke*, 11. See also, Evans, *Saint Luke*, 149. Fitzmyer, *The Gospel According to Luke*, 326, however, asserts that the reference to 'no wine or strong drink' is a call to the life of a Nazirite. Either position makes no difference to the present argument. What is important is Luke's construction which points to John being filled with the Holy Spirit.

34 The Semitic expression can refer to the time when the child is still in the womb (cf. Judg. 13:3-5) or to the time of emergence from the womb (from birth — cf. Ps. 22:10). However, based on the child's reaction in Luke 1:41, 'while the child is still in the womb' is more plausible here. Cf. Tannehill, *Narrative Unity*, Vol. 1, 23; Tatum, 'The Epoch of Israel', 186; Creed, *The Gospel According to St Luke*, 11.

35 Cf. the call of Jeremiah in Jer. 1:4, 5; and the call of Samson in Judg. 13:5-7. St Paul also referred to himself as being called from his mother's womb (cf. Gal. 1:15). The idea of God calling a person from the mother's womb would have been revived in the First Century. Cf. Bovon, *Luke 1: A Commentary*, 37.

36 Nolland, *Luke 1—9:20*, 34-36. See also Bock, *Luke 1:1—9:50*, 86.

role in Luke's narrative is explicitly prophetic (cf. Luke 1:76), Luke shows that John is more than a prophet (Luke 7:26) on two grounds: first, his reception of the Spirit from the womb, and second, his eschatological role. As Shepherd states, 'When John is explicitly described in prophetic terms and said to be filled with the prophetic Spirit, the Spirit is implicitly characterized as being the Spirit which inspired the Old Testament prophets (e.g. Gen. 41:38; Num. 11:24–30; 23:7 LXX; 24:2; 27:18; 1 Sam. 10:6; Isa. 61:1; Ezek. 2:2; Joel 2:28; Mic. 3:8)'.[37] The same phrase 'filled with the Spirit' foreshadows the characterisation of later prophetic figures: Jesus (Luke 4:1) and the followers of Jesus in Acts (for instance, 2:4; 4:8,31; 7:55; 9:17; 11:24; 13:9). From this beginning Luke has employed the authority of the Spirit of God to convey the certainty of the unfolding narrative, beginning with the ministry of John who has the duty of introducing Jesus onto the scene.

Luke's use of the terms ἔτι and ἐκ also emphasises the Spirit's role in John's ministry. Though ἔτι is read with ἐκ κοιλίας μητρὸς αὐτοῦ (from his mother's womb), the emphasis is on what takes places in the womb—'he will be filled with the Holy Spirit' (πνεύματος ἁγίου πλησθήσεται). Simply stated, 'he will be filled with the Holy Spirit from his mother's womb' already makes good sense. To qualify the expression with the word ἔτι (even) makes the whole expression emphatic. It gives the impression that the child in question is extraordinary; for no one in the past ever claimed to have been filled with the Spirit of God while still in the womb.[38] Luke's construction insists on the uniqueness of John's role in the realisation of the divine purpose, and shows that this role is legitimate.[39] The expression argues for the divine choice of John for a special mission. It is reasonable then to say that Luke employed ἔτι with the Spirit endowment to emphasise John's divine choice for the reader / community, which thus lends authorisation, authentication, and legitimation to John's mission.

Luke rewrites the narrative about John such that the one who knows and announces that Jesus will baptise with the Holy Spirit and with fire (Luke 3:16; cf. Matt. 3:11) will have to speak under the inspiration of the Holy Spirit. In this way, not only are John's words divinely inspired; his entire mission and identity have authority from the Holy Spirit who inspires him. For the reading community, this means the legitimation of John and his mission (and also of the later mission of the followers of Jesus). This narrative ingenuity also helps to strengthen John's message about the upcoming mission of Jesus (cf. Luke 3:16–18). Using this strategy, Luke points out from the outset, via the mouthpiece of the Spirit-inspired forerunner (John), how the story of Jesus fulfils God's plans.

4.2 Mary: Virgin Mother of the Messiah (Luke 1:35)

Luke's infancy narrative emphasises the role of Mary in the realisation of the divine purpose, a role (as Luke indicates) activated by the action of the Holy Spirit. The context is the annunciation by the angel to Mary about the birth of a son whom Mary is to name Jesus (Luke 1:26–38). This is solely

---

37 Shepherd, *Narrative Function*, 118.
38 While the phrase 'from his mother's womb' is not strictly Lukan, the infilling with the Spirit from the womb is a particularly Lukan trope. Prophets like Isaiah (Isa. 49:1) and Jeremiah (Jer. 1:5) and even Paul (Gal. 1:15) have claimed a calling from the womb; nevertheless, none of them made a claim to have been filled with the Holy Spirit from the womb. John also does not claim that as a character in the narrative. It is the voice of the angel of God who is an authorised and reliable spokesperson for God that makes that claim.
39 This is further corroborated by the remarks in verse 66 concerning John: 'All those who heard them pondered them and said: "what then will this child become?"' The question creates some expectations for the mission of John; but benefit of hindsight already tells the reader that the child was filled with the Holy Spirit even before his birth. Thus, even before John begins his ministry, the circumstances of his birth have already provided some authorisation for his mission.

Lukan material. Luke's narrative strongly argues that through the 'coming upon' (ἐπελεύσεται, will come upon) and the 'overshadowing' (ἐπισκιάσει, will overshadow) of the Holy Spirit, Mary conceives a son.[40]

4.2.1 The Puzzle of the Virgin Birth

In this pericope, Luke temporarily closes the curtain on Zechariah and Elizabeth and introduces Mary into the scene. Menzies suggests that this scene change ushers in a parallel between John and Jesus—a parallel which, Menzies argues, must have influenced Luke's inclusion of the Spirit's creative role (in Jesus' conception) into the narrative.[41] Changing scenes in this way highlights the superiority of Jesus, who (unlike John—the precursor) is not filled with the Spirit from the womb, but is conceived in a virgin's womb by the power of the Spirit (Luke 1:27,34; cf. Matt. 1:18).[42]

In Greek mythological thought the idea of the gods begetting divine offspring is prevalent.[43] Divine conceptions are said to be bestowed upon virgins (and Luke uses the word twice in 1:27). Where this is the case, it emphasises the divine begetting of the child involved—it is designed to privilege the resultant offspring. It is in this regard, for instance, that Zeus becomes the father of Arcas, with Callisto, the beautiful virgin, being the mother.[44] However, there are no precedents of virgin births in the OT, though there are improbable conceptions that are clearly attributed to divine agency (for instance, Gen. 18:9–10; 21:1–6).

Given that Luke writes to a predominantly Gentile audience, it is not unreasonable to suggest that Luke appeals to a known belief to address a seemingly difficult situation in the community. For just as some scholars today cast doubt on the historicity of the virgin birth,[45] it is also possible that some of Jesus' contemporaries (and by extension, Luke's) would have doubted the virgin birth. For instance, in Mark 6:3, Jesus comes to his hometown and the people ask, 'Is not this the carpenter, the son of Mary and brother of James, and Joses, and Judas, and Simon? And are not his sisters here with us?' The reference to his mother and not to his father is quite an unusual lineage for the era. Matthew and Luke, who use Mark as source, redacted the text such that Matthew reads, 'the carpenter's son whose mother is called Mary' (Matt. 13:55); and Luke refers to Jesus as 'Joseph's son' (Luke 4:22). By redacting Mark thus, Matthew and Luke seemingly attempt to avoid the implication of illegitimacy. In John's narrative, the Jews, in response to Jesus, assert: 'We were not born of fornication' (πορνείας, John 8:41). This statement coming from opposing Jews 'may

---

40 'Overshadowing' here recalls God's presence with God's people in the OT, especially in the Exodus event (Exod. 40:36–38), and in the Tent of Meeting (Exod. 40:34–35).
41 Menzies, *Empowered for Witness*, 112.
42 Debate on the exact meaning of the word virgin (παρθένος) has centred on its employment in Matt. 1:23 where the text of Isa. 7:14 (which uses the Hebrew word 'almah') is quoted. The word 'almah' means a 'young woman of marriageable and childbearing age' who may or may not still be a virgin, but who has not yet given birth to a child. See Lincoln, *Born of a Virgin?*, 75, 101. The Hebrew word used to signify a virgin would have been 'bethulah'. However, the LXX translates 'almah' with the Greek παρθένος which means a virgin (though Evans, *Saint Luke*, 159, argues that παρθένος in Greek primarily denotes the bloom of youth, and was used of a young girl with or without reference to virginity in the technical sense). This is the sense employed in the infancy narrative. Cf. Mullins, *The Gospel of Luke*, 121. Bovon, *Luke 1*, 49–50, argues that in official Judaism virginity was neither morally nor mystically of value. However, this is not official Judaism. Luke's narrative points to an interest in the miracle of the divine begetting, but also in Mary's status as a virgin. For further reading on the debate, see Landry, 'Narrative Logic', 65–79; and Legrand, *Doctrine of Virginity*.
43 See Burkert, *Greek Religion*, 183; Lincoln, *Born of a Virgin?*, 108–115. Some popular examples include Plato, Empedocles, Hercules, Pythagoras, Alexander the Great, and even Caesar Augustus, who were believed to have been begotten by the gods.
44 Burkert, *Greek Religion*, 150–151.
45 Borg, *The God We Never Knew*, 102; Tabor, *The Jesus Dynasty*, 50–71, 87–88, 140–148.

imply the illegitimacy of Jesus' birth', meant to provoke Jesus.[46] However, John's narrative has no infancy narrative, and elsewhere mentions Joseph twice as Jesus' father (1:45; 6:42). All these could be pointers to some really complicated situation that Luke wants to address—the virgin birth. This could explain the double use of the language in one verse (Luke 1:27) before the virgin is given a name.

This challenging and difficult state of affairs is expressed in Luke's narrative placed on the lips of Mary: 'How can this be since I am a virgin?' (Luke 1:34).[47] It is not the narrator this time who identifies Mary as a virgin; it is Mary who testifies to her virginal status. What follows from this point is the explanation of the possibility of the virgin birth. For Luke, the way out of the puzzle is the reference to the active / creative role of the Holy Spirit.

4.2.2 Unravelling the Puzzle

Luke refers to Mary's virginity three times in quick succession (1:27[2x],34) before drawing attention to the act of the Holy Spirit. This argues for the virginal conception as the central puzzle to be unravelled.[48] Luke also refers to Mary as engaged to Joseph (Luke 1:27; cf. Matt. 1:18; and Luke 2:5), of the house of David.[49] The depiction of Mary as an engaged virgin allows for the question 'how ... ?' which in turn provides the narrative opening for the role of the Holy Spirit. Matthew, writing for a predominantly Jewish audience, addresses this puzzle from two perspectives. First, Matthew makes a passive reference to the Holy Spirit: 'She was found to be with child from the Holy Spirit' (εὑρέθη Matt. 1:18). Second, Matthew presents it as a fulfilment of an OT prophetic text, Isaiah 7:14—'Look, the virgin shall conceive and bear a son, and they shall name him Emmanuel' (Matt. 1:23).

Luke, on the other hand, writing for a predominantly Gentile audience, addresses this problem by applying an accepted motif to the Christian story of Jesus, thereby shifting Mark's legitimation of Jesus at his baptism back to Jesus' conception / birth. The reliable agent of God announces that Mary's child yet to be conceived will be called 'Son of the Most High' (Luke 1:32). This is divine begetting which resonates with Luke's Gentile audience. Thus in 1:35, employing a future active voice, the angel announces to Mary: 'the Holy Spirit will come upon you' (πνεῦμα ἅγιον

---

46 Brown, *The Gospel according to John I–IX*, 364; Barrett, *The Gospel according to John*, 348.
47 Some interpreters find it impossible to make the question historically and psychologically credible on the lips of Mary. The argument is that if Mary is betrothed to Joseph, of the house of David, and the promised child is to be a descendant of David, it follows that Mary can marry Joseph in the near future and bear the child. On account of this, these scholars have concluded that it is a mere literary device by Luke to prepare the window for the announcement of the Holy Spirit activity in the next verse. For details of this argument, see for example Creed, *The Gospel of St Luke*, 19; Marshall, *The Gospel of Luke*, 60–70; Evans, *Saint Luke*, 162–63; Fitzmyer, *The Gospel according to Luke*, 348–50; Landry, 'Narrative Logic', 65–79.
48 As can be observed, Luke does not call Mary παῖς (girl; cf. 8:51) or παιδίσκη (little girl, maid; cf. 12:45) or κοράσιον (maiden; cf. 8:51). He rather calls her παρθένος (the normal understanding of which is virgin). This is a preparation for 1:34.
49 According to Jewish tradition of those days, engagement (betrothal) was already marriage awaiting consummation (cf. Deut. 22:23). It was legally binding and any sexual misconduct was interpreted as adultery. The completion of the marriage ceremony was when the bride was ceremoniously escorted to the husband's house. The narrative that Mary is engaged and yet a virgin indicates that she has exchanged consent with Joseph but has not been taken to live with him (cf. Matt. 1:18). For further reading on betrothal explained, see Brown, *The Birth of the Messiah*, 123–24. Jesus' lineage and ancestry is traced through Joseph to David (cf. 2:4; 3:23; 2 Sam. 7:12–16; 1 Chr. 17:11).

ἐπελεύσεται ἐπὶ σέ).[50] This is indicative of an action which is yet to take place. Shepherd points out that 'the active construction, with the Spirit as the subject of a future-tense verb, is rhetorically significant: it indicates to the reader the importance of this event'.[51] For the Jewish audience, the Lukan expression projects the profound experience of the action of the Holy Spirit, reminiscent of Isaiah 32:15—'Until a spirit from on high is poured out ... and the wilderness becomes a fruitful field'. In Luke, the Spirit is about to act on a virgin womb that will conceive and bear a child.[52] This also would be consonant with 'a theology of a new creation, wherein God's Spirit, active in the first creation of life (Gen. 1:2), was active again'.[53] Luke's narrative at this point highlights for the reader that (1), Jesus' conception is made possible by the action of the Holy Spirit, who is the power of the Most High (cf. Luke 24:49; Acts 1:8); (2), Jesus is holy, and (3), Jesus is Son of the Most High and is Son of God (1:32,35): titles which equally resonate with Luke's readers.[54] The characterisation of Mary as a virgin is thus a step into unravelling the status of the child yet to be conceived.

Thus appealing to the active / creative role of the Holy Spirit, Luke establishes that the virgin birth (which at this time in the narrative has not taken place) is not the work of any human action; it is entirely the result of divine initiative. In this way, Luke assures the reader (cf. 1:4) that the virginal conception is part of God's plan. The Spirit has here played a legitimatory role: one, on the virgin's conception; two, on the child conceived.

4.2.3 Mary's Prophetic Proclamation

The Holy Spirit coming upon Mary not only legitimates the virgin birth, it also prepares the reader for the significant prophetic proclamation in 1:46–55.[55] Mary, Like Zechariah, Elizabeth, and Simeon, speaks under the influence of the Holy Spirit (Zechariah, Elizabeth, and Simeon will be addressed below). As John was filled with the Holy Spirit from the womb but fulfils the prophetic role later in the narrative (cf. 1:44; 3:1–18), so also Mary experiences the 'generating function'[56] of the Spirit but then fulfils a prophetic role later in the narrative (1:46–55). Mary as a prophet is reinforced by her self-designation as the servant of the Lord (ἡ δούλη κυρίου, v.38; cf. Luke 2:29; Jer. 7:25; 25:4).[57] The Holy Spirit becomes the authority giving credence to the assertions in the proclamation.

---

50 A similar expression is used in Eph. 2:7 (ἐπερχομένοις, coming on); and James 5:1 (ἐπερχομέναις, coming upon). Outside of these two citations, the expression in confined to Luke-Acts — used about 7 times (Luke 11:22; 21:26; Acts 1:8; 8:24; 13:40; 14:19). In Acts 1:8, Luke employs the same term (ἐπελθόντος — a participle for ἐπέρχομαι ἐπί — to come upon) when speaking about the coming of the Spirit upon the disciples at Pentecost. Cf. also 1 Sam. 16:13 — the Spirit of the Lord came upon David. It is also reflective of Isa. 11:1–2 which describes the coming of the Spirit of the Lord upon the Davidic branch.
51 Shepherd, *Narrative Function*, 120.
52 Thus Luke 1:35, which spells out the action of the Spirit, proclaims a virginal conception for Mary. See Bock, *Luke 1:1—9:50*, 121.
53 Brown, *The Birth of the Messiah*, 298–309.
54 'Most High' (ὕψιστος) generally is a Lukan designation for God. (cf. Luke 1:35,76; 6:35; 8:28; Acts 7:8; 16:17); also, a common designation for God in Hellenistic Judaism. In this context, it expresses the preeminence of the divine begetting of Jesus. Cf. Bovon, *Luke* 1, 52.
55 Mary's prophetic praise spells out a lot of the recurrent themes in Luke, for example the place of the poor and lowly before God, God's faithfulness to promises, and fulfilment of God's plan. However, this article does not intend to go into details on Mary's proclamation. For details, see Tannehill, *Narrative Unity*, vol. 1, 26–32; Johnson, *The Gospel of Luke*, 43; Shepherd, *Narrative Function*, 121–22.
56 Shepherd, *Narrative Function*, 120.
57 Shepherd, *Narrative Function*, 121.

4.3 Elizabeth and Zechariah: Prophetic Recognition of the Messiah (Luke 1:41,67)

4.3.1 Elizabeth

The context within which Elizabeth is portrayed as 'filled with the Holy Spirit' is the visitation of Mary to Elizabeth (Luke 1:39–56).[58] Though Harrington sees the account as 'a complementary episode, a pendant to the diptych of annunciation (Luke 1:5–38)', it is nevertheless, a significant pericope, laden with biblical allusions.[59] The account opens with Mary setting out hastily to a Judaean town, where she enters Zechariah's house (1:39–40). Since Zechariah is of no importance to the development of the current story Mary says no word to him. The main characters in this encounter are Mary and Elizabeth, and their unborn babies in the womb.

Mary's greeting alerts Elizabeth to the presence of another, and so initiates a conversation. As can be observed, Luke's emphasis is not on Mary's greeting (for Luke does not even mention any words used by Mary), nor on anything that Mary says (at least not at this point). The focus is rather on Elizabeth's reaction to Mary's greeting, Elizabeth's endowment with the Holy Spirit, and what this means for her Spirit-inspired interpretation of what is about to happen within her (which bears the mark of prophetic utterances). This is Luke's interest in the current episode. Elizabeth's proclamation will further elucidate the identity of Mary's child and the profound role of Mary in the narrative.

a) The Effect of Mary's Greeting

Mary's greeting provokes two reactions: first, the child in Elizabeth's womb leaps (v.41a); second, Elizabeth is filled with the Holy Spirit (v.41b). There is a further reaction of Elizabeth's child in her womb (leapt for joy) as soon as she heard Mary's voice (v.44). The ἰδοὺ γάρ (for behold) at the beginning of verse 44 emphasises the hearing of Mary's voice and the resultant effect. The repetition of the 'leaping of the child' and the addition of ἐν ἀγαλλιάσει (for joy—which explains the reason for leaping), is thus an emphatic reference to the effect of Mary's greeting on Elizabeth and her unborn child. The episode recalls David who leaps and dances before the Ark of the Lord (2 Sam. 6:12–22). When rebuked by Michal, the daughter of Saul, David replied: 'It was before the Lord ... that I have danced' (2 Sam. 6:21). Recalling this OT narrative, it is not surprising then that the Lukan Elizabeth refers to Mary's unborn child as 'my Lord' (v.43). Luke in this pericope confirms and substantiates his earlier assertions about Mary and her unborn child—Mary overshadowed by the Holy Spirit bears a child in her womb; a child who is holy, the Son of the Most High, and Son of God (Luke 1:32,35).

b) Elizabeth: Filled with the Holy Spirit

Filled with the Holy Spirit, Elizabeth makes some thought-provoking utterances that buttress past events in the narrative and yet look to the future. Elizabeth recognises Mary as blessed (1:42a). This recalls Luke 1:28 where Mary is a favoured one. Luke uses εὐλογημένος for Mary and her unborn child (v.42b), a term which signifies 'being well spoken about, praised and honored for the position or favor bestowed on one by God'.[60] To be blessed among women is a 'Semitic way

---

58 The present focus is on the infilling with the Holy Spirit and how this serves a legitimatory purpose for the reader. The article will not concern itself much with the content of vv.46–56 which deal with Mary's song of praise, also known as the Magnificat.
59 Harrington, *Luke—Gracious Theologian*, 33.
60 Mullins, *The Gospel of Luke*, 129.

of saying "most blessed of women" since Hebrew or Aramaic do not have a superlative adjective or a superlative adjectival form of the participle'.[61] Further, Elizabeth acknowledges and praises Mary's faith. This is clarified in the use of the adjective μακαρία (blessed, 1:45) which emphasises Mary's blessedness for believing (πιστεύσασα) that what the Lord had spoken (λελαλημένοις) will be brought to completion / fulfilment (τελείωσις).[62] Here, the theme of promise and fulfilment is brought into relief. Furthermore, without being told, Elizabeth knows that Mary has a child in her womb and that Mary's child is special. This is a remarkable knowledge and insight. Elizabeth is Mary's kinswoman or relative, who is much older than Mary (cf. 1:36). Recognising Mary as the mother of her Lord, and most importantly, giving the child the title, 'my Lord' (a title which in the OT is generally used for God) is quite revealing.[63] Other than the angel who is a reliable character, Elizabeth becomes the first human character to possess such an amazing prophetic insight in the narrative. Even when the unborn child reacts in her womb, it is Elizabeth who gives expression to the reaction, and interprets it as dancing for joy.

Luke delays Elizabeth's utterances until she is 'filled with the Holy Spirit'. This implies that her words are Spirit-inspired. In the OT as well as in the Graeco-Roman religious world, the S/spirit's presence with individuals authenticates their utterances and mission. The belief is that a spirit-possessed / endowed individual has a connection with some super powers—gods and spirit—(in the case of the OT, God) which are not present for others.[64]

Luke applies this to Elizabeth's utterances which equal 'prophetic divination of events and their significance'.[65] Elizabeth's prophetic assertions, which deepen the readers' awareness of the identity of Jesus, also confirm the angel Gabriel's earlier statements. She has spoken prophetically; she communicates the mind of God. What is her authority? Here again Luke makes reference to the legitimating authority of the Holy Spirit who enables the utterances.[66] From this point, as Elizabeth and Mary (in the Magnificat) theologise and speak authoritatively about God's deeds, the reader is led to regard them as trustworthy characters and adopt their theological interpretation of the impending births.[67] This is because their utterances have come directly from the inspiration of the Holy Spirit. The Holy Spirit has served a legitimatory role.

---

61 Mullins, *The Gospel of Luke*, 129. Brown suggests that Mary is specially blessed by God, and not necessarily that Mary is the most blessed woman, since the same expression can be used of other women (cf. Deborah to Jael — Judg. 5:24; Uzziah to Judith — Jdt. 13:18). Brown, *The Birth of the Messiah*, 333.

62 μακαρία describes a deep, enduring state of happiness or blessedness essentially bound to one's standing before God, such a state that endures through changing and challenging situations and emotions. See Mullins, *The Gospel of Luke*, 130.

63 Cf. for instance, Gen. 15:2; Exod. 4:10; Isa. 3:15; Jer. 1:6. Lord, in the NT, refers usually to the Risen Christ. In the Gospel, Luke employs the term 'Lord' both for God (1:6,9,11,15,16,17,25) and for Jesus (2:11; 7:13; 10:1; 11:39; 12:42; 17:6; 18:6; 19:8,31; 24:3,34). However, in the infancy narrative, out of 26 usages, only two refer to Jesus (cf. 1:43; 2:11). But Luke uses it throughout Acts in reference to Jesus. Cf. Mullins, *The Gospel of Luke*, 130.

64 For several examples of spirit-possession and their effects in Graeco-Roman religion, see Gould, 'Making Sense of Greek Religion', 9–11.

65 Evans, *Saint Luke*, 169.

66 Brown suggests that 'it is through the prophetic action of John the Baptist in Elizabeth's womb that she knows Mary as the mother of my Lord': *The Birth of the Messiah*, 344. So also Creed, *The Gospel according to St Luke*, 21. However, even if the leaping of John the Baptist in the womb of Elizabeth raised an alarm for Elizabeth that there is something extraordinary here, Luke indicates that it is the infilling of the Spirit that ushered in the revelation concerning the identity of the child in Mary's womb. This is why Elizabeth speaks only after the infilling with the Holy Spirit. Yes, John bore witness to Jesus in the womb (1:41a), but Elizabeth divined the situation / witness through the inspiration of the Holy Spirit (1:41b) and thereafter utters her proclamation (1:42–45).

67 Reid, *Choosing the Better Part?*, 71.

4.3.2 Zechariah

Since the annunciation of John's birth, Zechariah has been silent. Even when Mary visited his house, Zechariah uttered no word. With John's birth and naming (Luke 1:57–66), the words of the angel are fulfilled. This fulfilment affirms the reliability of Luke's narrative: exactly what Luke wants to convey to the reader. Gabriel's earlier announcement concerning John's infilling with the Holy Spirit from the womb already depicts John's future mission. Now a human character within the narrative is going to elucidate this mission within the context of prophecy. The prophetic utterances will summarise the entire narrative of Luke-Acts: divine visitation from God (v.68), a mighty saviour raised (v.69; cf. v.71; 2:11), who is from the house of David (v.69; cf. 2:4); fulfilling earlier prophecy and promise (vv.70,71,73), and a call to serve God in holiness 'all our days' (vv.73–75). Zechariah has this role within the narrative, and so (like Elizabeth's insight into the identity of Jesus) foresees John's future mission and utters a prophecy which will be fulfilled within the story (vv.76–77; cf. 3:1–20). Johnson refers to this as a classic example of a programmatic prophecy which is meant to guide the reader's understanding of the narrative to follow.[68] The central question, however, is: what is it that guarantees the legitimacy of Zechariah's prophetic ministry and the reliability of his utterances?

For prophetic words to carry weight and be authoritative, the inspiration must also be authoritative. Therefore, although in Luke 1:64, after Zechariah regained his power of speech, he began to speak and praise God (the content of this speech is not recorded in the narrative), it is only now in preparation for these profound prophetic utterances that Luke indicates that Zechariah is filled with the Holy Spirit (ἐπλήσθη πνεύματος ἁγίου). In 1:67, Luke writes, 'Then his father, Zechariah, was filled with the Holy Spirit and spoke this prophecy' (καὶ Ζαχαρίας ὁ πατὴρ αὐτοῦ ἐπλήσθη πνεύματος ἁγίου καὶ ἐπροφήτευσεν λέγων). Luke is literally saying: this is the content of Zechariah's prophecy which he spoke under the inspiration of the Holy Spirit. Putting the prophetic words out to the reader in this way (as inspired by the Holy Spirit) assures the reader of the authenticity of Zechariah and his utterances.

In Luke 1:66, the neighbours and 'all who heard' about John's birth and the opening of Zechariah's vocal power (1:57–66) had asked: what then will this child be? (τί ἄρα τὸ παιδίον τοῦτο ἔσται). Verses 76–77 provide the answer to this question by declaring the prophetic role of John, as prophet of the Most High (προφήτης ὑψίστου), even as Jesus is Son of the Most High (υἱὸς ὑψίστου, 1:32). Verse 76 particularly confirms the words of the angel in verse 17, that John 'will go before the Lord to prepare his way'. This is proleptic of 3:4, where there is 'the voice of one crying in the desert: prepare the way of the Lord'. It equally anticipates 7:27 which quotes Malachi 3:1 thus, 'Behold I send my messenger before your face who will prepare your way before you'. Similarly, John's characterisation as 'prophet of the Most High' in verse 76 articulates the sentiments of Jesus in 7:26: 'A prophet? Yes, and I tell you, more than a prophet' (cf. also 16:16 which indicates that John is the last of the prophets).[69]

As Luke wants the reader to know, Zechariah gained all these insights through the inspiration of the Holy Spirit (1:67). By showing that Zechariah's prophetic insights and utterances concerning God's faithfulness to Israel are explicitly inspired by the Spirit, Luke gives them an extra degree of authority before both the hearer and the reader. In this way, Luke guarantees Zechariah and his words to be reliable, legitimate, and trustworthy.[70] This legitimation encompasses: (1) Zechariah's words, which point to (2) John's future role and ministry, and (3) Jesus' identity and mission.

---

68 Johnson, *The Gospel of Luke*, 45.
69 Brown, *The Birth of the Messiah*, 389.
70 Shepherd, *Narrative Function*, 119.

4.4 Simeon – Recognises / Announces Salvation and Mission to the World (Luke 2:22–28)

The presentation of the child Jesus in the Temple (found only in Luke) is the context in question. This will be the last mention of the Holy Spirit in the Lukan birth narrative. Here the scope of Jesus' mission will be defined. This episode follows just after the circumcision and naming ceremony of Jesus, just as it was with John (1:57–66). As law-abiding citizens, the parents of Jesus offer their sacrifice according to what is stated in the law of the Lord (v.24).[71]

Jesus, the central figure in the Gospel, is soon to begin his public ministry (4:14). Luke seeks to establish the certainty for the last time (within the birth narrative) concerning who Jesus is, and what his ministry entails just before he begins.[72] Luke now reiterates his earlier assertions through the mouthpiece of a devout and righteous Jerusalemite, Simeon, that Jesus is the Messiah (2:26; cf. 1:17,76), the salvation raised up for us (2:30; cf. 1:69). Luke further adds a new dimension to his presentation of Jesus which emphasises that Jesus' mission is not for a particular group of people; it is for all people (2:31), a light for revelation to the Gentiles (2:32), as well as the glory of Israel (2:32). This programmatic episode draws the mission of the Messiah (at this point infant Jesus). Simeon's insight also anticipates the acceptance of Jesus by the Gentiles and his rejection by a significant number of his own people. This provides some answers for Jesus' passion and death, and the later mission / persecution of the followers of Jesus in Acts.

For all of these to be substantiated, Luke introduces Simeon who identifies himself as a servant of God (τὸν δοῦλόν, just like Mary in 1:38), and speaks according to God's word (κατὰ τὸ ῥῆμά σου, 2:29). 'According to your word' here alludes to the theme of fulfilment. Simeon's identification as God's servant in verse 29 corroborates Luke's introduction in verse 25, where, as is characteristic of Lukan pneumatics, Simeon is introduced as δίκαιος (righteous; cf. Matt. 1:19) and εὐλαβής (devout), just like Zechariah and Elizabeth (1:6) in faithfulness to the law.[73] Three statements about Simeon are centred on the action of the Holy Spirit on Simeon, employing three different verbs:

- The Holy Spirit was upon Simeon (καὶ πνεῦμα ἦν ἅγιον ἐπ' αὐτόν, v.25c). This follows the OT language when the Spirit of the Lord is upon the prophets and inspires prophetic speech. The reader thus knows that what follows is under the inspiration of the Spirit, and so is reliable and trustworthy.
- The Holy Spirit had communicated something to Simeon (καὶ ἦν αὐτῷ κεχρηματισμένον ὑπὸ τοῦ πνεύματος τοῦ ἁγίου, v.26).[74] Luke, faithful to his passion for investigating everything from the beginning (Luke 1:3), tells the reader that the Holy Spirit had spoken to Simeon long before now, and so, what is happening now is a fulfilment of what was revealed earlier to Simeon. Therefore Simeon, who like Mary is a servant of God (2:29), speaks 'according to your word' (κατὰ τὸ ῥῆμά σου).

---

71 Mary and Joseph are shown to be law-abiding here in their fulfilling of two important customary duties: 1, the consecration or presentation of the child to the Lord (Exod. 13:1,11–16) and 2, the purification of the mother after the birth of the child with the traditional offering (Lev. 12:1–4).

72 Through reliable characters the reader already knows that Jesus is Son of the Most High, Davidic Messiah, Son of God (angel Gabriel); Jesus is the Lord (Elizabeth); Jesus is the Saviour, the Davidic king (Zechariah).

73 Similar introduction is used for Ananias in Paul's testimony of his own conversion (Acts 22:12; cf. also 10:1). This is indicative of a typical Lukan style.

74 This refers to an earlier revelation given to Simeon in the past, suggesting a good rapport between the Holy Spirit and Simeon before now.

- The first two verbs ('was upon', and 'had communicated / revealed') alert the reader to the third. If the Holy Spirit was upon Simeon, and had revealed to Simeon what was to be, it follows that Simeon had been in constant fellowship with the Holy Spirit. Hence, the Holy Spirit guides Simeon (καὶ ἦλθεν ἐν τῷ πνεύματι, v.27). The literal translation of the Greek is 'and he came by / in the Spirit'. That is to say, inspired (guided, led, prompted) by the Spirit, Simeon goes into the Temple, and sees the words of Isaiah fulfilled in Jesus.[75]

Before closing this scene, Luke makes a final reference to another character—a prophetess, Anna—who comes into the Temple at that time when Simeon was attending to the couple and their child (2:36–38). The title, prophetess, which comes before her name already indicates that Anna has the prophetic spirit. Contrary to Simeon who praises God and addresses the child's parents, Anna gives thanks to God (ἀνθωμολογεῖτο) and addresses the crowd, speaking about the child 'to all who were looking for the redemption of Jerusalem' (λύτρωσιν Ἰερουσαλήμ, v.38).[76] While Luke does not record Anna's words, Luke's construction suggests that her utterances are Spirit-inspired.

What becomes obvious here is that Luke, in keeping with his objective of establishing narrative assurance, tells the reader that Simeon and Anna take part in the divine initiative by the power of the Holy Spirit; it is the Holy Spirit that prompts Simeon's and Anna's prophetic declarations in the Temple. The same Spirit who inspires prophecy (2:26) effects the fulfilment (2:27). In Simeon's and Anna's utterances, Luke affirms that belief in Jesus (the salvation prepared for all peoples) is the answer to the expectation of the Jews (for Jesus is the glory and redemption of God's people, Israel). The accompaniment of the Holy Spirit gives the guarantee to this assertion. The Holy Spirit in this context serves to authenticate and legitimate (1) Simeon's and Anna's utterances, and (2) the future mission of Jesus now revealed through their Spirit-inspired words. The Holy Spirit is a strong factor in establishing this certainty.

5. Conclusion

The central question of the Gospel narrative is about the person of Jesus and his mission. Some teaching had already been handed down within the community about Jesus as the Messiah and Son of God (Luke 1:1–2). Luke wants to establish the certainty of what the community already knows.

Beginning with the infancy narrative, Luke introduces the person and mission of Jesus through the ministry of various characters who participate in the unfolding of the divine purpose fulfilled in Jesus. Each of these characters played a role that further reveals the identity and mission of Jesus. John as the forerunner of the Messiah necessarily has to come before the Messiah. Filled with the Holy Spirit he announces the one who is to baptise with the Holy Spirit and fire. Mary, a virgin overshadowed by the Holy Spirit, conceives and gives birth to Jesus: a divine initiative. Elizabeth recognises the presence of the Messiah even while still in the mother's womb; she proclaims Mary's unborn child as 'my Lord'. Zechariah recognises the birth of Jesus as a time of divine visitation, and declares him as saviour, while announcing the role of John as precursor of the Messiah. Simeon (and by association, Anna) makes it publicly known in the Temple that the mission of the Messiah extends beyond Israel to include the nations.

In these two chapters, Luke has crafted the preview of the entirety of the narrative of Luke-Acts:

---

75 For other instances where the Spirit leads people in the narrative of Luke-Acts, see Jesus (Luke 4:1); Philip (Acts 8:29); Peter (Acts 11:12); Paul and Barnabas (Acts 13:2); Paul (16:6–10; 20:22).
76 Bock, *Luke 1:1–9:50*, 252.

pre-Jesus (in John), Jesus' arrival (in Mary), Jesus' status and mission recognised (in Elizabeth and Zechariah), and the scope of his mission announced (in Simeon). These characters make very confronting and profound statements about Jesus' identity and his mission. This raises the question concerning their authority which also puts to test the legitimacy of their ministry and utterances. Luke addresses this by asserting for each of them the infilling with the Holy Spirit, the same Spirit of God which was the legitimating authority for those who acted in the name of God in the OT. The references to the Holy Spirit / Spirit of God for the Gentile reader already lends credence to the individuals possessed by this Spirit. Therefore, while earlier interpreters may be right that the Spirit empowers mission and / or inspires witnessing / prophecy, this article has argued that Luke does not simply narrate these accounts of the Spirit-filled individuals just to announce their relationship with the Spirit of God, or simply to state that they were inspired by the Spirit of God. Instead, Luke tells the story of their Spirit-endowment in order to demonstrate that who they are and what they embody / utter are authentic and legitimate. The empowerment and inspiration of the Spirit points to an end: legitimation. The Holy Spirit becomes the answer to every question of the reader. For every why, how, and what? Luke answers: it is by the authority of the Holy Spirit. Luke appeals to the Holy Spirit to provide justification and explanation to readers / hearers concerning the things about which they have been instructed (1:4). This is exactly what legitimation does. Even where it seems that the Spirit enables inspired speech, there must be the reason for appealing to the Spirit for that purpose. The legitimation of the pneumatic characters and their participation in the divine purpose provides that reason both here in the infancy narrative and in the rest of Luke-Acts.

Francis Innocent Otobo
Yarra Theological Union
University of Divinity
frotobo1@yahoo.com

Bibliography

Barrett, C. K. — *The Gospel according to John* (Philadelphia, PA: Westminster, 1978).

Berger, P. L. — *The Social Reality of Religion* (Ringwood, Victoria: Penguin Harmondsworth, 1973).

Berger, P., and L. Thomas — *The Social Construction of Reality: A Treatise in the Sociology of Knowledge* (London: Penguin, 1966).

Bock, D. L. — *Luke* (Downers Grove IL: IVP Academic, 1994).

Bock, D. L. — *Luke 1:1—9:50* (Grand Rapids, MI: Baker Academic, 1994).

Bonnah, G. K. A. — *The Holy Spirit: A Narrative Factor in the Acts of the Apostles* (Stuttgart: Verlag Katholisches Bibelwerk, 2007).

Borg, M. J. — *The God We Never Knew: Beyond Dogmatic Religion to a More Authentic Contemporary Faith* (New York, NY: HarperCollins, 1997).

Bovon, F. — *Luke 1: A Commentary on the Gospel of Luke 1:1—9:50* (Minneapolis, MN: Fortress, 2002).

Brown, R. E. — *The Birth of the Messiah: A Commentary on the Gospels of Matthew and Luke* (Garden City, NY: Image Books, 1979).

Brown, R. E. — *The Gospel according to John I—IX* (New Haven, CT: Yale University Press, 1966).

Burkert, W. — *Greek Religion* (Malden, MA: Blackwell Publishing, 1985).

Carroll, J. T. — *The Holy Spirit in the New Testament* (Nashville, TN: Abingdon, 2018).

Creed, J. M. — *The Gospel According to St. Luke: The Greek Text with Introduction, Notes and Indices* (London: Macmillan, 1953).

Dunn, J. D. G. — *The Acts of the Apostles* (Peterborough: Epworth Press, 1996).

Esler, P. F. — *Community and Gospel in Luke-Acts: The Social and Political Motivations of Lucan Theology* (Oakleigh, Melbourne: Cambridge University Press, 1987).

Evans, C. F. — *Saint Luke* (Philadelphia, PA: Trinity PressIntl, 1990).

Fitzmyer, J. A. — *The Gospel According to Luke I—IX* (AB 28; New York, NY: Doubleday, 1970).

Globe, A. — 'Some Doctrinal Variants in Matthew 1 and Luke 2, and the Authority of the Neutral Text', *Catholic Biblical Quarterly* 42.1 (1980), 52–72.

Godet, F. L. — *Commentary on the Gospel of Luke*. Vol. 1 (Grand Rapids, MI: Zondervan, 1887).

Green, J. B. — *The Gospel of Luke* (Grand Rapids, MI: Eerdmans, 1997).

Harrington, W. J. — *Luke—Gracious Theologian: The Jesus of Luke* (Dublin: Columba Press, 1997).

Hur, J. — *Dynamic Reading of the Holy Spirit in Luke-Acts* (London: T&T Clark International, 2004).

Johnson, L. T.	*The Acts of the Apostles* (Collegeville, MN: Liturgical Press, 1992).
Johnson, L. T.	*The Gospel of Luke* (Collegeville, MN: Liturgical Press, 1991).
Keener, C. S.	'Power of Pentecost: Luke's Missiology in Acts 1—2', *AJPS* 12.1 (2009), 47–73.
Keener, C. S.	'The Spirit and the Mission of the Church in Acts 1—2', *JETS* 62.1 (2019), 25–45.
Köstenberger, A. J.	*John* (Grand Rapids, MI: Baker Academic, 2004).
Kuecker, A.	*The Spirit and the 'Other': Social Identity, Ethnicity and Intergroup Reconciliation in Luke-Acts* (London: Bloomsbury, 2011).
Landry, D. T.	'Narrative Logic in the Annunciation to Mary (Luke 1:26–38)', *Journal of Biblical Literature* 114.1 (1995), 65–79.
Legrand, L.	*The Biblical Doctrine of Virginity* (London: G. Chapman, 1963).
Lincoln, A. T.	*Born of a Virgin? Reconceiving Jesus in the Bible, Tradition, and Theology* (Grand Rapids, MI: Eerdmans, 2013).
Lincoln, A. T.	'Theology and History in the Interpretation of Luke's Pentecost', *Expository Times* 96.7 (1985), 204–209.
Marshall, I. H.	*Commentary on Luke* (NIGTC; Grand Rapids, MI: Eerdmans, 1978).
Menzies, R. P.	*The Development of Early Christian Pneumatology with Special Reference to Luke-Acts* (JSNTSup 54; Sheffield: JSOT Press, 1991).
Menzies, R. P.	*Empowered for Witness: The Spirit in Luke-Acts* (Sheffield: Sheffield Academic Press, 1994).
Miller, D. R.	*Empowered for Global Mission: A Missionary Look at the Book of Acts* (Springfield, MO: Life, 2005).
Minear, P. S.	'Luke's Use of the Birth Stories', In Leander E. Keck and J. Louis Martyn (eds.), *Studies in Luke-Acts* (London: SPCK, 1968), 111–130.
Mullins, M.	*The Acts of the Apostles: A Commentary* (Dublin: Columba Press, 2013).
Mullins, M.	*The Gospel of Luke: A Commentary* (Dublin: Columba Press, 2010).
Na'Aman, N.	'The "Discovered Book" and the Legitimation of Josiah's Reform', *JBL* 130.1 (2011), 47–62.
Neyrey, J. H.	'The Symbolic Universe of Luke-Acts: "They Turn the World Upside Down"', in *The Social World of Luke-Acts: Models for Interpretation* (Peabody, MA: Hendrickson, 1991).
Nolland, J.	*Luke 1–9:20* (WBC; Dallas, TX: Word, 1989).
Oliver, H. H.	'The Lucan Birth Stories and the Purpose of Luke-Acts', *New Testament Studies* 10 (1964), 202–26.

Penney, J. M.	*The Missionary Emphasis of Lukan Pneumatology* (Sheffield: Sheffield Academic Press, 1997).
Reid, B. E.	*Choosing the Better Part?: Women in the Gospel of Luke* (Collegeville, MN: The Liturgical Press, 1996).
Shelton, J. B.	'"Filled with the Holy Spirit" and "Full of the Holy Spirit": Lucan Redactional Phrases', In Paul Elbert (ed.), *Faces of Renewal: Studies in Honor of Stanley M. Horton* (Peabody, MA: Hendrickson, 1988), 81–107.
Shelton, J. B.	*Mighty in Word and Deed: The Role of the Holy Spirit in Luke-Acts* (Peabody, MA: Hendrickson, 1991).
Shepherd, W. H.	*The Narrative Function of the Holy Spirit as a Character in Luke-Acts* (Atlanta, GA: Scholars, 1994).
Stronstad, R.	*The Charismatic Theology of St. Luke: Trajectories from the Old Testament to Luke-Acts* (Grand Rapids, MI: Baker Academic, 2012).
Tabor, J. D.	*The Jesus Dynasty: The Hidden History of Jesus, his Royal Family, and the Birth of Christianity* (New York, NY: Simon & Schuster, 2006).
Talbert, C. H.	*Reading Luke-Acts in its Mediterranean Milieu* (Leiden: Brill, 2003).
Tannehill, R. C.	*The Narrative Unity of Luke-Acts. Vol. 1: The Gospel According to Luke* (Philadelphia, PA: Fortress, 1986).
Tatum, W. B.	'The Epoch of Israel: Luke I—II and the Theological Plan of Luke-Acts', *New Testament Studies* 13.2 (1967), 184–95.
Turner, M. M. B.	*Power from on High: The Spirit in Israel's Restoration and Witness in Luke-Acts* (Eugene, OR: Wipf & Stock, 2000).
Turner, M. M. B.	'The Spirit of Christ and "Divine" Christology', In Joel B. Green and Max Turner (eds.), *Jesus of Nazareth Lord and Christ: Essays on the Historical Jesus and New Testament Christology* (Grand Rapids, MI: Eerdmans, 1994), 413–36.
Turner, M. M. B.	'The Spirit of Christ and Christology', In H. H. Rowdon (ed.), *Christ the Lord. Studies in Christology Presented to Donald Guthrie* (Leicester: Intervarsity Press, 1982), 168–90.

Global evangelism in Jesus' Temple destruction / last times discourse in Luke-Acts and in synoptic tradition
Confluence, congruence, intertextual linkages, and connective shaping

PATRICK COLE

Abstract

Jesus' temple destruction / last times discourse in Luke 21:5–36 shows very close narrative / structural confluence and linguistic congruence with Mark's account. Any Lukan editorial narrative abbreviations arguably allow him to import putatively 'reliable eyewitness' material distinct to him, which resonates with, enhances, but never contradicts, Mark's account.

While Luke's non-inclusion of Jesus' command in Mark 13:10 to evangelise all nations before the Parousia begs attention, the Luke 24:44–49//Acts 1:6–9 narrative 'hinge' between Luke's Gospel and Acts may provide a key to understanding this omission.

This 'hinge' material allows insertion of Lukan ascension narrative content including a parallel 'global evangelism' command from Jesus with post-resurrection kerygmatic content and focus. It also helps unlock a rich network of intertextual prophetic (principally Isaianic) references within Luke's putative 'eyewitness account' material inserted into Luke 21:14–28, locating the Lord's global evangelism command within Old Testament prophecies pointing to Jesus as the Servant Saviour 'light to the Gentiles'.

1. The Problem and Mapping the Terrain

If we adopt as our working hypothesis the broad post-Cadbury consensus that Luke-Acts is most likely a two-volume work, written by the same author,[1] why is it that Jesus' temple destruction / last times discourse ('the discourse') in Luke 21:5–36 does not include the explicit 'global evangelism imperative' seen in the parallel Matthean and Markan accounts (Mark 13:10//Matthew 24:14)? Why would the Gospel writer most engaged in documenting and celebrating the early church's proclamation of Jesus' gospel to the Gentile world in Acts omit this? In exploring solutions, we will examine the Lukan material (the discourse, plus other Lukan 'global evangelism imperative'-related texts) alongside the wider synoptic text tradition. We will see that close textual comparison[2] reveals extraordinarily high levels of *narrative confluence* (identifiable conceptual alignment, despite linguistic differences) and *literary congruence* (identical or near-identical phrases and / or words in Koine Greek). Parallel examination of possible specific Lukan intertextual linkages and connective shaping of material will suggest possible explanations for differing synoptic narrative approaches, notably the apparent Lukan 'omission' noted above.

On balance, a narrative-critical / revised literary-critical approach, such as espoused by Keener and Bauer for Acts, focusing on the text as received and as understood by the original readers / hearers,[3] seems most likely to be productive. That said, at times questions of sources, literary form and possible redactive activity will necessarily arise and be addressed, while minimising any disruption to the overall approach.

First, while mapping the Lukan terrain, the parallel Luke-Acts introductory dedications / introductions to Theophilus, the presumed sponsor (Luke 1:1–4 and Acts 1:1–2), suggest a close mutual literary relationship, broadly confirmed by reference to style and content. The working hypothesis of Lukan authorship of an inter-connected Luke-Acts initially underpins, and is then confirmed by, the sketching of resonances between arguably discourse-related 'global evangelism imperative' texts in Acts 1 and in Luke 24.

Secondly, the Gospel writer makes explicit claims about his research process and product (Luke 1:1–4), saying that 'many' predecessors have 'set their hand to the orderly compiling of an account' (πολλοὶ ἐπεχείρησαν ἀνατάξασθαι διήγησιν).[4] This 'orderly compiling' process by Luke's predecessors seems to have involved written products (as implied by ἐπεχείρησαν[5] and the technical meaning of διήγησις, denoting written narrative [see below]), that is an effort of 'many' to collect in writing fragmentary traditions of original oral and memory-based sources.[6]

Thirdly, although διήγησις was a well-established term in contemporary secular historiography, denoting a narrative history,[7] by describing *his* work as καθεξῆς γράψαι ('to write in order / an ordered account'), Luke may be signalling a subtle genre adjustment in his work *away* from the classical Hellenist / Roman usage of διήγησις (or its Latin equivalent '*narratio*') and the editorial / inventive wriggle-room inherent in both terms for writers at times to simply invent events or

---

1   See Morris, *Luke*, 14–22; Bock, *Luke*, 4–7; Nolland, *Luke 1–9:20*, xxxiii–xxxvii, Garland, *Luke*, 21–24; and Keener, *Acts*, 402–16.
2   Working with the SBLGNT Koine Greek text of Luke-Acts in Holmes, *The Greek New Testament*.
3   Keener, *Acts*, 18–20; Bauer, *Acts*, 12–14.
4   The natural sense of πολλοί arguably denotes at very least around five (and intuitively maybe more likely in the 10–20 range) predecessors and potential documentary sources. This seems borne out by textual analysis (for example identification various 'runs' of uniquely 'Lukan' material in his Gospel), consistent with the source complexity issues highlighted by commentators such as Bock, *Luke*, 915–17.
5   Bock, *Luke*, 56 n.11.
6   As *per* Nolland, *Luke 1–9:20*, 6.
7   Fitzmyer, *Luke I–IX*, 173 and 292; Bock, *Luke*, 53 and 56; Nolland, *Luke 1–9:20*, xxxi and 6. Fitzmyer in particular usefully tracks the use of διήγησις in detail in Hellenic and Roman authors.

dialogue.⁸ The latter looks distinctly at odds with both Luke's explicit authorial intentions (careful investigation and accurate reflection of eyewitness accounts of things actually 'completed among us')⁹ and his finished product. So, while retaining some traditional historiographical flexibility with linguistic expression, contextual descriptions, and editorial grouping of some teaching and events, Luke 'is not careless, nor is he a fabricator of events'.¹⁰ Nolland and Bruce both note (the latter especially referencing the discourse) that where we can cross-check with other sources, Luke seems especially conservative in reproducing the words of Jesus compared with surrounding narrative.¹¹

Consistent with this Gospel preamble editorial 'control language', our study will confirm that Luke appears wary of fundamentally reshaping what his research seems to have reliably suggested was a true reflection of what was *actually* said or done by Jesus himself. Even when he might have exercised some linguistic flexibility with accurate and sensitive Koine Greek reflection of speech or materials potentially made or recorded in Aramaic, the evidence seems to be of Luke giving weight to Koine Greek speech-reporting traditions and materials available to him from recognised elders / eyewitnesses, even when he is eminently capable of recasting / rephrasing this material in far better Koine Greek. Thus it does indeed appear that Luke seeks to operate in a narrative genre which is 'better' and more rigorous than διήγησις, precisely so that his patron, Theophilus, might know 'the truth / reliability' of 'the words' he has been taught (ἵνα ἐπιγνῷς περὶ ὧν κατηχήθης λόγων τὴν ἀσφάλειαν), by inference in particular of the spoken words of Jesus reported to Luke.

2. Looking at the 'Discourse' Koine Greek Texts in Luke-Acts and the Synoptic Gospels

In order to review the global evangelism imperative in the Lukan version of the temple destruction / last days discourse compared with synoptic tradition and related Luke-Acts material, some form of comparative textual analysis is needed, laying Luke 21:5–36 alongside the parallel narratives found (by and large) in Matthew 24:1–36//Mark 13:1–32. But a complete comparison arguably also requires inclusion of Luke 24:44–49 and Acts 1:6–9, which apparently draw on parallel and relevant narrative traditions and recollections.

First, setting the three directly parallel synoptic Gospel texts side by side, using graphic highlighting and text underlining (see Figures 1, 3 and 4), demonstrates an extraordinary degree of *structural symmetry*. Though some insertions are found only in Luke or Matthew compared with Mark, all three Synoptic Gospels follow an effectively identical sequence of thematically-centred clusters of sentences or pericopes, independent of precise linguistic content. This structural

---

8   Despite implicitly connecting his work with that of his predecessors by the words ἔδοξε κἀμοί ('it seemed good to me also'), he moves from speaking of διήγησις (with regard to the works of *others*) to describing *his work* as καθεξῆς γράψαι, 'to write in order/an ordered account'. Classical authors defined διήγησις / narratio as allowing the author to construct a narrative describing things which 'have happened <u>or as though they had happened</u>' (as per Aelius Theon, *Progymnasmata*, mid-late First Century AD) or 'setting forth of things as done <u>or as might have been done</u>' (Cicero, *De Inventione*, 1.19,27, 84BC) (Διήγημά ἐστι λόγος ἐκθετικὸς πραγμάτων γεγονότων ἢ ὡς γεγονότων, and 'narratio est rerum gestarum aut ut gestarum expositio' respectively): see Fitzmyer, *Luke I–IX*, 173, and Stavroula, 'Metaphrasis', 33.
9   Noting Luke's claims that his checking and editorial process aimed for an 'ordered account', requiring him to 'carefully investigate' (παρηκολουθηκότι ἄνωθεν πᾶσιν ἀκριβῶς) and check his sources for accurate eyewitness accounts of the life of Christ regarding the things *actually* 'completed among us' (περὶ τῶν πεπληροφορημένων ἐν ἡμῖν πραγμάτων).
10 Bock, *Luke*, 62–63.
11 Bruce, *Acts*, 18–19; Nolland, *Luke 1–9:20*, xxxi.

narrative coherence and symmetry is particularly marked in the first section of the discourse (Mark 13:1–10//Luke 21:5–13//Matthew 24:1–14).

Secondly, we see very high levels of *narrative congruence* (common elements) and *literary confluence* (common vocabulary and phrases), notably:

- *the context*: Jesus and the disciples in or leaving the Jerusalem temple, with interlocutors commending the building;
- *Jesus' initial response*: a warning that 'no stone will be left on another';
- *later questioning of Jesus* as to when this will happen and what signs will precede it;
- *Jesus' more detailed response* (with some nuanced synoptic differences):
  - the disciples are to be on careful watch so that they are not deceived;
  - many will come in Jesus' name, claiming to be him;
  - the disciples will hear of 'wars and rumours of wars', but they are not to be alarmed or afraid, because 'the end is still to come';
  - nations will rise against nations, and kingdoms against kingdoms;
  - there will be famines and earthquakes in various places;
  - there will be seizure, betrayal, persecution, and execution of believers;
  - followers of Jesus will be hated by everyone / all nations;
  - but faithful followers of Jesus who endure to the end will be saved;
  - a destructive desolating event will overtake Jerusalem and the temple, from which Christ-followers in Judaea must flee urgently and decisively, and which will cause enormous suffering;
  - there will be cosmic signs and frightening disturbance of the earthly order;
  - but the world will then see 'the Son of Man coming in a cloud with power and great glory';
  - like the fig tree shoots show that summer is coming, so these events will be a sign that 'it' (by inference the end of time and Jesus' restoration of God's kingdom on earth) is near; and,
  - an assurance that 'this generation' will not pass away until all these things happen.

Some of the above parallels may be debatable at the margins but this should not detract from the high level of congruence underscored by the three texts sharing: identical Koine Greek phrases at key points; Greek nouns and verbs with minor adjustments; and clauses reflecting directly parallel thoughts or statements (even when the actual Koine Greek vocabulary used differs).

That said, we also need to note some striking *differences*:

- *Matthew's inclusion of extra material* found in neither Mark or Luke, namely:
  - a warning from Jesus against false Christs (24:26);
  - a warning from Jesus that many followers will turn away from the faith (24:10–12)
  - an assurance from Jesus that the 'coming of the Son of Man' will be clearly visible to all (24:27); and,
  - Jesus' assurance that a sign of the coming of the Son of Man will appear in the heavens, which will cause 'mourning' amongst 'all the peoples of the earth' (24:30);

- *significant sections shared by Matthew and Mark* (but not Luke) covering:
  a requirement that 'the gospel' will / must be preached 'to all nations', prior to other things predicted or 'the end' (Matt. 24:14//Mark 13:10);
  - detail of the coming disaster to befall Jerusalem, that is an 'abomination' in the holy place / where it does not belong, which understanding readers will recognise when they see it

(Matt. 24:15//Mark 13:14); and a call to prayer that the disaster will not fall in winter, leading to unparalleled suffering, which the chosen could not survive unless God shortens its duration (Matt. 24:20–22//Mark 18–20);
- a short reference by Jesus to false messiahs 'at that time' deceiving believers (Matt. 24:23–25//Mark 13:21–22 and 23b);
- an assurance from Jesus that when the Son of Man comes 'on the clouds', he will send his angels to gather in the chosen (Matt. 24:31//Mark 13:27); and,
- Jesus' declaration that the timing of 'that day' (by inference, of the coming of the Son of Man in glory) is known only to God the Father, not to Jesus nor the angels (Matt. 24:36//Mark 13:32);

- *language shared by Mark and Luke* (but not Matthew), where Jesus tells the disciples:
  - they will testify to Jesus 'before kings and governors', and be given the right words by Jesus / the Holy Spirit when needed (Mark 13:11//Luke 21:13); and,
  - intimate family members will betray them (Mark 13:12//Luke 21:16);

- *Mark's declaration* (not shared by Matthew or Luke) that it was Peter, James, John, and Andrew who continued the questioning of Jesus about when the temple would be destroyed, and the sign of its imminence (Mark 13:3); and,

- *Luke's inclusion of material* not paralleled in Matthew or Mark, namely:
'pestilences' (Luke 21:11) being one earthly sign of cosmic distress, additional to the parallel listings in Matthew 24:7//Mark 13:8;
  - Jesus' assurance of providing the disciples with words and wisdom that adversaries will be unable to resist or contradict (Luke 21:15);
  - Jesus' assurance that 'not a hair of your head will perish' (Luke 21:18);
  - Jesus' warning that Jerusalem being 'surrounded by armies' will be the sign of the city's imminent destruction, a 'time of punishment in fulfilment of all that has been written', and a sign of 'wrath against this people' (Luke 21:20,22,23);
  - a curious prophetic saying by Jesus that 'this people' 'will fall by the sword and will be taken as prisoners to all the nations, and Jerusalem will be trampled on by the Gentiles until the times of the Gentiles are fulfilled' (Luke 21:24);
  - Jesus' encouragement to the disciples, when they see the signs he has prophesied taking place, to 'stand up and lift up your heads, because your redemption is drawing near' (Luke 21:28);
  - Jesus' warning the disciples to guard against self-indulgence and the anxieties of life so as to be ready for 'the day' of the coming of Jesus' end-days kingdom (Luke 21:34–35); and,
  - Jesus' call on the disciples to pray to 'escape' what is to happen, and to be able to 'stand' (as faithful followers who endure to the end) before the reigning Son of Man (Luke 21:36b).

Differences notwithstanding, the first two main sections of the Lukan discourse in particular show not just a very high level of structural confluence and textual congruence, but also apparent Lukan compression of Markan / proto-Markan material alongside the insertion of uniquely Lukan 'eyewitness account' material. We will see that this material sympathetically harmonises with, strengthens, and deeply enriches the Markan account, possibly by recovering memories of heavily intertextual elements of Jesus' speech, and of Jesus' pre-ascension explanations.

Our study will in particular suggest that these insertions transformatively reinforce Jesus' 'global evangelism' command / prediction in Mark 13:10//Matthew 24:14, even though omitted by Luke in that explicit format. Hinted at in Luke 21:13, the intertextual insertions make global evangelism not just a free-standing command from Jesus, but a divine imperative embedded in Old Testament Scripture, and given personally by the Father to Jesus. This imperative defines both Jesus' character and eternal work (including by the Spirit through the church) as the Isaianic Servant who 'must be' the 'light to the Gentiles'. For those with ears to hear, this enrichment points forward to when clear content and global focus to the 'gospel' message will be crystallised, along with repetition of the explicit global evangelism command from Jesus, in the ascension narratives at the end of 'volume one' (Luke's Gospel), and an 'it is written' programmatic schema and impetus for the start of 'volume two' (Acts). The disciples are then called to join, as Jesus' servants, in this servanthood-defining task.

3. Comparative Textual Analysis in a Narrative Framework

(A) The Discourse Part 1: Temple, Trials and Testimony (Mark 13:1–10; Luke 21:5–13; Matthew 24:1–14)

Dividing the discourse into three segments for analysis is somewhat arbitrary. But the discourse's first segment—set out with parallel synoptic texts in Figure 1—most graphically reflects extraordinarily high levels of structural symmetry, narrative confluence, and textual congruence, even compared with following segments.

There is considerable commentator debate over perceived Lukan versus Markan / Matthean discrepancies over the *context of the discourse* (location, interlocutors, and movement).[12] However, on balance, a natural narrative non-atomised reading of Luke 20:45—21:5, sensitive both to audience and movement 'markers' and to Luke's tendency to condense, compact, and remove detail not essential to his narrative purpose,[13] may resolve any question of synoptic conflict. So while Luke includes none of the explicit geographical / contextual markers of Mark 13:1–4//Matthew 24:1–3, a natural reading of Luke 21:5–7 does not necessarily *force* inconsistency with those accounts. Indeed, Luke's narrative can be plausibly read as moving with the Markan account.[14]

This is consistent with the strong structural confluence we see in the discourse's very first segment, despite significant linguistic / narrative variation, including between Mark and Matthew (Mark 13:1–3//Luke 21:5–6//Matthew 24:1–3a). Luke 21:6 directly repeats the vocabulary of Mark's 13:2b account of Jesus' prophecy of the temple stones being cast down (οὐ μὴ ἀφεθῇ ὧδε λίθος ἐπὶ λίθον ὃς οὐ μὴ καταλυθῇ), and almost exactly the Koine Greek words at the core of this (the rhythmic λίθος ἐπὶ λίθον, and λίθῳ ὃς οὐ μὴ καταλυθήσεται/ καταλυθῇ) ('stone on stone', and 'all will be thrown down').

Even more strongly in the rest of the first segment, we see precise parallels across all three Synoptics in the *ordering* of the subject material of Jesus' speech. Luke apparently edits out material shared between Mark and Matthew (Mark 13:1a//Matthew 24:1a; Mark 13:3a//Matthew 24:3a; Mark 13:6b//Matthew 24:5b; and Mark 13:10//Matthew 24:14). But Luke nowhere includes Matthean vocabulary or whole phrases not found in Mark (Matthew 24:3b; 24:8; and 24:10–12).

Figure 1 shows repeated examples of very close and even precise linguistic congruence of 'runs' of Koine Greek phrases and words in:

---

12 Noted in Fitzmyer, *Luke X–XXIV*, 1326 and 1330; Nolland, *Luke 18:35 — 24:53*, 987; Bock, *Luke*, 1661; Garland, *Luke*, 827; and Bovon, *Luke 3*, 102 n.2.
13 Bock, *Luke*, 1661.
14 Morris, *Luke*, 295–96.

Figure 1

Mark 13:1–10	Luke 21:5–13	Matthew 24:1–14
13 Καὶ ἐκπορευομένου αὐτοῦ ἐκ τοῦ ἱεροῦ λέγει αὐτῷ εἷς τῶν μαθητῶν αὐτοῦ·Διδάσκαλε, ἴδε ποταποὶ λίθοι καὶ ποταπαὶ οἰκοδομαί. ² καὶ ὁ Ἰησοῦς εἶπεν αὐτῷ· Βλέπεις ταύτας τὰς μεγάλας οἰκοδομάς; οὐ μὴ ἀφεθῇ ὧδε λίθος ἐπὶ λίθον ὃς οὐ μὴ καταλυθῇ. ³ Καὶ καθημένου αὐτοῦ εἰς τὸ Ὄρος τῶν Ἐλαιῶν κατέναντι τοῦ ἱεροῦ ἐπηρώτα αὐτὸν κατ' ἰδίαν Πέτρος καὶ Ἰάκωβος καὶ Ἰωάννης καὶ Ἀνδρέας· ⁴ Εἰπὸν ἡμῖν πότε ταῦτα ἔσται, καὶ τί τὸ σημεῖον ὅταν μέλλῃ ταῦτα συντελεῖσθαι πάντα. ⁵ ὁ δὲ Ἰησοῦς ἤρξατο λέγειν αὐτοῖς·Βλέπετε μή τις ὑμᾶς πλανήσῃ· ⁶ πολλοὶ ἐλεύσονται ἐπὶ τῷ ὀνόματί μου λέγοντες ὅτι Ἐγώ εἰμι, καὶ πολλοὺς πλανήσουσιν. ⁷ ὅταν δὲ ἀκούσητε πολέμους καὶ ἀκοὰς πολέμων, μὴ θροεῖσθε· δεῖ γενέσθαι, ἀλλ' οὔπω τὸ τέλος. ⁸ ἐγερθήσεται γὰρ ἔθνος ἐπ' ἔθνος καὶ βασιλεία ἐπὶ βασιλείαν, ἔσονται σεισμοὶ κατὰ τόπους, ἔσονται λιμοί·ἀρχὴ ὠδίνων ταῦτα. ⁹ βλέπετε δὲ ὑμεῖς ἑαυτούς·παραδώσουσιν ὑμᾶς εἰς συνέδρια καὶ εἰς συναγωγὰς δαρήσεσθε καὶ ἐπὶ ἡγεμόνων καὶ βασιλέων σταθήσεσθε ἕνεκεν ἐμοῦ εἰς μαρτύριον αὐτοῖς. ¹⁰ καὶ εἰς πάντα τὰ ἔθνη πρῶτον δεῖ κηρυχθῆναι τὸ εὐαγγέλιον.	21⁵ Καί τινων λεγόντων περὶ τοῦ ἱεροῦ, ὅτι λίθοις καλοῖς καὶ ἀναθήμασιν κεκόσμηται εἶπεν· ⁶ Ταῦτα ἃ θεωρεῖτε, ἐλεύσονται ἡμέραι ἐν αἷς οὐκ ἀφεθήσεται λίθος ἐπὶ λίθῳ ὃς οὐ καταλυθήσεται. ⁷ Ἐπηρώτησαν δὲ αὐτὸν λέγοντες Διδάσκαλε, πότε οὖν ταῦτα ἔσται, καὶ τί τὸ σημεῖον ὅταν μέλλῃ ταῦτα γίνεσθαι; ⁸ ὁ δὲ εἶπεν Βλέπετε μὴ πλανηθῆτε· πολλοὶ γὰρ ἐλεύσονται ἐπὶ τῷ ὀνόματί μου λέγοντες· Ἐγώ εἰμι καί·Ὁ καιρὸς ἤγγικεν·μὴ πορευθῆτε ὀπίσω αὐτῶν. ⁹ ὅταν δὲ ἀκούσητε πολέμους καὶ ἀκαταστασίας, μὴ πτοηθῆτε·δεῖ γὰρ ταῦτα γενέσθαι πρῶτον, ἀλλ' οὐκ εὐθέως τὸ τέλος. ¹⁰ τότε ἔλεγεν αὐτοῖς Ἐγερθήσεται ἔθνος ἐπ' ἔθνος καὶ βασιλεία ἐπὶ βασιλείαν, ¹¹ σεισμοί τε μεγάλοι καὶ κατὰ τόπους λιμοὶ καὶ λοιμοὶ ἔσονται, φόβητρά τε καὶ σημεῖα ἀπ' οὐρανοῦ μεγάλα ἔσται. ¹² Πρὸ δὲ τούτων πάντων ἐπιβαλοῦσιν ἐφ' ὑμᾶς τὰς χεῖρας αὐτῶν καὶ διώξουσιν, παραδιδόντες εἰς τὰς συναγωγὰς καὶ φυλακάς, ἀπαγομένους ἐπὶ βασιλεῖς καὶ ἡγεμόνας ἕνεκεν τοῦ ὀνόματός μου· ¹³ ἀποβήσεται ὑμῖν εἰς μαρτύριον.	24 Καὶ ἐξελθὼν ὁ Ἰησοῦς ἀπὸ τοῦ ἱεροῦ ἐπορεύετο, καὶ προσῆλθον οἱ μαθηταὶ αὐτοῦ ἐπιδεῖξαι αὐτῷ τὰς οἰκοδομὰς τοῦ ἱεροῦ· ² ὁ δὲ ἀποκριθεὶς εἶπεν αὐτοῖς· Οὐ βλέπετε ταῦτα πάντα; ἀμὴν λέγω ὑμῖν, οὐ μὴ ἀφεθῇ ὧδε λίθος ἐπὶ λίθον ὃς οὐ καταλυθήσεται. ³ Καθημένου δὲ αὐτοῦ ἐπὶ τοῦ Ὄρους τῶν Ἐλαιῶν προσῆλθον αὐτῷ οἱ μαθηταὶ κατ' ἰδίαν λέγοντες. Εἰπὸν ἡμῖν πότε ταῦτα ἔσται, καὶ τί τὸ σημεῖον τῆς σῆς παρουσίας καὶ συντελείας τοῦ αἰῶνος. ⁴ καὶ ἀποκριθεὶς ὁ Ἰησοῦς εἶπεν αὐτοῖς. Βλέπετε μή τις ὑμᾶς πλανήσῃ· ⁵ πολλοὶ γὰρ ἐλεύσονται ἐπὶ τῷ ὀνόματί μου λέγοντες· Ἐγώ εἰμι ὁ χριστός, καὶ πολλοὺς πλανήσουσιν. ⁶ μελλήσετε δὲ ἀκούειν πολέμους καὶ ἀκοὰς πολέμων ὁρᾶτε, μὴ θροεῖσθε·δεῖ γὰρ γενέσθαι, ἀλλ' οὔπω ἐστὶν τὸ τέλος. ⁷ ἐγερθήσεται γὰρ ἔθνος ἐπ' ἔθνος καὶ βασιλεία ἐπὶ βασιλείαν, καὶ ἔσονται λιμοὶ καὶ σεισμοὶ κατὰ τόπους· ⁸ πάντα δὲ ταῦτα ἀρχὴ ὠδίνων. ⁹ Τότε παραδώσουσιν ὑμᾶς εἰς θλῖψιν καὶ ἀποκτενοῦσιν ὑμᾶς, καὶ ἔσεσθε μισούμενοι ὑπὸ πάντων τῶν ἐθνῶν διὰ τὸ ὄνομά μου.* ¹⁰ καὶ τότε σκανδαλισθήσονται πολλοὶ καὶ ἀλλήλους παραδώσουσιν καὶ μισήσουσιν ἀλλήλους· ¹¹ καὶ πολλοὶ ψευδοπροφῆται ἐγερθήσονται καὶ πλανήσουσιν πολλούς· ¹² καὶ διὰ τὸ πληθυνθῆναι τὴν ἀνομίαν ψυγήσεται ἡ ἀγάπη τῶν πολλῶν. ¹³ ὁ δὲ ὑπομείνας εἰς τέλος οὗτος σωθήσεται. # ¹⁴ καὶ κηρυχθήσεται τοῦτο τὸ εὐαγγέλιον τῆς βασιλείας ἐν ὅλῃ τῇ οἰκουμένῃ εἰς μαρτύριον πᾶσιν τοῖς ἔθνεσιν, καὶ τότε ἥξει τὸ τέλος.

Key:
- Concepts shared by all 3 Synoptics
- Concepts shared by Mark/Luke
- Concepts shared by Luke/Matthew
- Concepts shared by Mark/Matthew
- Mark only
- Luke only
- Matthew only

Vocabulary shared
Exact words/phrases shared

* Matthew 24:9b seems to find its parallel in Mark 13:13a and Luke 21:17
\# Matthew 24:13 seems to find its parallel in Mark 13:13b

- Mark 13:2b//Luke 21:6b//Matthew 24:2b;
- Mark 13:5–6//Luke 21:8//Matthew 24:4–5;
- Mark 13:7//Luke 21:9//Matthew 24:6;
- Mark 13:8//Luke 21:10–11//Matthew 24:7; and,
- Mark 13:9//Luke 21:12–13//Matthew 24:9.[15]

Luke does seem to undertake relatively minor stylistic reshaping of some narrative material appearing also in Mark, around the edges of verbatim / near-verbatim Markan Koine Greek material reflecting Jesus' words. The most noticeable exception to this is probably the insertion of distinctly Lukan material in Luke 21:11–12, including words from Jesus. And while, as Bock notes, Luke 21:11 'provides the largest variation of wording of any verse in the discourse',[16] this is still within Fitzmyer's general observation that in the entire segment of Luke 21:8–11 (apart from the opening coda ὁ δὲ εἶπεν), 'Luke retains thirty-seven out of the fifty-one Marcan words'.[17]

Luke's abbreviated verse 8 opening coda compared with Mark—and even more so his inserted verse 10 opening coda—may (despite the close-to-identical Koine language of Mark 13:5–6a//Luke 21:8a) signal insertion of Lukan independently-sourced 'rounding out' words from Jesus in Luke 21:8b,9 and (as noted by Bovon) 11b and 12.[18] Bovon rightly highlights the linguistic significance of Luke's 21:11b insertion καὶ λοιμοὶ ἔσονται, φόβητρά τε καὶ σημεῖα ἀπ᾽ οὐρανοῦ μεγάλα ἔσται ('and there will be plagues, and there will be terrors and great signs from heaven'), namely 'the classical homonymous play on words, "famines and pestilences" (λιμοὶ καὶ λοιμοί) thereby introduced into this part of the discourse'.[19] But beyond being a 'classical homonymous play on words', this also seems to directly reflect the rhythmic cadences of the synoptically-shared λίθος ἐπὶ λίθον/ λίθῳ ('stone upon stone') words of Jesus in Mark 13:2//Luke 21:6//Matthew 24:2.

It is thus tempting to see here Lukan confidence that his putative independent eyewitness source for 21:8–12, running consistently alongside Mark 13:5–9, bears the marks of genuine consistency and authenticity seen in the Markan account, reflecting both the style and content of Jesus' oral teaching in Mark. His extra material is not just consistent with the Markan account, but suggestively rounds out / amplifies the Lord's words recorded in Mark, including by restoring an authentic rhythmic cadence in Luke 21:11 lost to Mark's interlocutor.[20]

Thus, where Luke does insert new language, it seems he is diligent to do so only when he is confident that eyewitness accounts available to him do not contradict the Markan (Petrine-sourced?) eyewitness account, and when they add important trustworthy and Mark-consistent material. He seems especially careful not to re-shape or materially re-cast Koine material which he judges authentically to convey the words and cadences of Jesus (even if conveying material possibly originally spoken in Aramaic).

So, despite Lukan introduction of material not found in Mark (Luke 21:1b,8b,11b,12a,12b), the overall impression from strictly comparative textual analysis of the parallel narrative texts is of a very close and most probably dependent (although not exclusive) text relationship between Luke and Mark (or at least a proto-Mark Koine Greek document). Comparative textual analysis also indicates Lukan co-dependence with Matthew on Mark, but not Lukan dependence on Matthew

---

15 Noting also that parts of Matthew 24:9b and Matthew 24:13 seem to find their full linguistic parallels 'out of sequence' in Mark 13:13a//Luke 21:17 and Mark 13:13b respectively.
16 Bock, *Luke*, 1688.
17 Fitzmyer, *Luke X–XXIV*, 1327.
18 Bovon, *Luke 3*, 106.
19 Bovon, *Luke 3*, 106.
20 This is even more probable if Bovon, *Luke 3*, 106, is right that 21:11b obviously reflects neither Luke's intentions nor his style.

(whose material is never favoured over Markan material).²¹ This of course generally aligns with the 'Mark first' and 'Lukan dependence on Markan material' theory broadly adopted by most commentators.²²

However, this raises even more acutely the question of why Luke apparently decides *not* to include some material shared by Mark and Matthew, crucially (for the purposes of this study) the clear 'global evangelism imperative' seen in Mark 13:10//Matthew 24:14.

(B) The Discourse Part 1: The 'Global Evangelism Imperative' and the Luke-Acts Narrative Hinge

The close Mark / Luke textual congruence seen above strongly suggests that Luke was both aware of the Markan text, and deferential to it, likely treating it as containing high-level reliable 'eyewitness testimony'. The direct textual congruence between Mark and Luke (but not Matthew) which resumes immediately afterwards in Mark 13:11–13//Luke 21:14–16 supports this conclusion. Yet not even the positive shades of near-repetition in Luke 21:13 of the final coda of Mark 13:9²³ adequately substitute for the imperative clarity of Mark 13:10, nor properly reflect the specific and focused Gentile mission interest in Luke's Gospel and Acts.

Setting Luke 24:44–48 and Acts 1:6–9 (narrating Jesus' ascension and a pre-ascension commissioning of his disciples) alongside Luke 21:5–13, and bringing these texts into direct engagement with key verses of Matthew 24:1–36 and Mark 13:1–32 (see **Figure 2**) may suggest a resolution.

The Luke-Acts ascension / commissioning narratives are unique to Luke, unreflected in Matthew, Mark, or John's Gospel (notwithstanding possible attenuated resonances with the 'longer endings' of Mark's Gospel (16:8b–20) and the Matthew 28:16–20 'Great Commission').²⁴ On closer examination, these narratives are not just one connective link between Luke and Acts,²⁵ but actually seem to be the *key narrative-connecting hinge*.²⁶ They form a narrative incident which unifies and connects, but also separates Luke's two volumes. The event appropriately both *closes* the account of Jesus' earthly life, and *opens* that of Jesus' work through the Holy Spirit to enable entry into his kingdom through the testimony of his disciples. The core of this narrative hinge is a global evangelism commissioning imperative from Jesus (making Luke's non-inclusion of Mark 13:10//Matthew 24:14 language in his version of Jesus' temple discourse even more intriguing).

---

21 The curious apparent Luke 21:6b//Matthew 24:2b agreement on the verbal form of a single word, the verb καταλύω (καταλυθήσεται compared with καταλυθῇ in Mark 13:2b), does not negate this. Luke has already gone a slightly different road to the shared Markan / Matthean formulation, with grammatical adjustment of their shared vocabulary (e.g. οὐκ ἀφεθήσεται rather than οὐ μὴ ἀφεθῇ ὧδε; and λίθος ἐπὶ λίθῳ rather than λίθος ἐπὶ λίθον). So he is not slavishly dependent on either (let alone Matthew over Mark) for grammatical form here. One might speculate on coincidental minor improvement of Mark's Koine Greek, or even shared usage of a trivially 'improved' Markan / proto-Markan text.
22 Morris, *Luke*, 59; Fitzmyer, *Luke I–IX*, 1326; Bock, *Luke*, 9; Nolland, *Luke 1 – 9:20*, xxix–xxx; Bauckham, *Jesus and the Eyewitnesses*, 146–47; Garland, *Luke*, 24; and Bovon, *Luke 3*, 103.
23 ἀποβήσεται ὑμῖν εἰς μαρτύριον / ἕνεκεν ἐμοῦ εἰς μαρτύριον αὐτοῖς, 'this will turn out for you to give testimony' / 'because of me as a testimony to them'.
24 Nolland, *Luke 18:35 – 24:53*, 1225–26.
25 Bock, *Acts*, 52.
26 Porter, 'The Unity of Luke-Acts', 135–36.

GLOBAL EVANGELISM IN JESUS' TEMPLE DESTRUCTION

Figure 2

Mark 13:10 & 32	Luke 24:44–48/Acts 1:6–8	Matthew 24:14 & 36
	24⁴⁴ Εἶπεν δὲ πρὸς αὐτούς· Οὗτοι οἱ λόγοι μου οὓς ἐλάλησα πρὸς ὑμᾶς ἔτι ὢν σὺν ὑμῖν, ὅτι δεῖ πληρωθῆναι πάντα τὰ γεγραμμένα ἐν τῷ νόμῳ Μωϋσέως καὶ προφήταις καὶ ψαλμοῖς περὶ ἐμοῦ. ⁴⁵ τότε διήνοιξεν αὐτῶν τὸν νοῦν τοῦ συνιέναι τὰς γραφάς, ⁴⁶ καὶ εἶπεν αὐτοῖς ὅτι οὕτως γέγραπται παθεῖν τὸν χριστὸν καὶ ἀναστῆναι ἐκ νεκρῶν τῇ τρίτῃ ἡμέρᾳ,	
13¹⁰ καὶ εἰς πάντα τὰ ἔθνη πρῶτον δεῖ κηρυχθῆναι τὸ εὐαγγέλιον	⁴⁷ καὶ κηρυχθῆναι ἐπὶ τῷ ὀνόματι αὐτοῦ μετάνοιαν καὶ ἄφεσιν ἁμαρτιῶν εἰς πάντα τὰ ἔθνη— ἀρξάμενοι ἀπὸ Ἰερουσαλήμ. ⁴⁸ ὑμεῖς ἐστε μάρτυρες τούτων.	24¹⁴ καὶ κηρυχθήσεται τοῦτο τὸ εὐαγγέλιον τῆς βασιλείας ἐν ὅλῃ τῇ οἰκουμένῃ εἰς μαρτύριον πᾶσιν τοῖς ἔθνεσιν, καὶ τότε ἥξει τὸ τέλος.
13³² Περὶ δὲ τῆς ἡμέρας ἐκείνης ἢ τῆς ὥρας οὐδεὶς οἶδεν, οὐδὲ οἱ ἄγγελοι ἐν οὐρανῷ οὐδὲ ὁ υἱός, εἰ μὴ ὁ πατήρ	¹⁶ Οἱ μὲν οὖν συνελθόντες ἠρώτων αὐτὸν λέγοντες· Κύριε, εἰ ἐν τῷ χρόνῳ τούτῳ ἀποκαθιστάνεις τὴν βασιλείαν τῷ Ἰσραήλ; 7 εἶπεν δὲ πρὸς αὐτούς· Οὐχ ὑμῶν ἐστιν γνῶναι χρόνους ἢ καιροὺς οὓς ὁ πατὴρ ἔθετο ἐν τῇ ἰδίᾳ ἐξουσίᾳ, ⁸ ἀλλὰ λήμψεσθε δύναμιν ἐπελθόντος τοῦ ἁγίου πνεύματος ἐφ' ὑμᾶς, καὶ ἔσεσθέ μου μάρτυρες ἔν τε Ἰερουσαλὴμ καὶ ἐν πάσῃ τῇ Ἰουδαίᾳ καὶ Σαμαρείᾳ καὶ ἕως ἐσχάτου τῆς γῆς.	24³⁶ Περὶ δὲ τῆς ἡμέρας ἐκείνης καὶ ὥρας οὐδεὶς οἶδεν, οὐδὲ οἱ ἄγγελοι τῶν οὐρανῶν οὐδὲ ὁ υἱός, εἰ μὴ ὁ πατὴρ μόνος.
13¹⁰ καὶ εἰς πάντα τὰ ἔθνη πρῶτον δεῖ κηρυχθῆναι τὸ εὐαγγέλιον		24¹⁴ καὶ κηρυχθήσεται τοῦτο τὸ εὐαγγέλιον τῆς βασιλείας ἐν ὅλῃ τῇ οἰκουμένῃ εἰς μαρτύριον πᾶσιν τοῖς ἔθνεσιν, καὶ τότε ἥξει τὸ τέλος.

Key:
- Concepts shared by all 3 Synoptics
- Concepts shared by Mark/Luke
- Concepts shared by Luke/Matthew
- Concepts shared by Mark/Matthew
- Mark only
- Luke only
- Matthew only

- Vocabulary shared
- Exact words/phrases shared

Commentators note that the uniquely Lukan material in both versions of the ascension / commissioning event (like the immediately preceding Emmaus Road encounter with the risen Lord, Luke 24:13–35) bear signs of Lukan editorial shaping.[27] The Emmaus Road and Luke 24:44–48 ascension / commissioning narrative also seemingly form a pair of closely-related narrative panels. Notably, in both Jesus 'opens the Scriptures' (law, prophets, and psalms) regarding himself, explaining the divine necessity of fulfilment of these Scriptures, a key Lukan theme.[28] The level of Lukan 'shaping' may reflect personal collecting / recording of these unique witness accounts, for example from the named Cleopas for the Emmaus Road narrative.[29]

Bock and Porter usefully summarise the debate whether Luke 24:44–49 and Acts 1:6–9 record the *same event* in the *same locale* (or if Luke manufactures a fictitious event).[30] On balance, Porter's analysis of geography and timelines / timing indicators in Luke 24 seems persuasive that there can be no clear presumption that in his Gospel Luke is asserting the ascension happened on the resurrection evening (and thus not 'after forty days', as per the Acts 1 account), or at a different place.[31] It is thus reasonable to presume that Luke is just applying narrative compression in Luke 24:44–53, and the same ascension event is being referenced in Luke 24//Acts 1, even if narratively presented slightly differently.[32]

We need not be surprised if Luke records Jesus' words from the same 'event' (likely extending well beyond the summaries in Luke 24//Acts 1) in different formulations, while still functioning as a single narrative hinge: given different narrative contexts (wrapping up Jesus' earthly ministry and gospel message; and mapping the start of the Holy Spirit's post-ascension ministry), Luke does not seemingly feel bound to record the same conversation for the same audience in full, or in identical terms.

That said, Figure 2 shows very close Koine Greek parallels between Luke 24 and Acts 1 and the global evangelism imperative recorded in Mark 13:10//Matthew 24:14. Notably, in Luke 24 Jesus is recorded as *commanding the preaching* of a specific message *to all the world*.

Luke 24:47, Mark 13:10, and Matthew 24:14 all use the phrase καὶ κηρυχθῆναι/ κηρυχθήσεται ('and is to be preached' / 'will be preached'). Luke 24:47 and Mark 13:10 carry an *identical* Koine formulation, using the aorist passive infinitive of κηρύσσω (to preach / proclaim as a herald). Matthew by contrast uses the future passive indicative of the same verb. While a close linguistic similarity is shared by all three Synoptics, Matthew's use of the future passive indicative could be read as indicating that (at least in that narrative context) Jesus was simply saying that preaching his gospel *would happen* in the future, ahead of 'the end'. If so, Luke 24:47 (with Mark 13:10) accentuates a significant if subtle difference compared with Matthew.

First, arguably an isolated 'natural reading' of all three of the 24:46–47 infinitives *already* demands (*contra* Bovon and Dupont)[33] that they be read as suggestive imperatives, with the sense '*must* suffer, *must* rise again, *must* be proclaimed', as per Bock, Fitzmyer, Garland, and Nolland.[34]

But secondly we note that in Luke 24:47, καὶ κηρυχθῆναι directly follows two other aorist infinitives in Luke 24:46 (παθεῖν, to suffer, and ἀναστῆναι, to rise again). All three immediately

---

27 Fitzmyer, *Luke X–XXIV*, 1554–56, and 1578–81; and Bock, *Luke*, 1904–05.
28 Garland, *Luke*, 974–75.
29 Bauckham, *Jesus and the Eyewitnesses*, 47.
30 Bock, *Luke*, 1927–30; and Porter, 'The Unity of Luke-Acts', 124–29.
31 Porter, 'The Unity of Luke-Acts', 125–29.
32 Bock, *Luke*; Garland, *Luke*, 969.
33 Bovon, *Luke 3*, 395 n.57.
34 Fitzmyer, *Luke X–XXIV*, 1579–80; Nolland, *Luke 18:35 – 24:53*, 1219; Bock, *Luke*, 1931, 1938; and Garland, *Luke*, 966–68; 974–75.

follow, and are dependent on, the ὅτι οὕτως γέγραπται ... τὸν χριστόν ('thus it is written ... the Christ') construction in Luke 24:46. Moreover, in terms of logical connection, natural 'narrative flow', and repetition of Koine language (γέγραπται/ γεγραμμένα), the Luke 24:46 construction and the following infinitives almost certainly should also be read as dependent on the ὅτι δεῖ πληρωθῆναι πάντα τὰ γεγραμμένα ἐν τῷ νόμῳ Μωϋσέως καὶ προφήταις καὶ ψαλμοῖς περὶ ἐμοῦ construction in 24:44 (the first six words in particular, literally 'that *must* be fulfilled all that is written'). Thus the 'natural reading' of the Luke 24:46–47 infinitives is arguably confirmed and strengthened by the narrative connection of Luke 24:46 with the preceding ὅτι δεῖ (the emphatic additional 'must be') in 24:44.[35]

Commentators have similarly noted the close correspondence of Luke 24:47 with Mark 13:10,[36] where the natural sense of the aorist passive infinitive is the same suggestive imperative 'must be preached', similarly strengthened by the preceding πρῶτον δεῖ ('first must be') formulation.[37] Thus Luke 24:47 seemingly completely shares Mark's understanding that Jesus had explicitly instructed his disciples that his message *must* be proclaimed.[38]

As to the message's *content*, Mark 13:10 and Matthew 24:14 record Jesus saying that this is to be τὸ εὐαγγέλιον (the gospel/good news). Luke 24 does not use that word, instead having Jesus (in the ascension / commissioning narrative context) commanding, more richly, ἐπὶ τῷ ὀνόματι αὐτοῦ μετάνοιαν καὶ ἄφεσιν ἁμαρτιῶν ('that repentance and forgiveness of sins in his name') is to be proclaimed, giving *content* to τὸ εὐαγγέλιον.

As to the *geographic / theopolitical focus of proclamation*,[39] Luke in Luke 24:47 understands this as *identical* to Mark 13:10's Koine Greek record of Jesus' words, namely εἰς πάντα τὰ ἔθνη ('to all nations'). The extra Lukan gloss to the focus of mission in Acts 1:8 is striking, spelling out its starting point, transition, and final reach.[40] The direct word-for-word LXX Isaianic reverberations of the last phrase (καὶ ἕως ἐσχάτου τῆς γῆς, 'and to the ends of the earth') are highly suggestive of a hyperlink to the Isaianic 'Servant' (especially to Isaiah 49) and his global 'good news' remit, thereby pointing to a rich substratum of submerged global evangelism commands which we will examine in Part 2 of the discourse.

So, despite the absence of 'global evangelism command' language directly reflecting Matthew 24:14//Mark 13:10 in Luke's version of Jesus' discourse, Luke 24:47 shows that Luke indeed shares Mark's understanding of the existence and reliability of such an eyewitness-based command. In light of this, Lukan omission of the Mark 13:10 language in the identical narrative context might be because:

- knowing and trusting the authority of Mark 13:10, Luke is not inclined to tamper with or edit it by importing words that are not part of a received high-level reliable eyewitness account;

---

35 This detailed flow of the Koine Greek is noted also by Pao, *Acts*, 87–88.
36 Nolland, *Luke 18:35 – 24:53*, 1219.
37 Lane, *Mark*, 459–62; Evans, *Mark 8:27 – 16:20*, 310; and Edwards, *Mark*, 393. That said, given Matthew's 24:14 reference καὶ τότε ἥξει τὸ τέλος (that this preaching would be a necessary precondition for 'the end' to come), and his recording of Jesus' 'Great Commission' mandate, it may be wise at this stage not to conclude from this a Mark / Luke versus Matthew 'difference', but rather to consider the possibility of a Matthean difference of localised editorial emphasis.
38 Maybe repeatedly, as with Luke's recording Jesus repeatedly telling his 'slow to understand' disciples of his coming betrayal, death, and resurrection in Jerusalem.
39 Pao, *Acts*, 94–96, perceptively notes that the missional focus is not just geographic, but also (he would argue primarily) theo-political, in terms of the extension of the kingdom of God beyond the Jewish nation to the Gentiles, both by ethnically-inclusive salvation and by global establishment of the Jewish Messiah's rule.
40 καὶ ἔσεσθέ μου μάρτυρες ἔν τε Ἰερουσαλὴμ καὶ ἐν πάσῃ τῇ Ἰουδαίᾳ καὶ Σαμαρείᾳ καὶ ἕως ἐσχάτου τῆς γῆς, 'and you will be my witnesses in Jerusalem and in all Judea and Samaria and to the ends of the earth'.

- but equally he may be reluctant to simply repeat the Markan wording in light of personal and audience-in-mind editorial concerns, as suggested by Fitzmyer.[41] While necessarily conjecture on the reasons for a concrete and observable linguistic phenomenon, it seems plausible that Luke avoids the bald use of εὐαγγέλιον because of potentially misleading and offensive resonances the word carried for Gentile and Jewish readers alike (and maybe personally for Luke's ostensible patron Theophilus), due to its usage in the pagan emperor cult[42] or other contemporary secular contexts;
- in any case, prior to the betrayal, suffering, death and resurrection of Jesus, the content of the message to be proclaimed is not yet fully clear;
- simultaneously, Luke's own 'reliable eyewitness' post-resurrection material, containing the two linked Emmaus Road and the commissioning / ascension narrative panels, tell him that the risen Christ *repeated* the Markan temple discourse global evangelism command, this time filling out εὐαγγέλιον with specific post-resurrection message content; and,
- this material was ideal to form a narrative hinge between the Gospel and Acts, setting out clearly the gospel message of the personal significance of the life, death, and resurrection of Christ (repentance, forgiveness from the risen Lord, and proclamation in his name), and then sketching out the missional proclamation agenda for Jesus' followers (to the ends of the earth).

So, although both Luke and Matthew add minor glosses to a shared synoptic understanding of the key aspects of the good news message entrusted by Jesus to his disciples, the evidence seems to show that Luke explicitly shares the Markan understanding that Jesus commanded that his good news '*must* be preached' 'to the ends of the earth'.

(C) The Discourse Part 2: Persecution, Destruction of Jerusalem and Times of Suffering / Subjugation, End-times Signs, Watchfulness and the Return of the Son of Man (Mark 13:11–27; Luke 21:14–28; Matthew 24:15–31)

Figure 3's comparative text table for the second section of Jesus' discourse shows:
- noticeably greater Lukan and Matthean departure from the Markan text (omission of Markan material, and insertion of unique Lukan or Matthean material);
- but also very strong structural and linguistic narrative congruence.

Linguistic markers suggest a few minor Matthean *structural* editorial changes, e.g.:
- conceptually / linguistically identical material in Mark 13:13a//Luke 21:17 is seemingly moved forward to Matthew 24:9b;

---

41 Fitzmyer, *Luke I–IX*, 148 and 172–174, notes that, while the verb εὐαγγελίζω (to announce good news) is a Lukan favourite, he never uses the noun εὐαγγέλιον in his Gospel, and only twice in Acts (15:7; 20:24), when apostles (Peter and Paul) are speaking. Moreover, even here it is rounded out and does not stand alone. In Acts 15:7 the Koine formulation reads, τὸν λόγον τοῦ εὐαγγελίου καὶ πιστεῦσαι ('the message of the good news and become believers'); and in Acts 20:24, τὸ εὐαγγέλιον τῆς χάριτος τοῦ θεοῦ ('the good news of the grace of God'). Even when Luke uses the verb εὐαγγελίζω in his Gospel, except where it is part of a quotation from or allusion to Isaiah, it does not stand alone, but carries an object. Thus Fitzmyer's conjecture seems entirely plausible that Luke studiously avoided the bald and unqualified use of εὐαγγέλιον because of potentially misleading and offensive resonances the word carried for Gentile and Jewish readers alike (including potentially specifically for 'Theophilus', the ostensible patron of Luke's work), due to its usage in the pagan emperor cult (or even contemporary vulgar, secular, or dramatic comedy contexts).

42 Brent, 'Imperial Cult', 412, 432–33, in particular suggests that the contemporary development of the Imperial Cult and its values likely formed a significant part of the immediate historical and social context for 'Theophilus and his circle', in which εὐαγγελία ('good news') meant most of all good news of events reassuring dispersed Graeco-Roman cities of continuing peaceful powerful rule emanating from Rome for 'the rising beneficiaries of the Augustan revolution'. He notes also that the granting of an Imperial Cult to a city such as Sardis led to that city being described as 'evangelised'.

Figure 3

Mark 13:11–27	Luke 21:14–28	Matthew 24:15–31
¹¹ καὶ ὅταν ἄγωσιν ὑμᾶς παραδιδόντες, μὴ προμεριμνᾶτε τί λαλήσητε, ἀλλ' ὃ ἐὰν δοθῇ ὑμῖν ἐν ἐκείνῃ τῇ ὥρᾳ τοῦτο λαλεῖτε, οὐ γάρ ἐστε ὑμεῖς οἱ λαλοῦντες ἀλλὰ τὸ πνεῦμα τὸ ἅγιον. ¹² καὶ παραδώσει ἀδελφὸς ἀδελφὸν εἰς θάνατον καὶ πατὴρ τέκνον, καὶ ἐπαναστήσονται τέκνα ἐπὶ γονεῖς καὶ θανατώσουσιν αὐτούς· ¹³ καὶ ἔσεσθε μισούμενοι ὑπὸ πάντων διὰ τὸ ὄνομά μου*. ὁ δὲ ὑπομείνας εἰς τέλος οὗτος σωθήσεται. §

¹⁴ "Οταν δὲ ἴδητε τὸ βδέλυγμα τῆς ἐρημώσεως ἑστηκότα ὅπου οὐ δεῖ, ὁ ἀναγινώσκων νοείτω,

τότε οἱ ἐν τῇ Ἰουδαίᾳ φευγέτωσαν εἰς τὰ ὄρη, ¹⁵ ὁ ἐπὶ τοῦ δώματος μὴ καταβάτω μηδὲ εἰσελθάτω τι ἆραι ἐκ τῆς οἰκίας αὐτοῦ, ¹⁶ καὶ ὁ εἰς τὸν ἀγρὸν μὴ ἐπιστρεψάτω εἰς τὰ ὀπίσω ἆραι τὸ ἱμάτιον αὐτοῦ.

¹⁷ οὐαὶ δὲ ταῖς ἐν γαστρὶ ἐχούσαις καὶ ταῖς θηλαζούσαις ἐν ἐκείναις ταῖς ἡμέραις. ¹⁸ προσεύχεσθε δὲ ἵνα μὴ γένηται χειμῶνος· ¹⁹ ἔσονται γὰρ αἱ ἡμέραι ἐκεῖναι θλῖψις # οἵα οὐ γέγονεν τοιαύτη ἀπ' ἀρχῆς κτίσεως ἣν ἔκτισεν ὁ θεὸς ἕως τοῦ νῦν καὶ οὐ μὴ γένηται. ²⁰ καὶ εἰ μὴ ἐκολόβωσεν κύριος τὰς ἡμέρας, οὐκ ἂν ἐσώθη πᾶσα σάρξ. ἀλλὰ διὰ τοὺς ἐκλεκτοὺς οὓς ἐξελέξατο ἐκολόβωσεν τὰς ἡμέρας. ²¹ καὶ τότε ἐάν τις ὑμῖν εἴπῃ· Ἴδε ὧδε ὁ χριστός, Ἴδε ἐκεῖ, μὴ πιστεύετε· ²² ἐγερθήσονται γὰρ ψευδόχριστοι καὶ ψευδοπροφῆται καὶ δώσουσιν σημεῖα καὶ τέρατα πρὸς τὸ ἀποπλανᾶν εἰ δυνατὸν τοὺς ἐκλεκτούς· ²³ ὑμεῖς δὲ βλέπετε· προείρηκα ὑμῖν πάντα. | ¹⁴ θέτε οὖν ἐν ταῖς καρδίαις ὑμῶν μὴ προμελετᾶν ἀπολογηθῆναι, ¹⁵ ἐγὼ γὰρ δώσω ὑμῖν στόμα καὶ σοφίαν ᾗ οὐ δυνήσονται ἀντιστῆναι ἢ ἀντειπεῖν ἅπαντες οἱ ἀντικείμενοι ὑμῖν. ¹⁶ παραδοθήσεσθε δὲ καὶ ὑπὸ γονέων καὶ ἀδελφῶν καὶ συγγενῶν καὶ φίλων, καὶ θανατώσουσιν ἐξ ὑμῶν, ¹⁷ καὶ ἔσεσθε μισούμενοι ὑπὸ πάντων διὰ τὸ ὄνομά μου.* ¹⁸ καὶ θρὶξ ἐκ τῆς κεφαλῆς ὑμῶν οὐ μὴ ἀπόληται. ¹⁹ ἐν τῇ ὑπομονῇ ὑμῶν κτήσασθε τὰς ψυχὰς ὑμῶν.

²⁰ "Οταν δὲ ἴδητε κυκλουμένην ὑπὸ στρατοπέδων Ἰερουσαλήμ, τότε γνῶτε ὅτι ἤγγικεν ἡ ἐρήμωσις αὐτῆς.

²¹ τότε οἱ ἐν τῇ Ἰουδαίᾳ φευγέτωσαν εἰς τὰ ὄρη, καὶ οἱ ἐν μέσῳ αὐτῆς ἐκχωρείτωσαν, καὶ οἱ ἐν ταῖς χώραις μὴ εἰσερχέσθωσαν εἰς αὐτήν, ²² ὅτι ἡμέραι ἐκδικήσεως αὗταί εἰσιν τοῦ πλησθῆναι πάντα τὰ γεγραμμένα.

²³ οὐαὶ ταῖς ἐν γαστρὶ ἐχούσαις καὶ ταῖς θηλαζούσαις ἐν ἐκείναις ταῖς ἡμέραις· ἔσται γὰρ ἀνάγκη μεγάλη ἐπὶ τῆς γῆς # καὶ ὀργὴ τῷ λαῷ τούτῳ, ²⁴ καὶ πεσοῦνται στόματι μαχαίρης καὶ αἰχμαλωτισθήσονται εἰς τὰ ἔθνη πάντα, καὶ Ἰερουσαλὴμ ἔσται πατουμένη ὑπὸ ἐθνῶν, ἄχρι οὗ πληρωθῶσιν καιροὶ ἐθνῶν. | ¹⁵ "Οταν οὖν ἴδητε τὸ βδέλυγμα τῆς ἐρημώσεως τὸ ῥηθὲν διὰ Δανιὴλ τοῦ προφήτου ἑστὸς ἐν τόπῳ ἁγίῳ, ὁ ἀναγινώσκων νοείτω,

¹⁶ τότε οἱ ἐν τῇ Ἰουδαίᾳ φευγέτωσαν ἐπὶ τὰ ὄρη, ¹⁷ ὁ ἐπὶ τοῦ δώματος μὴ καταβάτω ἆραι τὰ ἐκ τῆς οἰκίας αὐτοῦ, ¹⁸ καὶ ὁ ἐν τῷ ἀγρῷ μὴ ἐπιστρεψάτω ὀπίσω ἆραι τὸ ἱμάτιον αὐτοῦ.

¹⁹ οὐαὶ δὲ ταῖς ἐν γαστρὶ ἐχούσαις καὶ ταῖς θηλαζούσαις ἐν ἐκείναις ταῖς ἡμέραις.

²⁰ προσεύχεσθε δὲ ἵνα μὴ γένηται ἡ φυγὴ ὑμῶν χειμῶνος μηδὲ σαββάτῳ· ²¹ ἔσται γὰρ τότε θλῖψις μεγάλη # οἵα οὐ γέγονεν ἀπ' ἀρχῆς κόσμου ἕως τοῦ νῦν οὐδ' οὐ μὴ γένηται. ²² καὶ εἰ μὴ ἐκολοβώθησαν αἱ ἡμέραι ἐκεῖναι, οὐκ ἂν ἐσώθη πᾶσα σάρξ· διὰ δὲ τοὺς ἐκλεκτοὺς κολοβωθήσονται αἱ ἡμέραι ἐκεῖναι. ²³ τότε ἐάν τις ὑμῖν εἴπῃ· Ἰδοὺ ὧδε ὁ χριστός, ἤ Ὧδε, μὴ πιστεύσητε· ²⁴ ἐγερθήσονται γὰρ ψευδόχριστοι καὶ ψευδοπροφῆται, καὶ δώσουσιν σημεῖα μεγάλα καὶ τέρατα ὥστε πλανῆσαι εἰ δυνατὸν καὶ τοὺς ἐκλεκτούς· ²⁵ ἰδοὺ προείρηκα ὑμῖν. ²⁶ ἐὰν οὖν εἴπωσιν ὑμῖν· Ἰδοὺ ἐν τῇ ἐρήμῳ ἐστίν, μὴ ἐξέλθητε· Ἰδοὺ ἐν τοῖς ταμείοις, μὴ πιστεύσητε· ²⁷ ὥσπερ γὰρ ἡ ἀστραπὴ ἐξέρχεται ἀπὸ ἀνατολῶν καὶ φαίνεται ἕως δυσμῶν, οὕτως ἔσται ἡ παρουσία τοῦ υἱοῦ τοῦ ἀνθρώπου· ²⁸ ὅπου ἐὰν ᾖ τὸ πτῶμα, ἐκεῖ συναχθήσονται οἱ ἀετοί. |

Figure 3 (continued)

Mark 13:11–27	Luke 21:14–28	Matthew 24:15–31
²⁴ Ἀλλὰ ἐν ἐκείναις ταῖς ἡμέραις μετὰ τὴν θλῖψιν ἐκείνην ὁ ἥλιος σκοτισθήσεται, καὶ ἡ σελήνη οὐ δώσει τὸ φέγγος αὐτῆς, ²⁵ καὶ οἱ ἀστέρες ἔσονται ἐκ τοῦ οὐρανοῦ πίπτοντες, καὶ αἱ δυνάμεις αἱ ἐν τοῖς οὐρανοῖς σαλευθήσονται.	²⁵ Καὶ ἔσονται σημεῖα ἐν ἡλίῳ καὶ σελήνῃ καὶ ἄστροις, καὶ ἐπὶ τῆς γῆς συνοχὴ ἐθνῶν ἐν ἀπορίᾳ ἤχους θαλάσσης καὶ σάλου, ²⁶ ἀποψυχόντων ἀνθρώπων ἀπὸ φόβου καὶ προσδοκίας τῶν ἐπερχομένων τῇ οἰκουμένῃ, αἱ γὰρ δυνάμεις τῶν οὐρανῶν σαλευθήσονται.	²⁹ Εὐθέως δὲ μετὰ τὴν θλῖψιν τῶν ἡμερῶν ἐκείνων ὁ ἥλιος σκοτισθήσεται, καὶ ἡ σελήνη οὐ δώσει τὸ φέγγος αὐτῆς, καὶ οἱ ἀστέρες πεσοῦνται ἀπὸ τοῦ οὐρανοῦ, καὶ αἱ δυνάμεις τῶν οὐρανῶν σαλευθήσονται. ³⁰ καὶ τότε φανήσεται τὸ σημεῖον τοῦ υἱοῦ τοῦ ἀνθρώπου ἐν τῷ οὐρανῷ, καὶ τότε κόψονται πᾶσαι αἱ φυλαὶ τῆς γῆς
²⁶ καὶ τότε ὄψονται τὸν υἱὸν τοῦ ἀνθρώπου ἐρχόμενον ἐν νεφέλαις μετὰ δυνάμεως πολλῆς καὶ δόξης.	²⁷ καὶ τότε ὄψονται τὸν υἱὸν τοῦ ἀνθρώπου ἐρχόμενον ἐν νεφέλῃ μετὰ δυνάμεως καὶ δόξης πολλῆς.	καὶ ὄψονται τὸν υἱὸν τοῦ ἀνθρώπου ἐρχόμενον ἐπὶ τῶν νεφελῶν τοῦ οὐρανοῦ μετὰ δυνάμεως καὶ δόξης πολλῆς·
²⁷ καὶ τότε ἀποστελεῖ τοὺς ἀγγέλους καὶ ἐπισυνάξει τοὺς ἐκλεκτοὺς ἐκ τῶν τεσσάρων ἀνέμων ἀπ' ἄκρου γῆς ἕως ἄκρου οὐρανοῦ.		³¹ καὶ ἀποστελεῖ τοὺς ἀγγέλους αὐτοῦ μετὰ σάλπιγγος μεγάλης, καὶ ἐπισυνάξουσιν τοὺς ἐκλεκτοὺς αὐτοῦ ἐκ τῶν τεσσάρων ἀνέμων ἀπ' ἄκρων οὐρανῶν ἕως τῶν ἄκρων αὐτῶν.
	²⁸ ἀρχομένων δὲ τούτων γίνεσθαι ἀνακύψατε καὶ ἐπάρατε τὰς κεφαλὰς ὑμῶν, διότι ἐγγίζει ἡ ἀπολύτρωσις ὑμῶν.	

Key:
- Concepts shared by all 3 Synoptics
- Concepts shared by Mark/Luke
- Concepts shared by Luke/Matthew
- Concepts shared by Mark/Matthew
- Mark only
- Luke only
- Matthew only

Vocabulary shared
Exact words/phrases shared

Note also that Mark 13:13a and Luke 21:17 (*) seem to find their conceptual and linguistic parallel in Matthew 24:9b; Mark 13:13b (§) and Matthew 24:13 are linguistically identical; and Luke 21:23b seems to run linguistically parallel with Mark 13:19a and Matthew 24:21a (#).

- that seen in Mark 13:13b//Luke 21:18 is seemingly postponed to Matthew 24:13; and,
- (less certainly) the linguistic harmony of Mark 13:19a//Luke 21:23b//Matthew 24:21a (the 'distress' language), suggests minor structural narrative rearrangement.

But these minor deletions / insertions / rearrangements aside, Figure 3 shows the three texts effectively marching together in *narrative confluence* and *structural lock-step*. It also graphically illustrates continuing high levels of *linguistic congruence* (linguistic similarity, or even exact reproduction of Koine Greek phrases, or words), especially between Mark and Luke. That said, Luke seems to be *compressing* this part of the Markan account (including largely editing out Mark 13:18–23//Matthew 24:20–28 material, perhaps because of his Luke 17:20–37 report of an earlier parallel pronouncement by Jesus), while also *expanding / elaborating* the Markan account by interleaving additional material, apparently from his separate 'eyewitness accounts'.[43]

Comparative textual analysis indicates insertion of distinctly Lukan material in Luke 21:15,20,22,24,25b,26,28, and Luke's introduction of different phraseology (for example, vv.14,19,21b) even when verses run directly parallel *conceptually* with the Markan account. *Pace* Fitzmyer,[44] Bovon and Bock may be right that in 21:10–28, Luke is drawing on a complete parallel account of the discourse,[45] or at least a parallel source for this section.[46]

Linguistically, Luke 21:14–16 closely reflects Mark 13:11–12. However, as for Luke's insertion of 21:11b, we should note carefully the new rhythmic balances and alliterations introduced via the inserted non-Markan texts in 21:15 and 21:16,[47] even if the inserted text in some respects does not meet what we know to be personal interests of Luke (notably the work of the Holy Spirit).[48] Indeed, Bovon similarly detects a 'rhythmic, almost poetic character of 21:20–24', which he declares is found nowhere else in Luke.[49]

We can thus venture to suggest again that in his non-Markan 'eyewitness account' material Luke has detected compelling reflections of the authentic tone, oral rhythms, and flow of Jesus' voice, resonating with the λίθος ἐπὶ λίθον / λίθῳ cadences earlier in the discourse at 21:6.[50] Thus he confidently inserts as reliable the other material from his 'eyewitness accounts' contained in 21:18,20,24,25b,26,28.

Arguably, the most important insertions are in verses 2–28: Jerusalem being surrounded by armies (v.20); the time of punishment and wrath (vv.22,23b); the times of destruction and 'of the Gentiles' (v.24); and the time of 'your redemption' (v.28). Luke's own eyewitness material, interleaved with that of Mark / Peter, has Jesus speaking of the (apparently sequential) impending traumatic physical destruction of Jerusalem as part of Scripturally-prophesied divine judgement, a period of Gentile supremacy, a time of frightening global apocalyptic signs of a disturbed creation, finally followed by the return of the Son of Man (Jesus) in glory, and the redemption / deliverance (ἀπολύτρωσις, 21:28) of the saints. Closer analysis will highlight how this interleaving results in

---

43 Nolland, *Luke 18:35– 24:53*, 1000.
44 Fitzmyer, *Luke X–XXIV*, 1326.
45 Bovon, *Luke 3*, 106–08.
46 Bock, *Luke*, 1678.
47 ἐγὼ γὰρ δώσω ὑμῖν στόμα καὶ σοφίαν ᾗ οὐ δυνήσονται ἀντιστῆναι ἢ ἀντειπεῖν ἅπαντες οἱ ἀντικείμενοι ὑμῖν ('for I will give you a mouth and wisdom which none of your enemies will be able to resist or contradict') in 21:15, and καὶ συγγενῶν καὶ φίλων to round out καὶ ὑπὸ γονέων καὶ ἀδελφῶν ('and (you will be betrayed / handed over) by parents and brothers and relatives and friends' in 21:16 (although admittedly these new alliterations are at the expense of Luke removing an original alliteration in Mark 13:12 (καὶ παραδώσει ἀδελφὸς ἀδελφὸν, 'and a brother will betray / hand over a brother')
48 Bock, *Luke*, 1671.
49 Bovon, *Luke 3*, 107.
50 And also previously in Luke 19:44, Jesus' pronouncement of the fate of the temple as part of his lament over Jerusalem.

the global evangelism imperative infusing this part of the discourse, and confirming synoptic confluence, notwithstanding Luke's omission of Mark 13:10.

Luke 21:20–28 effectively duplicates the Markan / Matthean accounts in shorter form. But Luke 21:22 records Jesus saying (making explicit the Old Testament resonances underlying the Markan / Matthean accounts) that all that is to come, notably destruction of Jerusalem and the temple, will be 'in fulfilment of everything that is written [in Old Testament Scripture]' (πλησθῆναι πάντα τὰ γεγραμμένα). Nolland notes that despite variation of the verbs used to describe 'fulfilment', πάντα τὰ γεγραμμένα links back to Luke 18:31 (the phrase's first appearance in Luke's Gospel) and probably here also *forward* to Luke 24:44.[51] Jesus links what is to come (destruction / judgement, and Parousia / redemption) directly with Old Testament prophecy which 'must' be fulfilled.

Luke 21:20–24 seemingly has Jesus finally answering directly the disciples' question from 21:7 (provoked by Jesus' v.6 'casting down' prophecy), 'When will these things happen, and what will be the sign that they are about to take place?' But narrative analysis also challenges us to see 21:8–19 as part of Jesus' answer, placing a definite future destruction of Jerusalem and its temple within 'an escalating pattern of wars and disturbances, along with earthquakes, famines, and plagues and with dreadful portents and signs from heaven [as part of a] divinely appointed process'.[52] As in the Markan account, implicitly from the time of Jesus speaking (and certainly before major escalation of events within this pattern), there will be deceptive messiahs / prophecies and intense persecution of believers (Luke 21:8,12–19//Mark 13:5 and 9-13). These will be at the very start of the birthing of a new world order (Mark 13:8b), equivalent to Jesus' words in Luke 21:12a Πρὸ δὲ τούτων πάντων ('But before all this').

(D) The 'Global Evangelism Imperative' in Part 2 of the Discourse: 'The Times of the Gentiles', Intertextual Resonances, Metalepsis and the Luke-Acts Narrative Hinge

In Luke's account, it seems that Jesus was also warning that the physical destruction of Jerusalem would be the start of a new period of waiting, ἄχρι οὗ πληρωθῶσιν καιροὶ ἐθνῶν ('until the times of the Gentiles are fulfilled', Luke 21:24b), ahead of the Parousia seemingly in mind in 21:25–28. The plurality of καιροὶ ἐθνῶν seems to indicate a period, not a point in time, and many Gentile dominators, not just Rome. The 'trampling on Jerusalem' is thus a *period*, as well as a specific destruction event. And in saying this waiting period is to be 'fulfilled' (πληρωθῶσιν), Luke seems to imply Jesus is referring not just to a future *chronological* end to this period, but also an end which by its nature will see all Old Testament Scripture 'fulfilled', in ways that reach well beyond any Jerusalem destruction event.

With the πίμπλημι / πληρόω 'fulfilment' language of 21:22/24b and its 'fulfilment of all that is written' interpretative lens in mind, we need implicitly to scan Luke's version of the discourse (particularly 21:9–28) to identify key LXX Scriptures Jesus may have been referencing,[53] using the online German Bible Society edition (Rahlfs edition).[54]

---

51 Nolland, *Luke 18:35 – 24:53*, 1001.
52 Nolland, *Luke 18:35 – 24:53*, 990.
53 Consistent with general commentary opinion (for example Morris, *Luke*, 26–27) that the 'go to' Old Testament source underlying Luke's Gospel (and Jesus' words recorded there) is a version of the Septuagint.
54 Rahlfs, *Septuagint (LXX)*.

This 'fulfilment of all that is written' interpretative lens suggests we also need to move to a mode of narrative analysis more closely and specifically attentive to intertextual resonances, and likely hearer understanding of the narrative in that context. Beers and Hays usefully set out a spectrum of intertextual indicators potentially drawing Old Testament meanings, texts, and prophecies into New Testament texts (ranging from 'it is written' style 'quotation' or 'citation', through 'allusion' (by way of repeating a specific Koine phrase or Biblical name), down to an 'echo' which may contain a single specific Koine word or a meaning-congruent evocative phrase).[55] Hays also highlights the possible use of *metalepsis* (where the echoing of a small piece of a precursor text requires the reader to recover 'the original context from which the fragmentary echo came [...] reading the two texts in dialogical juxtaposition').[56] Beyond the use of citation and allusion in this section of the discourse, the discernment of echo and metalepsis arguably emerges as particularly important: intertextual sensitivity becomes an essential narrative-critical tool in understanding how the Lukan narrative was actually heard and understood, especially by a Hellenistic Jewish audience.

As our study proceeds, we see strong suggestions that Luke is not just writing with an intertextual style (although he certainly does in narrative passages). Rather it seems he enthusiastically brings us eyewitness accounts which portray a Jesus who both explicitly lived and routinely spoke intertextually, conscious of and pointing to the fulfilment of Old Testament Scriptures in himself.

A simplified listing of potential intertextual connections in Appendix 1 reflects commentator observations, but specially focuses on uniquely Lukan insertions into the discourse, including:

- 21:10 (some conceptual 'nation against nation' echoes of 2 Chronicles 15:6 / Isaiah 19:2 language);
- 21:11 (conceptual and possible linguistic echoes of 'earthquakes, famines, pestilence, and fearful events' language in Isaiah 5:13–14 (and often elsewhere in Isaiah), Ezekiel 38:19–22, and Haggai 2:6);
- 21:20a (linguistic resonance with Isaiah 29:3 / conceptual resonance with Jeremiah 6:6);
- 21:20b (multiple direct linguistic resonance of the judgement / apocalyptic 'trigger word' 'desolation' (ἐρήμωσις), with 'destruction of Jerusalem' passages in Jeremiah and seemingly pre-eminently (given the explicit Luke 21:27 invocation of Daniel 7:13) in Daniel 8:13; (9:2,) 9:27; 12:11);[57]
- 21:22 (multiple direct linguistic resonance of 'time of vengeance' language with passages in Jeremiah; one linguistic and other conceptual resonances with verses in Isaiah, and hybrid linguistic / conceptual resonance with Hosea 9:7);
- 21:23b ('great distress and wrath against this people' finds conceptual resonance with Daniel

---

55   Beers, *Followers*, 23–25; Hays, *Echoes*, 10–11.
56   Hays, *Echoes*, 11.
57   ἐρήμωσις occurs 16 times in 14 LXX verses: twice in Leviticus (Leviticus 26:34,35, warning of the consequences of covenantal disobedience); twice in 2 Chronicles (30:7; 36:21, recalling the consequences of covenantal disobedience and describing the final fall of Jerusalem); once in Psalm 73:19 (LXX 72:19), describing the fate of the ungodly; 5 times in 3 verses in Daniel as indicated above, and 6 times in Jeremiah (4:7; 7:34; 22:5; 25:18 (LXX 32:18); 44:6 (LXX 51:6); 44:22 (LXX 51:22)). The latter 11 occurrences are all specific to the desolation of Jerusalem and the land and cities of Judah following covenantal disobedience. Overall, this pattern is highly suggestive of the Koine word 'desolation' functioning as a specialised metaleptic trigger word here in Luke's Gospel, invoking a renewed fulfilment cycle of LXX prophecy of imminent judgement on Judaea and God-ordained foreign destruction of Jerusalem (see below). This judgement — and the broad number of Danielic occurrences of ἐρήμωσις — hold good if using the 'Old Greek' LXX text rather than the Theodotion LXX text apparently favoured by Rahlfs for Daniel 9:2 (one extra reference), or the Theodotion LXX text rather than the 'Old Greek' text apparently favoured by Rahlfs for Daniel 9:27 (one less reference).

12:1, and linguistic / conceptual resonance with Isaiah 13:9);
- 21:24a (linguistic and conceptual resonance of 'fall by the sword / taken as prisoners to all the nations' with Jeremiah 24:4–6 and Deuteronomy 28:64);
- 21:24b ('Jerusalem will be trampled on by the Gentiles' finds a striking degree of linguistic resonance at least seven times in Isaiah, once in Daniel 8:13, and once with Zechariah 23:3);
- 21:25a ('signs in the sun, moon, and stars' seems to resonate linguistically with Isaiah 13:10 and 34:4, amongst other texts);
- 21:25b seems to resonate thematically and linguistically with Psalm 46:2–3 and Isaiah 24:18–19 respectively;
- 21:26a seems to resonate with the terror motif in Isaiah 2:10,19,21; 24:19, including with the broader 'shaking of the earth' language of Isaiah 2:21;
- 21:26b seems to resonate thematically with the 'shaking of the heavenly bodies' in Isaiah 13:13, parallel with verse 25a resonances;
- 21:27 (strong allusion to Daniel 7:13); and,
- 21:27b/28 (apparent linguistic / thematic links to Isaiah 40:26; 49:18; 51:6; 60:1–4).

Focusing more closely on the major Lukan insertions (21:20,22,23b,24,28), together with 21:27, we can discern some strong and consistent invocation in Luke's account of Jesus' speech of particular LXX prophetic texts which 'are to be fulfilled'. Appendix 1 shows Jesus in Luke's (Markan-consistent) additional material invoking specific prophetic texts in Isaiah, Jeremiah, and Daniel in an arguably clearer, more coherent, and mutually interlocking manner compared with Mark or Matthew.

The inserted Lukan 'day of vengeance' language of 21:22 resonates strongly linguistically with repeated prophetic passages in Jeremiah, and somewhat strongly with passages from Isaiah, as well as Hosea 9:7. Indeed, the divine 'vengeance' or 'day(s) of vengeance' seemingly invoked by Luke 21:22's 'days of vengeance' (ἡμέραι ἐκδικήσεως) could be described as a thematic favourite in Jeremiah (ἐκδίκησις and ἡμέρα/καιρὸς ἐκδικήσεως, or close non-verbal cognates), occurring in no less than twelve LXX verses.[58] While Isaiah is *conceptually* directly parallel in five verses (34:8; 35:4; 59:17; 61:2; 63:4), the LXX text prefers κρίσεως ('judgement') and ἀνταποδόσεως ('retribution') in its 'vengeance' / 'days of vengeance' formulations (34:8; 35:4; 61:2; 63:4), only using ἐκδικήσεως to describe the Lord's 'garment' when coming in judgement (59:17).[59] But Hosea 9:7's direct rhythmic combination of αἱ ἡμέραι τῆς ἐκδικήσεως and αἱ ἡμέραι τῆς ἀνταποδόσεώς strongly suggests the direct equivalence of the variant Isaianic κρίσεως / ἀνταποδόσεως LXX terminology with Luke 21:22's ἡμέραι ἐκδικήσεως.[60]

So Luke's inserted material here tends to suggest eyewitness understanding that, parallel with Danielic prophecies, the coming destruction of Jerusalem will also fulfil 'what is written' in Isaiah, Jeremiah, and Hosea, and be a divine act of 'vengeance', avenging justice, 'against this people'. There are hints through a number of the Jeremiah and Isaiah texts to a balancing and subsequent post-destruction redemptive 'vengeance' on Israel's enemies (Isa. 34:8, 59:17; 63:4; Jer. 46:10,21; 50:15,27,28,31; 51:6,11,36—LXX 26:10,21; 27:15,27,28,31; 28:6,11,36), including specifically in Jer. 51:11—LXX 28:11 retribution for the destruction of 'his temple'.

---

58 Corresponding in ten instances directly with נְקָמָה (neqamah) (Strong's Hebrew 5360) in the Westminster Leningrad Codex text (Jeremiah 1:20; 20:12; 46:10; 50:15; 50:28 (twice); 51:6; 51:11 (twice); and 51:36). Pao and Schnabel, 'Luke', 376, note the very close Hebrew / Greek linguistic resonance (and contextual resonance for 51:6 particularly).

59 All five of these LXX usages correspond directly with נָקָם (naqam) (Strong's Hebrew 5359, and the masculine form of the Jeremiah texts' נְקָמָה (neqamah)) appearing in these verses in the Westminster Leningrad Codex text.

60 As indeed does the linguistically <u>directly</u> parallel naqam / naqamah Isaiah / Jeremiah usage in the Westminster Leningrad Codex Hebrew text already noted. This language potentially underlies the Lukan Koine Greek.

But in the discourse context, the main thrust of the allusions (keyed to Jeremiah 5:29; 11:20; 20:12; and Hosea 9:7) is that the coming destruction of the temple (Luke 21:20) will not simply be Roman cruelty, but an act of God in judgement on his people. Luke portrays Jesus as invoking Old Testament Scripture to say that the God of Israel does not admire the beauty of the stones and dedicated gifts, but (astoundingly) declares them to be objects of wrath, judgement, and impending destruction. Divine vengeance and destruction prophesied and experienced previously after Israel's rebellion (Jeremiah 20:2) will be experienced again through other raised-up 'Gentiles'.

Lukan insertions in 21:20 seem to show his special eyewitness source providing an additional snippet from Jesus,[61] combining with an abbreviated (compared with Mark and Matthew) but no less clear primary reference in 21:20b to prophecies in Daniel 8:13; (9:2); 9:27; 12:11 through the 'trigger word' 'desolation' (ἐρήμωσις / ἐρημώσεως). Along with the 21:20a resonances with Isaiah 29:3 and Jeremiah 6:6 (linguistic for the former (κυκλουμένην / κυκλώσω, 'encircled'), thematic for the latter), it appears Luke's special source is pointing to Jesus' intertextual warning that all these prophetic passages, fulfilled dramatically in the past, will imminently come to life in another cycle of fulfilment.[62] Once again, the forthcoming destruction of Jerusalem, and butchering of its population, will not be another act of Roman political bastardry, but an act of the God of Israel, 'according to Scripture'.

Another significant Lukan insertion from his special source is 21:24–25, rich in Old Testament allusion. In verse 24a, as commentators note,[63] there are compelling linguistic resonances with Jeremiah 20:4–6[64] and with Deuteronomy 28:64. Jewish readers would likely hear Jesus referencing the Law's divine warning that covenantal disobedience would bring judgement, exile, and scattering among the nations. Meanwhile, the echo of Jeremiah 20:4–6 in Jesus' words hints at another fulfilment cycle of Jeremiah's prophecy of Babylonian domination and exiling of Judah into captivity. Once again, future destruction will not be random Roman action, but the deliberate and predicted action of Israel's God in judgement.

However, as far as Luke is concerned, it seems that Jesus' words in 21:24b ('Jerusalem will be trampled underfoot by the Gentiles until the times of the Gentiles are fulfilled') are close to the heart of the discourse. Fitzmyer and others rightly detect a resonance with Zechariah 12:3, although maybe not as close linguistically as Fitzmyer suggests.[65] Hosea 5:11 ('Ephraim trampled in judgement') has a similar linguistic cognate and thematic resonance (πατουμένη / κατεπάτησεν). Probably more significant, given other parallel linguistic linkages to it in the discourse passage, is the similarly linguistic (cognate) resonance (πατουμένη / καταπάτημα) with Daniel 8:13 (desolation / raising of the desolating abomination), and with the Danielic tableau of the Son of Man's glorious return (see below).

---

61 These point to the looming fulfilment of prophecies in Isaiah 29:3 and Jeremiah 6:6 in a way particularly useful to pre-AD 70 readers, the 21:20a injunction to flee being apparently linked to seeing the besieging army gathering, not post-destruction: Ὅταν δὲ ἴδητε κυκλουμένην ὑπὸ στρατοπέδων Ἰερουσαλήμ ('When you see Jerusalem being encircled by armies').

62 The metaleptic 'desolation' reference, for example, provides the lens whereby successive LXX covenantal warnings (Lev. 26:34,35), records of judgement on Jerusalem (2 Chron. 30:7; 36:21), and fulfilled prophecies of judgement on / foreign destruction of Jerusalem (Jeremiah 4:7; 7:34; 22:5; 25:18 [LXX 32:18]; 44:6 [LXX 51:6]; 44:22 [LXX 51:22]) are refocused through re-invocation of the Danielic prophecies to foreshadow forthcoming historical as well as apocalyptic judgement and destruction.

63 Marshall, *Luke*, 773; Fitzmyer, *Luke X–XXIV*, 1346; and Nolland, *Luke 18:35 – 24:53*, 1002.

64 Luke 21:24a's καὶ πεσοῦνται στόματι μαχαίρης καὶ αἰχμαλωτισθήσονται ('and they will fall [by the mouth of] the sword and be led away captive') compared with Jeremiah 20:4–6 καὶ πεσοῦνται ἐν μαχαίρᾳ ... ἐν αἰχμαλωσίᾳ ('and they will fall by the sword ... be led away into captivity').

65 Fitzmyer, *Luke X–XXIV*, 1346; Nolland, *Luke 18:35 – 24:53*, 1002.

But the slew of Isaianic texts (Isaiah 5:5; 10; 22:5; 28:3; 63:6; 63:18) with linguistic cognate resonance (the compounded LXX καταπατέω, in place of Luke's simpler but directly-equivalent πατέω) seems even more significant, *pace* Marshall.[66] 'Being trampled down' (καταπατέω and cognates) seems a favoured and distinctive Isaianic LXX expression, occurring seven times in passages of prophetic texture related to God's person. Elsewhere in the Old Testament, other than possibly in Psalm 56:2 and 57:4 (LXX 55:2–3 and 56:4 respectively), καταπατέω is used more prosaically. Since the LXX Jeremiah text nowhere uses καταπατέω or its cognates, verse 24b becomes all the more strongly resonant with Isaianic prophecy.

So what might Jesus be invoking through these Isaianic 'trampling' resonances?

- for Isaiah 5:5, in the famous 'Song of the Vineyard', the emphasis is on a personally offended God of Israel destroying his vineyard / Israel, breaking down its wall and arranging for its trampling by calling in 'distant nations' (5:6), in a time when 'the mountains will shake' (5:25), and there will be roaring 'like the roaring of the seas', 'darkness', 'distress', and darkening of the sun (contrast with Luke 21:11,25,26). Jerusalem may be 'trampled on' by the Gentiles, but this will be, according to Scripture, an action of deliberate judgement, organised by the God of Israel;
- for Isaiah 10:6, the resonance is to the God of Israel bringing the Assyrians, the 'rod of my anger', to 'trample down' the godless nation of Israel and Jerusalem, but yet also to the God who promises the restitution of a repentant remnant, and the redirection of his wrath against their oppressors (10:21–25);
- for Isaiah 22:5, the resonance is to a 'Lord's day' of 'trampling' in the valleys surrounding Jerusalem (ἐν φάραγγι Σιων) and destruction of Jerusalem's walls by a Babylonian army, moving at the God of Israel's instigation (with no immediate hope of redemption);
- for Isaiah 28:3, the resonance is to the God of Israel's promise to Ephraim / Judah that he will 'trample underfoot' Jerusalem, their pride, but also (through metaleptic linking to its wider context) to a counter-balancing prophecy that he will be 'a glorious crown' for the (faithful) remnant of his people (Isaiah 28:5), and that he will 'lay a stone in Zion'[67] as a foundation for righteous rule and life (Isaiah 28:16–18, contrasting with Luke 21:6's 'not one stone on another' language). This 'trampling-resonant' text flows into Isaiah 29's divine lament over Jerusalem, and 29:3's reference to Jerusalem being encamped against on all sides by a besieging army; and,
- for Isaiah 62:3,6,18, the triple 'trampling' resonance invokes the picture first of the God of Israel as a vengeful warrior trampling down 'the nations in my anger' to save Israel (62:3,6), and secondly of the people of God complaining of their enemies having 'trampled down your sanctuary' after a period of Jewish possession, leading to a call to the God of Israel to 'rend the heavens and come down' (Isaiah 64).

These rich and parallel resonances link Jerusalem's destruction to the Isaianic 'trampling' passages so as to arguably engage two pairs of hinged prophecies: firstly, *judgement* (on Israel / Jerusalem; and on the nations), and secondly *redemption / deliverance* (of the righteous remnant; but also of at least some Gentiles who come to see Jesus, the Jewish Messiah, as the light of the world). While the second wing of the second hinge is yet to emerge more clearly in Luke 21:27–28, hints of this may come with the phrase 'until the times of the Gentiles are fulfilled' (ἄχρι οὗ πληρωθῶσιν καιροὶ ἐθνῶν).

---

66 Marshall, *Luke*, 773.
67 Ἰδοὺ ἐγὼ ἐμβαλῶ εἰς τὰ θεμέλια Σιων λίθον πολυτελῆ ἐκλεκτὸν ἀκρογωνιαῖον ἔντιμον εἰς τὰ θεμέλια αὐτῆς ('See, I lay in Zion a foundation stone, selected as a costly and valued cornerstone for its foundation').

Nolland (amongst others) concludes that this phrase refers to a period of God's judgement on the nations, corresponding to the devastation visited on Jerusalem.[68] However, reading the phrase with closer attention to the range of Isaianic redemptive resonances noted above should lead us to reconsider that view.

We argued above that Jesus speaks in 21:24b of a period of Gentile (not just Roman) oppressive domination, and thus of a 'trampling' temporal continuum after the actual historical destruction of Jerusalem, for which it will be an ongoing metaphor. The trampling will continue after the 'desolation', 'falling by the sword', and deporting of prisoners 'to all the nations' (21:20,24a). It is not until these 'times' end (ἄχρι οὗ πληρωθῶσιν, 'until they are fulfilled') that Jesus in Luke's account goes on to speak of the start of a new season of apocalyptic / end times events and his return in glory (21:25–28).

But a period of oppressive Gentile domination does not exclude it being simultaneously a time of gospel proclamation, repentance, and entry by faith into the coming kingdom, noting, in line with Bovon's comments, the positive 'making full' / Scripture-fulfilment nuances of πληρόω (when Jesus / Luke could have used another word).[69] Pauline Isaiah-related understandings set out in Romans 10:18–11:32, along with Jesus' Mark 13:10-consistent command recorded in Luke 24 / Acts 1, give rise to long-standing Christian interpretative tradition[70] and reasonable modern commentary[71] which recognise or support this view.

It is helpful to examine the next major Lukan insertion (21:28) along with 21:27, which follows Mark 13:26 word-for-word in Koine Greek, aside from minor a change in one word (Luke's νεφέλῃ ['in a cloud'], compared with Mark's νεφέλαις ['in the clouds']). Fitzmyer correctly takes these verses as a block with verses 25–26, Jesus moving smoothly from the 'times of the Gentiles' to describe 'another "end", to "what is coming upon the world" (v.26)'.[72]

Intertextually, Luke 21:27's linguistic resonance with Daniel 7:13 is closer to short-hand quotation than to just allusion (see Appendix 1). Taken together with the earlier Daniel 8:13 and 12:11 resonances in 21:20b, in 21:27 Jesus seems to be deliberately invoking a rich canvas of Danielic end-times prophecy.

In the context of the ending of the 'times of the Gentiles' and the onset of a series of apocalyptic signs of cosmic disturbance (with a host of LXX linguistic and thematic resonances), Jesus seems:

- by appealing to the Daniel 7:13, to appropriate to himself (as the self-designated 'Son of Man') a prophecy which foreshadows both a post-resurrection heavenly vindication / enthronement, and an earthly reflection of this in the 'end times'.[73] This return will, in Danielic terms, follow unprecedented distress (Daniel 12:1–2//Matthew 24:21//Mark 13:19//Luke 21:23b); and,
- to be pointing, via the Danielic internal connections, and the earlier 8:13 and 12:11 resonances with the 'desolation' language in Luke 20b, to the enigmatically-explained prophecies in Daniel that:

---

68 Nolland, *Luke 18:35 – 24:53*, 1002–1003; Nolland, 'Times', 146.
69 Bovon, *Luke 3*, 115–16. Pao, *Acts*, 87–88 and 87 n.100, makes this same point with regard to πληρόω, explicitly in Luke 24:44, but noting also the Luke 21:24 occurrence in this same sense.
70 Bovon, *Luke 3*, 116 n.82.
71 Marshall, *Luke*, 773–74; Bock, *Luke*, 1680; and Garland, *Luke*, 834.
72 Fitzmyer, *Luke X–XXIV*, 1348.
73 Bock, *Proclamation*, 136–37; Nolland, *Luke 18:35 – 24:53*, 1006; and Bock, *Luke*, 1684–86, notwithstanding the contrasting view adopted in Walton, 'The End', 387.

- the Anointed One will be put to death (Daniel 9:26);
- Jerusalem / the temple will be trampled upon / desecrated as judgement on the sins of God's people (Daniel 8:9–13 and 9:26); and,
- final divine judgement on the enemies of God and reward for the faithful will be held off into an uncertain future time (Daniel 2:5–13).

In other words, Luke 21:27's short-hand quote of Daniel 7:13 and the earlier Daniel resonances prophesy 1) a time of 'trampling' and judgement on Israel / the temple; and 2) with the return of Jesus as glorified and risen Lord, a time of judgement upon the Gentiles and opponents of God's rule alongside deliverance for the faithful, after an indefinite period of waiting / distress under Gentile oppression.

Within the discourse, 21:28 stands out as distinctively Lukan, most likely from his separate eyewitness source.[74] It is also suggestively linked through ἀρχομένων δὲ τούτων γίνεσθαι ('when these things begin to take place') to the apocalyptic post-'time of the Gentiles' trampling described in verses 25–26, rather than the Jerusalem destruction event or the generalised 'signs' in 21:9–17.[75] Jesus seems to be telling his disciples to discern and greet joyfully the signs of his return, and of their imminent deliverance / redemption from earthly evil and cosmic collapse.

But if Luke's special source consistently portrays Jesus as highlighting Old Testament Scriptures 'to be fulfilled', what potential Scriptures are identifiable here? Marshall points to the probable resonance of 21:28's ἀπολύτρωσις ('deliverance') with Isaiah 63:4's καὶ ἐνιαυτὸς λυτρώσεως πάρεστιν ('a year of deliverance was at hand').[76] But given the Isaianic prophetic resonances noted already, a wider search for Isaianic resonances with Luke 21:27b's 'power and great glory' and 28's 'stand up and lift up your heads', and 'your redemption is drawing near' seems warranted. Appendix 1 admittedly shows no direct *linguistic resonance* between the 'stand up and lift your heads' (ἀνακύψατε καὶ ἐπάρατε τὰς κεφαλὰς ὑμῶν) of Luke 21:28 and the 'raise your eyes' (ἀναβλέψατε εἰς ὕψος τοὺς ὀφθαλμοὺς ὑμῶν / ἆρον κύκλῳ τοὺς ὀφθαλμούς σου / ἄρατε εἰς τὸν οὐρανὸν τοὺς ὀφθαλμοὺς ὑμῶν / ἆρον κύκλῳ τοὺς ὀφθαλμούς σου) of LXX Isaiah 60:1–4; 49:18; 51:6; and 26:3. But a strong *conceptual equivalence* looks at least likely.

Interestingly, while for all of these Isaiah passages the central theme (and main flow of any resonance in the discourse) is the joyful final deliverance of the faithful people of God, a parallel theme is also discernible of at least some Gentiles responding positively to the Jewish Messiah. Set in the powerful context of the Isaiah 49 'Servant Song', Isaiah 49:18 and surrounds arguably exemplify this pattern. The 'lifting of eyes and looking around' of 49:18 falls under the chapeau of the promised liberation and deliverance of God's people by God himself, prophesied in 49:8–13 (the 'day of salvation', ἐν ἡμέρᾳ σωτηρίας, of v.8) in his capacity as 'Deliverer' (ὁ ῥυσάμενος, v.7). But this hope of deliverance is specifically in the context of God's call to a particular 'Servant of the Lord', whose identity is at the outset announced in a divine call to 'the islands and Gentile nations' (Ἀκούσατέ μου, νῆσοι, καὶ προσέχετε, ἔθνη, 49:1). While the Servant is tasked to restore / re-gather the judgement-dispersed people of Israel, his parallel and specific divine commission will be as a 'light to the nations and an instrument of deliverance to the ends of the earth' (εἰς φῶς ἐθνῶν τοῦ εἶναί σε εἰς σωτηρίαν ἕως ἐσχάτου τῆς γῆς, 49:6b). 'Ends of the earth' certainly refers to the promised ingathering of the globally-dispersed Israel, but the primary sense here appears to be the Servant's redemptive work as the 'light to the Gentiles'.

---

74   Marshall, *Luke*, 777; Nolland, *Luke 18:35 – 24:53*, 1006.
75   Garland, *Luke*, 835.
76   Marshall, *Luke*, 777.

If this proposed intertextual / metaleptic resonance is correct, Luke 21:28 becomes an appeal by Jesus to his followers to greet the coming 'fulfilment' of Isaiah 49:1–7, both of Jesus' personal mission as the Servant / 'light to the Gentiles', and of the Spirit-empowered mission of the 'servant church' of Acts in proclaiming 'salvation, to the ends of the earth'. The prophetic 'light to the Gentiles' linkage is of course well-known to Luke through the Song of Simeon, recorded in Luke 2:29–32, strengthening the likelihood that an Isaianic messianic redemptive 'mission to the Gentiles', suggestively invoked by Jesus, is indeed a rich intertextual sub-stratum to Luke 21:28.

But, like resolution of Luke's non-inclusion of Mark 13:10 in the first part of the discourse, confirmation of intertextual 'Gentile mission' references in the discourse's second part (Luke 21:14–28) is to be found in the Luke 24//Acts 1 interlocking ascension narratives.

Hays highlights how Luke 24 and Acts 1 'bring to life' Isaianic intertextual resonances in Luke's Gospel.[77] In the parallel panels in Luke 24 (the Emmaus Road in 24:13–35; the pre-ascension / ascension narrative in 24:36–53) the risen Christ explains that everything written about him in the Old Testament Scripture 'must be fulfilled', and he then 'opens the minds of the disciples' (τότε διήνοιξεν αὐτῶν τὸν νοῦν) so they can 'understand the Scriptures' (τοῦ συνιέναι τὰς γραφάς). It is no exaggeration to say he seems to be explaining exactly those intertextual resonances we are tracking in the discourse.

The Gentile mission is the particular focus of Jesus' pre-ascension words, *in content* and *in missional scope*. Furthermore, the Acts 1:8 (in this synoptic context) uniquely Lukan phrase 'my witnesses [...] to the ends of the earth' (καὶ ἔσεσθέ μου μάρτυρες [...] ἕως ἐσχάτου τῆς γῆς) seems to bring, with the complete and exact phrase ἕως ἐσχάτου τῆς γῆς, a clear, powerful, direct, and near-exclusive Koine Greek corpus resonance with Isaiah 8:9; 48:20; 49:6; 62:11,[78] an 'allusion' rather than just an 'echo' in Hays' and Beers' intertextual spectrum.[79] The Paul / Barnabas' direct quotation in Acts 13:47 of Isaiah 49:6's 'light to the Gentiles' language as central to the Lord's 'command' to them (apparently applying to themselves the Luke 24:44–49//Acts 1:6–9 commissioning) makes the ascension narratives' Isaianic linkages (especially to Isaiah 49) secure,[80] and credibly *intentionally* metaleptic.[81]

As we 'recover the original context from which the fragmentary echo came',[82] Acts 13:47 shows how the early church unpacked Jesus' metaleptic appeal to Isaiah 49:6 and its surrounds in two directions. First, *towards Jesus* as the Isaianic 'Servant' / Judge of Israel's oppressors (Isaiah 49:1–2 and 24–26), the Deliverer ending oppression (Isaiah 49:8–20), Restorer of Israel / 'the kingdom', and God's 'light to the Gentiles' (Isaiah 49:6, responding to Acts 1:6b). Secondly, *towards themselves* as ones called by Jesus to be his 'witnesses' (Acts 1:8), joining with him in his Servant task to proclaim God's deliverance in Gentile mission, gathering in non-Jewish believers 'in his

---

77 Hays, *Echoes*, 272.
78 Keener, *Acts*, 703, drawing on Tannehill, notes: 'Just as Acts 1:8 alludes to Isaiah for "my witnesses," it also alludes to Isaiah for the geographic range of the testimony of God's salvation (Isa. 41:5,9; 42:10; 43:6; 48:20; 49:6; 52:10; 62:11). That Luke depends on Isaiah's language here is clear: although mention of the ends of the earth is common in ancient literature, Luke's complete and exact phrase ἕως ἐσχάτου τῆς γῆς appears four or five times in the LXX (Isa. 8:9; 48:20; 49:6; 62:11; also *Pss. Sol.* 1:4) and only twice in the NT (Acts 13:47 and here); it also appears in Christian writings dependent on Isaiah or Acts, "but nowhere else in the immense range" of literature in the *Thesaurus linguae graecae* (TLG)'.
79 Hays, *Echoes*, 10–11.
80 Keener, *Acts*, 703.
81 Thus Pao, *Acts*, 97, notes that 'One can therefore conclude that the Isaianic text that lies behind Luke 24:47 and Acts 1:8 finally appears without significant alteration in Acts 13:47'.
82 Hays, *Echoes*, 11.

name'.[83] This 'allusion'-level metaleptic connection to Isaiah 49, confirmed by the 'quotation'-level connection in Acts 13:47, tends to support our earlier proposed 'suggestive echo'-level resonance between Luke 21:28 and Isaiah 49.

In terms of the 'Gentile mission' imperative, consistent with Wilson's observation, this seems to be how Luke records Jesus making clear that 'the inclusion of the Gentiles is not the result of a mere quirk of history [...]; rather it is grounded in the eternal will of God and an integral part of his promises to Israel'.[84] Jesus is pointing intertextually to Isaiah 49 not just as another Old Testament prophecy, but one integral to his life's divine calling, and to his future work through his disciples (Luke 24:4–49//Acts 1:8).

Thus any Isaiah 48:20 and 62:11 echo resonances of the Acts 1:8 ἕως ἐσχάτου τῆς γῆς phrase should also probably be read as invoking respectively: the same Isaiah 49 Servant Song complex (including the suggested 'raising of eyes' echo reference in 49:18), and the 'lift up your eyes' complex of chapters 60—62. Both thus invoke the message of global Gentile *as well as* Jewish deliverance.

(E) The Discourse Part 3: Fig Tree and Coming Kingdom (Mark 13:28-32; Luke 21:29-36; Matthew 24:32-36)

Completing our survey, the final portion (Luke 21:29–36, see Figure 4) again shows very strong conceptual and linguistic congruence with the two other synoptics (Mark 13:28–32//Matthew 24:32–36).

For the initial segment (Luke 21:29–31) there is only very minor reshaping of the Markan account in verses 29 and 30a, and the insertion of Lukan glosses in 29b and 31b respectively.[85] The 21:29b broadening of the fig tree reference (Israel?) to 'all the trees' may point to an eschatological period of redemptive fruitfulness shared in parallel by both Gentile and Jewish believers, a Lukan version of the eschatological gathering of 'the elect' by the angels, recorded in Mark 13:27//Matthew 24:31, but not specifically reflected in Luke. If so, quite aside from thematic melding with Jesus' preceding prophecies of the signs of coming eschatological judgement (not just the fall of Jerusalem) and redemption (including via potential 1 Enoch-resonance of this Koine Greek phrase),[86] the 'Gentile mission' is again unobtrusively reflected. As **Figure 4** demonstrates, the final segment (Luke 21: 34–36) appears largely peculiar to Luke / his special source.[87]

---

83 Beers, *Followers*, 130–33.
84 Wilson, *Gentiles*, 53.
85 καὶ πάντα τὰ δένδρα ('and all the trees') in 29b and ἡ βασιλεία τοῦ θεοῦ ('the kingdom of God') in 31b.
86 See Bolt, 'Breathing in Enoch', 175–182.
87 That the single word command in 21:36a to 'stay awake' (γρυπνετε) also appears in Mark 13:33 is most likely coincidental. The differing language and context of the wider Mark 13:33//Matthew 24:42 formulations compared with Luke may suggest two independent commands from Jesus, both keyed to the same initial imperative verb or expression, as we can note elsewhere in synoptic recording of Jesus' rhetorical teaching.

Figure 4

Mark 13:28–32	Luke 21:29–36	Matthew 24:32–36
²⁸ Ἀπὸ δὲ τῆς συκῆς μάθετε τὴν παραβολήν· ὅταν ἤδη ὁ κλάδος αὐτῆς ἁπαλὸς γένηται καὶ ἐκφύῃ τὰ φύλλα, γινώσκετε ὅτι ἐγγὺς τὸ θέρος ἐστίν· ²⁹ οὕτως καὶ ὑμεῖς, ὅταν ἴδητε ταῦτα γινόμενα, γινώσκετε ὅτι ἐγγύς ἐστιν ἐπὶ θύραις.	²⁹ Καὶ εἶπεν παραβολὴν αὐτοῖς· Ἴδετε τὴν συκῆν καὶ πάντα τὰ δένδρα· ³⁰ ὅταν προβάλωσιν ἤδη, βλέποντες ἀφ' ἑαυτῶν γινώσκετε ὅτι ἤδη ἐγγὺς τὸ θέρος ἐστίν· ³¹ οὕτως καὶ ὑμεῖς, ὅταν ἴδητε ταῦτα γινόμενα, γινώσκετε ὅτι ἐγγύς ἐστιν ἡ βασιλεία τοῦ θεοῦ.	³² Ἀπὸ δὲ τῆς συκῆς μάθετε τὴν παραβολήν· ὅταν ἤδη ὁ κλάδος αὐτῆς γένηται ἁπαλὸς καὶ τὰ φύλλα ἐκφύῃ, γινώσκετε ὅτι ἐγγὺς τὸ θέρος· ³³ οὕτως καὶ ὑμεῖς, ὅταν ἴδητε πάντα ταῦτα, γινώσκετε ὅτι ἐγγύς ἐστιν ἐπὶ θύραις.
³⁰ ἀμὴν λέγω ὑμῖν ὅτι οὐ μὴ παρέλθῃ ἡ γενεὰ αὕτη μέχρις οὗ ταῦτα πάντα γένηται. ³¹ ὁ οὐρανὸς καὶ ἡ γῆ παρελεύσονται, οἱ δὲ λόγοι μου οὐ μὴ παρελεύσονται.	³² ἀμὴν λέγω ὑμῖν ὅτι οὐ μὴ παρέλθῃ ἡ γενεὰ αὕτη ἕως ἂν πάντα γένηται. ³³ ὁ οὐρανὸς καὶ ἡ γῆ παρελεύσονται, οἱ δὲ λόγοι μου οὐ μὴ παρελεύσονται. ³⁴ Προσέχετε δὲ ἑαυτοῖς μήποτε βαρηθῶσιν ὑμῶν αἱ καρδίαι ἐν κραιπάλῃ καὶ μέθῃ καὶ μερίμναις βιωτικαῖς, καὶ ἐπιστῇ ἐφ' ὑμᾶς αἰφνίδιος ἡ ἡμέρα ἐκείνη ³⁵ ὡς παγίς· ἐπεισελεύσεται γὰρ ἐπὶ πάντας τοὺς καθημένους ἐπὶ πρόσωπον πάσης τῆς γῆς. ³⁶ ἀγρυπνεῖτε δὲ ἐν παντὶ καιρῷ δεόμενοι ἵνα κατισχύσητε ἐκφυγεῖν ταῦτα πάντα τὰ μέλλοντα γίνεσθαι, καὶ σταθῆναι ἔμπροσθεν τοῦ υἱοῦ τοῦ ἀνθρώπου.	³⁴ ἀμὴν λέγω ὑμῖν ὅτι οὐ μὴ παρέλθῃ ἡ γενεὰ αὕτη ἕως ἂν πάντα ταῦτα γένηται. ³⁵ ὁ οὐρανὸς καὶ ἡ γῆ παρελεύσονται, οἱ δὲ λόγοι μου οὐ μὴ παρέλθωσιν.
³² Περὶ δὲ τῆς ἡμέρας ἐκείνης ἢ τῆς ὥρας οὐδεὶς οἶδεν, οὐδὲ οἱ ἄγγελοι ἐν οὐρανῷ οὐδὲ ὁ υἱός, εἰ μὴ ὁ πατήρ.		³⁶ Περὶ δὲ τῆς ἡμέρας ἐκείνης καὶ ὥρας οὐδεὶς οἶδεν, οὐδὲ οἱ ἄγγελοι τῶν οὐρανῶν οὐδὲ ὁ υἱός, εἰ μὴ ὁ πατὴρ μόνος.

Key:

Concepts shared by all 3 Synoptics
Concepts shared by Mark/Luke
Concepts shared by Luke/Matthew
Concepts shared by Mark/Matthew
Mark only
Luke only
Matthew only

Vocabulary shared
Exact words/phrases shared

4. Conclusions

While the *text* of the Lukan version of Jesus' temple destruction / last times discourse is not identical with its synoptic parallels, the *narrative structure* is. With strong conceptual and structural congruences, supported by repeated significant 'runs' of identical Koine phrases and words, the Lukan version seems to share and even absorb into itself an underlying synoptic (overwhelmingly Markan) tradition. Luke simultaneously apparently edits in special (apparently reliable eyewitness) material, which resonates with and improves (but never contradicts or materially amends) the Markan material. Luke seems fully conversant with, and respectful of, the Markan / proto-Markan text, and is especially conscious of the Danielic and Isaianic resonances of Jesus' words.

The puzzling omission by Luke of Jesus' direct global evangelism imperative (Mark 13:10) that, pre-Parousia, the 'gospel must first be preached to all nations' is explicable. Hinted at in Luke 21:13, the imperative is richly woven into the discourse through multiple intertextual references apparently made by Jesus according to Luke's separate 'eyewitness account' material. Luke 24:44–49//Acts 1:6–9 (the 'hinging' ascension event connecting Luke-Acts) then provide the hermeneutical key which makes explicit and unlocks the discourse's global evangelism substratum in a new and powerful way.

As regards Luke 21:5–13, Luke 24:44–49//Acts 1:6–9 show that, far from excising or reformulating Mark 13:10, Luke is aware of a parallel and later command from Jesus that gives both new kerygmatic content summarising Jesus' saving work, and the global mission strategy narrative and theological schema which will drive intentional global gospel proclamation in Acts.

For the discourse's second section (Luke 21:14–28), these same hinging passages help confirm, especially through 'explanatory' intertextual references to global Gentile mission in Isaiah, the rich network of intertextual quotes, allusions and echoes of LXX texts drawn into this section by Luke. These firmly locate Jesus' Gentile mission imperative (and the curious 21:24b phrase 'the times of the Gentiles') within an interlocking network of balanced pairs of scriptural prophecies that 'must be fulfilled' regarding world events and Jesus as Judge, Redeemer, and Servant Saviour. Most significantly, metaleptic connection of the words of Jesus to Isaiah 49 emphasises that his 'mission to the Gentiles' command is grounded in nothing less than God's eternal and explicit commissioning of Jesus to be his Servant / Redeemer and 'light to the Gentiles'.[88]

Any Lukan connective shaping in the discourse arguably reflects not so much personal stylistic preferences, as a desire to reflect faithfully the words and works of a Jesus whom his sources said was above all *personally* intertextual, deliberately and consistently living, ministering, and speaking to fulfil 'all that is written about me in the Law, the Prophets and the Psalms'.

Patrick Cole
Research Student, St Mark's National Theological Centre, CSU
pandncole@bigpond.com

---

88 Wilson, *Gentiles*, 53.

Bibliography

Bauckham, R. — *Jesus and the Eyewitnesses: the Gospels as Eyewitness Testimony* (Grand Rapids, MI: Eerdmans, 2006).

Bauer, D. R. — *The Book of Acts as Story. A Narrative-Critical Study* (Grand Rapids, MI: Baker Academic, 2021).

Beers, H. — *The Followers of Jesus as the 'Servant'—Luke's Model from Isaiah for the Disciples in Luke-Acts* (London: Bloomsbury T&T Clark, 2016).

ben Ya'akov, S. and A. b-M. ben-Asher (eds.) — *The Tanach: Leningrad Codex* (2024) <https://tanach.us/Tanach.xml> [accessed via <https://biblehub.com/> July/August 2024]

Bock, D. L. — *Acts* (Grand Rapids, MI: Baker Academic, 2007).

Bock, D. L. — *Luke* (Grand Rapids, MI: Baker Academic, 1994).

Bock, D. L. — *Proclamation from Prophey and Pattern: Lucan Old Testament Christology* (Sheffield: JSOT Press, 1987).

Bolt, P. G. — 'Breathing in Enoch to breathe out Jesus. Two Examples of Luke's Apocalypticism', in P. G. Bolt (ed.), *The Future of Gospels and Acts Research* (CGAR Series 3; Macquarie Park: SCD Press, 2021), 153–188.

Bovon, F. — *Luke 3: A Commentary on the Gospel of Luke 19:28—24:53* (Minneapolis, MN: Fortress, 2012).

Brent, A. — 'Luke-Acts and the Imperial Cult in Asia Minor', *Journal of Theological Studies* 48:2 (1997), 411–38.

Bruce, F. F. — *The Acts of the Apostles* (London: Tyndale, 1951).

Edwards, J. R. — *The Gospel According to Mark* (Grand Rapids, MI: Eerdmans, 2002).

Evans, C. E. — *Mark 8:27—16:20* (Nashville, TN: Thomas Nelson, 2001).

Fitzmyer, J. A. — *The Gospel According to Luke I—IX: Introduction, Translation, and Notes* (New York, NY: Doubleday, 1979).

Fitzmyer, J. A. — *The Gospel According to Luke X—XXIV: Introduction, Translation, and Notes* (New York, NY: Doubleday, 1985).

Garland, D. E. — *Luke* (Grand Rapids, MI: Zondervan Academic, 2011).

Hays, R. B. — *Echoes of Scripture in the Gospels* (Waco, TX: Baylor University Press, 2016).

Holmes, M. W. — *The Greek New Testament: SBL Edition* (2010) <https://www.biblegateway.com/> [accessed June-December 2023].

Keener, C. S. — *Acts: An Exegetic Commentary* (Grand Rapids, MI: Baker Academic, 2012).

Lane, W. L. — *The Gospel According to Mark* (Grand Rapids, MI: Eerdmans, 1974).

Marshall, I. H.	*The Gospel of Luke: A Commentary on the Greek Text* (Exeter: Paternoster, 1978).
Morris, L.	*The Gospel According to St Luke* (Grand Rapids, MI: Eerdmans, 1974).
Nolland, J.	'"The Times of the Nations" and a Prophetic Pattern in Luke 21', in T. R. Hatina (ed.), *Interpretation in Early Christian Gospels. Vol. 3: The Gospel of Luke* (London: T&T Clark, 2010), 133–47.
Nolland, J.	*Luke 1—9:20* (Nashville, TN: Thomas Nelson, 2000).
Nolland, J.	*Luke 18:35—24:53* (Nashville, TN: Thomas Nelson, 1993).
Pao, D. W. and E. J. Schnabel	'Luke', in G. K.Beale and D. A. Carson (eds.), *Commentary on the New Testament use of the Old Testament* (Grand Rapids, MI: Baker Academic, 2007), 251–414.
Pao, D. W.	*Acts and the Isaianic New Exodus* (Eugene, OR: Wipf & Stock, 2016).
Porter, S. E.	'The Unity of Luke-Acts and the Ascension Narratives', in D. K. Bryan and D. W. Pao (eds.), *Ascent into Heaven in Luke-Acts: New Explorations of Luke's Narrative Hinge* (Minneapolis, MN: Fortress, 2016), 111–36.
Rahlfs, A.	*Septuagint (LXX)* (Stuttgart: Deutsche Bibel Gesellschaft, 2006) <https://www.academic-bible.com/en/scholarly-bible-editions/scholarly-bible-editions/the-septuagint-lxx> [accessed June-December 2023].
Stavroula, C.	'Metaphrasis: Mapping Premodern Rewriting', in C. Stavroula, C. and C. Høgel, *Metaphrasis: A Byzantine Concept of Rewriting and Its Hagiographical Products* (Brill, 2020), 3–60 <https://brill.com/downloadpdf/display/book/9789004438453/BP000010.pdf> [downloaded 20 October 2023 02:37:58AM].
Walton, S.	'The End: What and When? Eschatology in Luke-Acts', in Hilary Marlow, Karla Pollman, and H. van Noorden (eds.), *Eschatology in Antiquity: Forms and Functions* (Oxford UK, and New York, NY: Abingdon and Routledge, 2021), 383–95.
Wilson, S. G.	*The Gentiles and the Gentile Mission in Luke-Acts* (Cambridge: Cambridge University Press), 1973.

Appendix 1: Old Testament LXX Resonances of Selected Luke 21 Discourse Verses

Luke 21 verse	Referenced Words	Possible Old Testament LXX Reference
10	Nation against nation, kingdom against kingdom Ἐγερθήσεται ἔθνος ἐπ' ἔθνος καὶ βασιλεία ἐπὶ βασιλείαν	Isa. 19:2 καὶ ἐπεγερθήσονται Αἰγύπτιοι ἐπ' Αἰγυπτίους, καὶ πολεμήσει ἄνθρωπος τὸν ἀδελφὸν αὐτοῦ καὶ ἄνθρωπος τὸν πλησίον αὐτοῦ, πόλις ἐπὶ πόλιν καὶ νομὸς ἐπὶ νομόν (God at work to trouble the Egyptian empire) 2 Chron. 15:6 καὶ πολεμήσει ἔθνος πρὸς ἔθνος καὶ πόλις πρὸς πόλιν (God at work to trouble the pagan nations)
11	Earthquakes, famines, pestilences and fearful events <u>σεισμοί τε μεγάλοι</u> καὶ κατὰ τόπους <u>λιμοὶ</u> καὶ <u>λοιμοὶ</u> ἔσονται, <u>φόβητρά</u> τε καὶ σημεῖα ἀπ' οὐρανοῦ μεγάλα ἔσται.	Isa.5:13–14 ¹³τοίνυν αἰχμάλωτος ὁ λαός μου ἐγενήθη διὰ τὸ μὴ εἰδέναι αὐτοὺς τὸν κύριον, καὶ πλῆθος ἐγενήθη νεκρῶν διὰ <u>λιμὸν</u> καὶ δίψαν ὕδατος. ¹⁴καὶ ἐπλάτυνεν ὁ ᾅδης τὴν ψυχὴν αὐτοῦ καὶ διήνοιξεν τὸ στόμα αὐτοῦ τοῦ μὴ διαλιπεῖν, καὶ καταβήσονται οἱ ἔνδοξοι καὶ οἱ μεγάλοι καὶ οἱ πλούσιοι καὶ οἱ λοιμοὶ αὐτῆς Ezek. 38:19–22 καὶ ὁ ζῆλός μου. ἐν πυρὶ τῆς ὀργῆς μου ἐλάλησα Εἰ μὴν ἐν τῇ ἡμέρᾳ ἐκείνῃ ἔσται <u>σεισμὸς μέγας</u> ἐπὶ γῆς Ισραηλ, καὶ <u>σεισθήσονται</u> ἀπὸ προσώπου κυρίου … ²⁰ πάντες οἱ ἄνθρωποι οἱ ἐπὶ προσώπου τῆς γῆς, καὶ ῥαγήσεται τὰ ὄρη, καὶ πεσοῦνται αἱ φάραγγες, καὶ πᾶν τεῖχος ἐπὶ τὴν γῆν πεσεῖται. ²¹ καὶ καλέσω ἐπ' αὐτὸν πᾶν <u>φόβον</u>, λέγει κύριος· μάχαιρα ἀνθρώπου ἐπὶ τὸν ἀδελφὸν αὐτοῦ ἔσται. ²²καὶ κρινῶ αὐτὸν <u>θανάτῳ</u> καὶ αἵματι καὶ ὑετῷ κατακλύζοντι καὶ λίθοις χαλάζης, καὶ πῦρ καὶ θεῖον βρέξω ἐπ' αὐτὸν καὶ ἐπὶ πάντας τοὺς μετ' αὐτοῦ καὶ ἐπ' ἔθνη πολλὰ μετ' αὐτοῦ. Hag. 2:6 διότι τάδε λέγει κύριος παντοκράτωρ Ἔτι ἅπαξ ἐγὼ <u>σείσω</u> τὸν οὐρανὸν καὶ τὴν γῆν καὶ τὴν θάλασσαν καὶ τὴν ξηράν

20a	Jerusalem being surrounded by armies Ὅταν δὲ ἴδητε <u>κυκλουμένην</u> ὑπὸ στρατοπέδων Ἰερουσαλήμ	Isa. 29:3 καὶ <u>κυκλώσω</u> ὡς Δαυιδ ἐπὶ σὲ καὶ βαλῶ περὶ σὲ χάρακα καὶ θήσω περὶ σὲ πύργους Jer. 6:6 ὅτι τάδε λέγει κύριος Ἔκκοψον τὰ ξύλα αὐτῆς, ἔκχεον ἐπὶ Ιερουσαλημ δύναμιν· ὦ πόλις ψευδής, ὅλη καταδυναστεία ἐν αὐτῇ
20b	Its desolation is near τότε γνῶτε ὅτι ἤγγικεν ἡ <u>ἐρήμωσις</u> αὐτῆς	Only word Luke has in common with Mark is 'desolation', but note Daniel 'trampling' and 'abomination' refs. too in parallel. Dan. 8:13 καὶ ἡ ἁμαρτία <u>ἐρημώσεως</u> ἡ δοθεῖσα, καὶ τὰ ἅγια ἐρημωθήσεται εἰς <u>καταπάτημα</u> Dan. 9:2 (Old Greek text) εἰς συμπλήρωσιν <u>ἐρημώσεως</u> Ιερουσαλημ ἑβδομήκοντα ἔτη Dan. 9:27 (OG text) καὶ ἀφαιρεθήσεται ἡ <u>ἐρήμωσις</u> / καὶ ἐπὶ τὸ ἱερὸν βδέλυγμα τῶν <u>ἐρημώσεων</u> ἔσται ἕως συντελείας / καὶ συντέλεια δοθήσεται ἐπὶ τὴν <u>ἐρήμωσιν</u> Dan. 12:11 καὶ ἑτοιμασθῇ δοθῆναι τὸ βδέλυγμα τῆς <u>ἐρημώσεως</u> Lev. 26:34,35 τὰς ἡμέρας τῆς <u>ἐρημώσεως</u> αὐτῆς 2 Chron. 30:7 καὶ παρέδωκεν αὐτοὺς εἰς <u>ἐρήμωσιν</u> 2 Chron. 36:21 πάσας τὰς ἡμέρας τῆς <u>ἐρημώσεως</u> Ps. 73:19 (LXX 72:19) πῶς ἐγένοντο εἰς <u>ἐρήμωσιν</u> Jer. 4:7 τοῦ θεῖναι τὴν γῆν εἰς <u>ἐρήμωσιν</u> Jer. 7:34 ὅτι εἰς <u>ἐρήμωσιν</u> ἔσται πᾶσα ἡ γῆ Jer. 22:5 ὅτι εἰς <u>ἐρήμωσιν</u> ἔσται ὁ οἶκος οὗτος Jer. 25:18 (LXX 32:18) τοῦ θεῖναι αὐτὰς εἰς <u>ἐρήμωσιν</u> Jer. 44:6 (LXX 51:6) καὶ ἐγενήθησαν εἰς <u>ἐρήμωσιν</u> Jer. 44:22 (LXX 51:22) ἡ γῆ ὑμῶν εἰς <u>ἐρήμωσιν</u>

22	This is the <u>time of vengeance</u> ...	Isa. 34:8	ἡμέρα γὰρ <u>κρίσεως</u>
		Isa. 35:4	ἰδοὺ ὁ θεὸς ἡμῶν <u>κρίσιν ἀνταποδίδωσιν</u> καὶ <u>ἀνταποδώσει</u>
	ὅτι <u>ἡμέραι ἐκδικήσεως</u>	Isa. 59:17	καὶ περιεβάλετο ἱμάτιον <u>ἐκδικήσεως</u> καὶ τὸ περιβόλαιο (garment of vengeance)
		Isa. 61:2	καὶ <u>ἡμέραν ἀνταποδόσεως</u>
		Isa. 63:4	<u>ἡμέρα γὰρ ἀνταποδόσεως</u>
		Jer. 5:29	ἢ ἐν ἔθνει τῷ τοιούτῳ οὐκ <u>ἐκδικήσει</u> ἡ ψυχή μου
		Jer. 11:20	σοῦ <u>ἐκδίκησιν</u> ἐξ αὐτῶν
		Jer. 20:12	παρὰ σοῦ <u>ἐκδίκησιν</u> ἐν αὐτοῖς
		Jer. 46:10 (LXX 26:10)	καὶ ἡ ἡμέρα ἐκείνη κυρίῳ τῷ θεῷ ἡμῶν <u>ἡμέρα ἐκδικήσεως</u> τοῦ <u>ἐκδικῆσαι</u> τοὺς ἐχθροὺς αὐτοῦ
		Jer. 46:21 (LXX 26:21)	ὅτι ἡμέρα ἀπωλείας ἦλθεν ἐπ᾽ αὐτοὺς καὶ <u>καιρὸς ἐκδικήσεως</u> αὐτῶν
		Jer. 50:15 (LXX 27:15)	ὅτι <u>ἐκδίκησις</u> παρὰ θεοῦ ἐστιν, ἐκδικεῖτε ἐπ᾽ αὐτήν· καθὼς <u>ἐποίησεν</u>, ποιήσατε αὐτῇ (vengeance against Babylon)
		Jer. 50:27,28,31 (LXX 27:27, 28, 31)	²⁷ὅτι ἥκει ἡ <u>ἡμέρα</u> αὐτῶν καὶ <u>καιρὸς ἐκδικήσεως</u> αὐτῶν ²⁸τὴν <u>ἐκδίκησιν</u> παρὰ κυρίου θεοῦ ἡμῶν ³¹ ἡ <u>ἡμέρα</u> σου καὶ ὁ <u>καιρὸς ἐκδικήσεώς</u> σου
		Jer. 51:6 (LXX 28:6)	ὅτι <u>καιρὸς ἐκδικήσεως</u> αὐτῆς ἐστιν παρὰ κυρίου, ἀνταπόδομα αὐτὸς ἀνταποδίδωσιν αὐτῇ
		Jer. 51:11 (LXX 28:11)	ὅτι <u>ἐκδίκησις</u> κυρίου ἐστίν, <u>ἐκδίκησις</u> λαοῦ αὐτοῦ ἐστιν (vengeance on Babylon, vengeance for temple)
		Jer. 51:36 (LXX 28:36)	καὶ <u>ἐκδικήσω</u> τὴν <u>ἐκδίκησίν</u> σου
		Hos. 9:7	αἱ <u>ἡμέραι</u> τῆς <u>ἐκδικήσεως</u>, ἥκασιν αἱ <u>ἡμέραι</u> τῆς <u>ἀνταποδόσεώς</u> σου

23b	Great distress and wrath against this people ἔσται γὰρ ἀνάγκη μεγάλη ἐπὶ τῆς γῆς καὶ <u>ὀργὴ</u> τῷ λαῷ τούτῳ	Dan. 12:1 ἐκείνη ἡ ἡμέρα θλίψεως, οἵα οὐκ ἐγενήθη ἀφ' οὗ ἐγενήθησαν ἕως τῆς ἡμέρας ἐκείνης (NB. connection with Mark 13:19/Matt 24:21) Isa. 13:9 ἰδοὺ γὰρ ἡμέρα κυρίου ἀνίατος ἔρχεται θυμοῦ καὶ <u>ὀργῆς</u> θεῖναι τὴν οἰκουμένην ὅλην ἔρημον καὶ τοὺς ἁμαρτωλοὺς ἀπολέσαι ἐξ αὐτῆς
24a	Fall by the sword and be taken as prisoners to all the nations: <u>καὶ πεσοῦνται</u> στόματι <u>μαχαίρης</u> καὶ <u>αἰχμαλωτισθήσονται</u> <u>εἰς τὰ ἔθνη πάντα</u>	Jer. 20:4–6 ⁴διότι τάδε λέγει κύριος Ἰδοὺ ἐγὼ δίδωμί σε εἰς μετοικίαν σὺν πᾶσι τοῖς φίλοις σου, <u>καὶ πεσοῦνται ἐν μαχαίρᾳ</u> ἐχθρῶν αὐτῶν, καὶ οἱ ὀφθαλμοί σου ὄψονται, καὶ σὲ καὶ πάντα Ιουδαν δώσω εἰς χεῖρας βασιλέως Βαβυλῶνος, καὶ μετοικιοῦσιν αὐτοὺς καὶ κατακόψουσιν αὐτοὺς ἐν μαχαίραις· ⁵καὶ δώσω τὴν πᾶσαν ἰσχὺν τῆς πόλεως ταύτης καὶ πάντας τοὺς πόνους αὐτῆς καὶ πάντας τοὺς θησαυροὺς τοῦ βασιλέως Ιουδα εἰς χεῖρας ἐχθρῶν αὐτοῦ, καὶ ἄξουσιν αὐτοὺς εἰς Βαβυλῶνα. ⁶καὶ σὺ καὶ πάντες οἱ κατοικοῦντες ἐν τῷ οἴκῳ σου πορεύσεσθε <u>ἐν αἰχμαλωσίᾳ</u>, καὶ ἐν Βαβυλῶνι ἀποθανῇ καὶ ἐκεῖ ταφήσῃ, σὺ καὶ πάντες οἱ φίλοι σου, οἷς ἐπροφήτευσας αὐτοῖς ψευδῆ Deut. 28:64 καὶ διασπερεῖ σε κύριος ὁ θεός σου <u>εἰς πάντα τὰ ἔθνη</u>
24b	'Jerusalem <u>will be trampled on</u> by the Gentiles' καὶ Ἰερουσαλὴμ ἔσται <u>πατουμένη</u> ὑπὸ ἐθνῶν	Isa. 5:5 καταπάτημα (καταπατέω) Isa. 10:6 καταπατεῖν (καταπατέω) Isa. 22:5 καταπατήματος (καταπατέω) Isa. 28:3 καταπατηθήσεται (καταπατέω) Isa. 63:3,6 καταπεπατημένης (καταπατέω) κατεπάτησα (καταπατέω) Isa. 63:18 κατεπάτησαν (καταπατέω) Dan. 8:13 καταπάτημα (καταπατέω) (see also note on v.20b above) Zech. 12:3 (LXX) καὶ ἔσται ἐν τῇ ἡμέρᾳ ἐκείνῃ θήσομαι τὴν Ιερουσαλημ λίθον <u>καταπατούμενον</u> πᾶσιν τοῖς ἔθνεσιν Hos. 5:11 <u>κατεπάτησεν</u> κρίμα

25a	Signs in the sun, moon and stars Καὶ ἔσονται σημεῖα ἐν <u>ἡλίῳ</u> καὶ <u>σελήνῃ</u> καὶ <u>ἄστροις</u>	Isa. 13:10 οἱ γὰρ <u>ἀστέρες</u> τοῦ οὐρανοῦ καὶ ὁ Ὠρίων καὶ πᾶς ὁ κόσμος τοῦ οὐρανοῦ τὸ φῶς οὐ δώσουσιν, καὶ σκοτισθήσεται τοῦ <u>ἡλίου</u> ἀνατέλλοντος, καὶ ἡ <u>σελήνη</u> οὐ δώσει τὸ φῶς αὐτῆς. Isa. 34:4 καὶ ἑλιγήσεται ὁ οὐρανὸς ὡς βιβλίον, καὶ πάντα τὰ <u>ἄστρα</u> πεσεῖται ὡς φύλλα ἐξ ἀμπέλου καὶ ὡς πίπτει φύλλα ἀπὸ συκῆς
25b	Anguish and perplexity at the roaring and tossing of the sea καὶ ἐπὶ τῆς γῆς συνοχὴ ἐθνῶν ἐν <u>ἀπορίᾳ</u> ἤχους θαλάσσης καὶ σάλου	Psa. 46:2–3 ³διὰ τοῦτο οὐ φοβηθησόμεθα ἐν τῷ ταράσσεσθαι τὴν γῆν καὶ μετατίθεσθαι ὄρη ἐν καρδίαις θαλασσῶν. ⁴ἤχησαν καὶ ἐταράχθησαν τὰ ὕδατα αὐτῶν, ἐταράχθησαν τὰ ὄρη ἐν τῇ κραταιότητι αὐτοῦ. Isa. 24:18–19 ¹⁸ καὶ ἔσται ὁ φεύγων τὸν φόβον ἐμπεσεῖται εἰς τὸν βόθυνον, ὁ δὲ ἐκβαίνων ἐκ τοῦ βοθύνου ἁλώσεται ὑπὸ τῆς παγίδος, ὅτι θυρίδες ἐκ τοῦ οὐρανοῦ ἠνεῴχθησαν, καὶ σεισθήσεται τὰ θεμέλια τῆς γῆς. ¹⁹ ταραχῇ ταραχθήσεται ἡ γῆ, καὶ <u>ἀπορίᾳ</u> ἀπορηθήσεται ἡ γῆ·
26a	People will faint from terror ἀποψυχόντων ἀνθρώπων ἀπὸ <u>φόβου</u> καὶ προσδοκίας τῶν ἐπερχομένων τῇ οἰκουμένῃ	Isa. 2:10 καὶ νῦν εἰσέλθετε εἰς τὰς πέτρας καὶ κρύπτεσθε εἰς τὴν γῆν ἀπὸ προσώπου <u>τοῦ φόβου κυρίου</u> Isa. 2:19 εἰσενέγκαντες εἰς τὰ σπήλαια καὶ εἰς τὰς σχισμὰς τῶν πετρῶν καὶ εἰς τὰς τρώγλας τῆς γῆς ἀπὸ προσώπου <u>τοῦ φόβου κυρίου</u> καὶ ἀπὸ τῆς δόξης τῆς ἰσχύος αὐτοῦ, ὅταν ἀναστῇ θραῦσαι τὴν γῆν. Isa. 2:21 <u>τοῦ φόβου κυρίου</u> καὶ ἀπὸ τῆς δόξης τῆς ἰσχύος αὐτοῦ, ὅταν ἀναστῇ θραῦσαι τὴν γῆν (NB. in context of rising to shake the earth) Isa. 24:17 <u>φόβος</u> καὶ βόθυνος καὶ παγὶς ἐφ᾽ ὑμᾶς τοὺς ἐνοικοῦντας ἐπὶ τῆς γῆς

26b	Heavenly bodies will be shaken	
	αἱ γὰρ δυνάμεις τῶν οὐρανῶν σαλευθήσονται	Isa. 13:13 ὁ γὰρ οὐρανὸς θυμωθήσεται καὶ ἡ γῆ σεισθήσεται ἐκ τῶν θεμελίων αὐτῆς διὰ θυμὸν ὀργῆς κυρίου
27	The Son of Man coming in a cloud with power and great glory	
	καὶ τότε ὄψονται <u>τὸν υἱὸν τοῦ ἀνθρώπου</u> ἐρχόμενον <u>ἐν νεφέλῃ</u> μετὰ δυνάμεως καὶ δόξης πολλῆς	Dan. 7:13 καὶ ἰδοὺ <u>ἐπὶ τῶν νεφελῶν</u> τοῦ οὐρανοῦ <u>ὡς υἱὸς ἀνθρώπου</u> ἤρχετο, καὶ ὡς παλαιὸς ἡμερῶν παρῆν
27b/28	With power and great glory. Stand up, and lift your heads, because your redemption is drawing near.	Isa. 40:26 <u>ἀναβλέψατε εἰς ὕψος τοὺς ὀφθαλμοὺς ὑμῶν</u> καὶ ἴδετε· τίς κατέδειξεν πάντα ταῦτα; ὁ ἐκφέρων κατὰ ἀριθμὸν τὸν κόσμον αὐτοῦ πάντας ἐπ' ὀνόματι καλέσει·ἀπὸ <u>πολλῆς δόξης</u> καὶ ἐν κράτει ἰσχύος οὐδέν σε ἔλαθεν
	...μετὰ δυνάμεως καὶ <u>δόξης πολλῆς</u>. ἀρχομένων δὲ τούτων γίνεσθαι ἀνακύψατε <u>καὶ ἐπάρατε τὰς κεφαλὰς ὑμῶν</u>, διότι ἐγγίζει ἡ ἀπολύτρωσις ὑμῶν διότι ἐγγίζει ἡ <u>ἀπολύτρωσις</u> ὑμῶν	Isa. 49:18 <u>ἆρον κύκλῳ τοὺς ὀφθαλμούς σου</u> καὶ ἰδὲ πάντας, ἰδοὺ συνήχθησαν καὶ ἤλθοσαν πρὸς σέ· ζῶ ἐγώ, λέγει κύριος, ὅτι πάντας αὐτοὺς ἐνδύσῃ καὶ περιθήσῃ αὐτοὺς ὡς κόσμον νύμφης Isa. 51:6 <u>ἄρατε εἰς τὸν οὐρανὸν τοὺς ὀφθαλμοὺς ὑμῶν</u> καὶ ἐμβλέψατε εἰς τὴν γῆν κάτω, ὅτι ὁ οὐρανὸς ὡς καπνὸς ἐστερεώθη, ἡ δὲ γῆ ὡς ἱμάτιον παλαιωθήσεται, οἱ δὲ κατοικοῦντες τὴν γῆν ὥσπερ ταῦτα ἀποθανοῦνται, τὸ δὲ σωτήριόν μου εἰς τὸν αἰῶνα ἔσται, ἡ δὲ δικαιοσύνη μου οὐ μὴ ἐκλίπῃ Isa. 60:1,4 ¹ Φωτίζου φωτίζου, Ιερουσαλημ, ἥκει γάρ σου τὸ φῶς, <u>καὶ ἡ δόξα κυρίου</u> ἐπὶ σὲ ἀνατέταλκεν. ²ἰδοὺ σκότος καὶ γνόφος καλύψει γῆν ἐπ' ἔθνη· ἐπὶ δὲ σὲ φανήσεται κύριος, <u>καὶ ἡ δόξα αὐτοῦ</u> ἐπὶ σὲ ὀφθήσεται. ³καὶ πορεύσονται βασιλεῖς τῷ φωτί σου καὶ ἔθνη τῇ λαμπρότητί σου. ⁴ <u>ἆρον κύκλῳ τοὺς ὀφθαλμούς σου</u>

'Wonders in the heaven above' (Acts 2:19)

The graeco-roman portent mentality and *terata* in luke-acts

JAMES R. HARRISON

Abstract

This article examines Luke's adapted citation from LXX Joel 2:30 ('wonders from the heavens above') in Acts 2:19 against the backdrop of Jewish and Graeco-Roman literary accounts of prodigies and portents. While there are similarities between this literary corpus and Luke-Acts, Lukan distinctives emerge, reflecting the impact of Luke's Christology and realised eschatology upon his presentation of apocalyptic portents in the Gospel, as well as his focus on the ministry outcomes of portents in Acts. Two case studies—Luke's supra-cephalic fire portents (Acts 2:3) and the meteorite statue from heaven in the temple of Artemis (19:35)—are investigated in their Jewish and Graeco-Roman context. Luke's transcultural focus and his awareness of the first-century constriction of portents to the Roman ruler are explored. Not only does Luke bring out the cross-cultural significance of the Pentecost fire portents in regards to the outworking of Joel's prophecy in Acts, but he also highlights the continuing threat of indigenous gods such as Artemis to the Christian mission, while exposing their ultimate powerlessness for his auditors.

In his adapted citation of Joel's prophecy in Acts 2:16–21 (LXX Joel 2:28–32), Luke specifies by means of his addition to Acts 2:19 exactly where the 'wonders' (τέρατα) accompanying the last days would take place, in contrast to the truncated version found in LXX Joel 2:30. By adding the word 'above' (ἄνω) to the phrase 'in the heaven' (ἐν τῷ οὐρανῷ) in Acts 2:19,[1] Luke airs tantalisingly the expectation of portents 'in the heaven above' for his readers.[2] However, throughout the book of Acts, Luke consistently links τέρατα with σημεῖα as a description of

---

1 On the role of Joel's prophecy in Acts 2:16–21 in relation to Graeco-Roman revelatory phenomena, Harrison, 'Prophecy, Divination, and Oneirology'.
2 Luke's strategic addition of ἄνω to Joel's phrase mentioning portents appears not to be replicated in the Graeco-Roman literature. For example, in the case of comets, different formulae and motifs are used. Direction of comet: 'in [ἀφ'] the west'; 'towards [πρός] the north'; 'in [περί] the equinoctial zone'; 'from [ἀπό] the south towards [πρός] the north', etc. Location of comet: 'in [κατά] the sky'; 'over [ὑπέρ] the sea'; 'over [ὑπέρ] Rome'; 'over [ὑπέρ] the city'. Time of comet's appearance: 'around [πρός] the time of the winter solstice'; 'for [ἐπί] a long time'; 'from [ἀπό] the third to [ἕως] the fifth hour', etc. For 63 Latin and Greek samples, see Barrett, 'Observations of Comets'. Seemingly, in view of this selection of ancient evidence, Luke is not only stylistically clarifying the location of Joel's heavenly portents by means of his τέρατα addition of ἄνω to ἐν τῷ οὐρανῷ (Acts 2:19), but he is also differentiating to some degree his phraseology from the routine concerns and formulae associated with Graeco-Roman portents.

miracles,[3] recalling the Deuteronomic 'salvation' motifs of the LXX.[4] It could be viably argued that Luke has subordinated any interest in portents to the motif of 'signs on the earth'. But such an unqualified conclusion makes Luke's addition of ἄνω in Acts 2:19 even more puzzling, placing as it does a heavier emphasis on Joel's distinction between 'heavenly' wonders and 'earthly' signs. Why is such an intensification of the distinction necessary on Luke's part if the σημεῖα καὶ τέρατα phrase merely denotes the miraculous, infused with Old Testament soteriological echoes?

Furthermore, such a conclusion would be premature, given the strong Jewish tradition of signs heralding the eschatological messianic age.[5] It is also unlikely that Luke, sensitive to Graeco-Roman cultural interests, would have totally ignored the pervasive tradition of prodigies and portents which feature so prominently in the pages of Livy, Dio, Tacitus, Suetonius, Dionysius of Halicarnassus, and Plutarch.[6] A closer examination of Luke-Acts confirms this. One strand of Lukan evidence regarding portents, culled from his Markan source (Luke 21:25–27; cf. Mark 13:24–26) and a Q logion (Luke 17:24; cf. Mark 24:21), mirrors traditional Jewish apocalyptic expectations concerning the great tribulation and the inauguration of the messianic age. By contrast, in Acts 19:26b,35b, Luke presents the Christian gospel as colliding with the 'portent mentality' of the worshippers of Ephesian Artemis, creating deep concern on the part of the Ephesian silversmiths over the loss of their income (19:24-26a). Furthermore, the supra-cephalic 'fire' portents of Acts 2:3 reflect Jewish intertextual echoes and Graeco-Roman legitimation rhetoric in their narration. In sum, although portents in Luke-Acts do not appear with the prominence and regularity of those recorded in the writings of ancient historians and biographers, the Lukan τέρατα are worth pursuing in their Jewish and Graeco-Roman context for any insights that they may provide into the outworking of Joel's prophecy in the narrative of Acts, including its presaging in Luke's Gospel.[7]

New Testament scholars, however, have only paid minimal attention to portents in Luke-Acts, with the exceptions of Edwin A. Judge and John Squires.[8] Judge has discussed prodigies in Lucan's *Pharsalia*,[9] focusing on the poem's celestial (*Phars.* 526–44) and terrestrial signs (545–83), comparing the results with the book of Acts. Judge concludes:

> In contrast to Lucan's concentrated mass of portent material, generically arranged, and worked up with rhetorical detail, Acts treats its portents along with the rest of the narrative, making no very clear distinction between incidents that are portentous or miraculous and those that are not.[10]

---

3   τέρατα: Acts 2:19,22,43; 4:30; 5:12; 6:8; 7:36; 14:3; 15:12. σημεῖα: Acts 2:19,22,43; 4:30; 5:12; 6:8; 7:36; 8:13; 14:3; 15:12. There is only one stylistic variation and one addition to the phrase σημεῖα καὶ τέρατα in the book of Acts: respectively, 2:22: δυνάμεσι καὶ τέρασι καὶ σημείοις; 8:13: σημεῖα καὶ δυνάμεις μεγάλας.
4   LXX τέρατα: Deut. 4:34; 6:22; 7:19; 13:2; 28:46; 34:11; cf. Neh. 9:10; Isa. 8:18; 20:3.
5   See Allison, *The End of the Ages*, 5–25; Berger, 'Hellenistich-heidnische Prodigien'. On Josephan portents, see McCasland, 'Portents in Josephus'. On the Gospel of Mark, see Vette, 'The Omens at Jesus's Death'.
6   On Graeco-Roman signs generally, see McCartney, 'Thunder and Lightning'; Bloch, *Les prodiges dans l'antiquité Classique*; Flaceliere, *Greek Oracles*; Whittaker, '"Signs and Wonders"'; Rasmussen, *Public Portents in Republican Rome*. On portents specifically, see Krauss, *Omens, Portents and Prodigies*; Rogers, 'The Neronian Comets'; Hammond, 'Portents, Prophecies, and Dreams'; Brenk, 'Omens and Portents'; Bosman, 'Signs and Narrative Design in Plutarch's *Alexander*'; Engels, 'Dionysius of Halicarnassus on Roman Religion, Divination and Prodigies'; Stewart, 'Imperial Fortunes'; Kamezis, Bailey, and Poletti (eds.), *The Intellectual Climate of Cassius Dio*, 301–23; Satterfield, 'Livy, Cassius Dio, and Prodigies'; Antoniou, 'Athena Spits Blood'.
7   See the insightful discussion of Schnabel, *Acts*, 137–39.
8   See Judge, '"Signs of the Times"'; Squires, *The Plan of God in Luke-Acts*.
9   On prodigies in Lucan's *Pharsalia*, see Dick, 'The Technique of Prophecy'.
10 Judge, '"Signs of the Times"', 420.

By contrast, Squires has explored the role of 'wonders and signs' in the plan of God as unfolded in Luke-Acts, concentrating more on the miraculous in the ministry of Jesus and the apostles than on portents *per se*,[11] though the latter are briefly mentioned in his monograph.[12] In this regard, Squires has helpfully analysed portents in Hellenistic historiography and in the writings of Josephus,[13] focusing upon divine signs, divine providence, and the LXX pairing of 'signs and wonders' in Josephus. Neither Judge nor Squires considers the role of τέρατα in Joel's prophecy in Acts 2:19, bypassing entirely the intriguing addition of ἄνω to the LXX text.[14]

A problem, however, emerges for our investigation precisely at this point. If Joel's prophecy is so thematically programmatic for Acts[15]—paralleling the pivotal positioning of the Isaianic citation at the beginning of Luke's Gospel (Isa 61:1–2 [Luke 4:18–19])—why does Luke seemingly pay so little attention to portents (τέρατα), traditionally understood, in the book of Acts, as opposed to their more prominent appearance in the Gospel? Indeed, it needs to be appreciated that the genre of miraculous 'signs' performed by Jesus and his apostles 'on the earth below' (Acts 2:19: σημεῖα ἐπὶ τῆς γῆς κάτω) garner little attention in ancient literature: in antiquity, portents, where the gods communicated their will and guidance to human beings, were considered the real realm of the 'miraculous'. And how do portents in both Luke and Acts interconnect, if at all? Our answers to these questions will need to be carefully nuanced, paying close attention to the presence and absence of τέρατα terminology in relation to portents in Acts, listening carefully to other terminological clues that might be present, while recognising the significance of the inter-textual echoes from Exodus[16] and Deuteronomy (*supra*, n.4), considering the authorial intention and reader-reception of the texts themselves, and recognising the Lukan distinctives distinguishing his text from contemporary 'portent' narratives in the Graeco-Roman world.

Finally, before we embark upon our investigation of the Lukan 'wonders in heaven above', brief consideration should be given to an important transition that occurred in the annalistic 'prodigy' tradition from the late Roman republic to the early imperial era in Rome and provincial Italy. From the time of Hannibal's invasion of Italy onwards, the Roman senate classified all public prodigies (*prodigia publica*) that occurred, referring them to the Roman priests for their recommendations as to what expiatory acts were required for violations of the *pax deorum* ('peace of the gods'). It is likely that public prodigies not only functioned as signs of divine wrath requiring propitiation but also as expressions of the compassion of the gods in providing warnings regarding the city's future.[17] But, by the time of the late republic, the reporting of public prodigies had either dramatically diminished or had vanished entirely, with Cicero and Livy, it is argued, not citing any

---

11 Squires, *The Plan of God in Luke-Acts*, 89–101.
12 Squires, *The Plan of God in Luke-Acts*, 95–96.
13 Squires, *The Plan of God in Luke-Acts*, 78–89.
14 Acts 2:19 is mentioned three times by Squires, *The Plan of God in Luke-Acts*, 64, 78, 97.
15 Luke carefully charts the central elements of Joel's prophecy (i.e. prophecy, dreams and visions, wonders and signs) throughout Acts. προφεύσουσιν: 2:17,18; 11:28; 19:6; 21:9. προφήτης: Acts 11:27; 13:1; 15:22,32; 21:10. ὁράσεις and ἐνυπνίοις: Acts 2:17. ὀπτασία: Acts 26:19 (cf. Luke 1:22; 24:23). ὅραμα: Acts 9:10,12; 10:3,7,19; 11:5; 12:9; 16:9,10; 18:19. σημεῖα and τέρατα, *supra* n.3.
16 Squires, *The Plan of God in Luke-Acts*, 85, notes that the phrase σημεῖα καὶ τέρατα referred to the plagues in Egypt (Exod. 7:3,9; 11:9–10). In the case of τέρατα, the word appears 'alone at Exod. 15:11; Wis. 19:8'. By contrast, σημεῖα, appears alone occasionally (Exod. 8:23; 10:1,2; 11:9), but refers 'most often to the Exodus itself (Deut. 4:34; 6:22; 7:19; 11:3; 26:28; 29:3; 34:11; Neh. 9:10; Ps. 77 (78):43; 104(105):27; 134(135):9; Jer. 39(42):20–21; Bar. 2:11'.
17 Satterfield, 'Prodigies', 443.

portents from the *Annales Maximi*.[18] The result was that *omina imperii* (signs that the gods had chosen the recipient to be the Roman ruler) flourished as their replacement, the nature of the omens invoked meeting the precise political needs of each ruler.[19]

The foregoing observations do not impinge directly upon our consideration of the Lukan τέρατα, but the Roman context of public prodigies must be factored in as much as the writings of Hellenistic historiography and Josephus. While changes in the official Roman recording of portents occurred with the advent of the imperial age—prodigies now largely confined to the political interests of the Roman ruler—continuities with the republican past nevertheless remained, facilitated by the involvement of the Roman senate and the priestly colleges. Notwithstanding, the literary evidence points to various prodigy reports and expiations still occurring during the early imperial period.[20] Consequently, we can confidently expect that the Lukan portents would have provoked the interest of Roman auditors as much as the intrigue of Greek auditors in the First Century AD.

1. The Gospel of Luke, Portents, and the Eschatological Age

At two points in the Gospel of Luke Jesus speaks of the signs preceding the inauguration of his eschatological messianic reign. The time of great tribulation preceding his return as the Son of Man is characterised in Luke 21:25–27 as follows:

> And there will be signs (σημεῖα) in sun and moon and stars, and upon the earth distress of nations in perplexity at the roaring of the sea and the waves, men fainting with fear and with foreboding of what is coming on the world; for the powers of the heavens will be shaken. And then they will see the Son of Man coming in a cloud with power and great glory. The inception of his messianic reign, according to Luke 17:24, will be apparent to all: 'as the lightning flashes and lights up the sky from one side to the other, so will the Son of Man be in his day'.

Finally, the crucifixion itself was attended by eschatological portents: 'about the sixth hour there was darkness over the whole land until the ninth hour, while the sun's light failed; and the curtain of the temple was torn in two' (Luke 23:44–45). How would Jewish readers, familiar with descriptions of the catastrophic events surrounding the eschaton in apocalyptic literature, have reacted to this? What elements of Luke's presentation diverge from the popular stereotypes in Judaism? Further, how intelligible would the Lukan portents have been to a Graeco-Roman audience? What points of contact and divergence emerge?

1.1 Jewish Signs of the Eschatological Age

Jewish apocalyptic literature spoke of the culmination of the present world being heralded by a great tribulation (the 'messianic woes').[21] A variety of terrifying portents would attend the

---

18 On the debate when Roman writers ceased to use the *Annales maximi*, see Rawson, 'Prodigy Lists'; Frier, *Libri Annales Pontificum Maximorum*; Drews, 'Pontiffs, Prodigies'; Satterfield, 'The Prodigies of 17 B.C.E.'. See Chalupa, 'The Religio-Political Change', 60–65, on the many reasons suggested by scholars for the disappearance of prodigies.
19 See Lorsch, *Omnia imperii*.
20 See Chalupa, 'The Religio-Political Change'; Santangelo, 'Prodigies in the Early Principate?'; Antoniou, 'Athena Spits Blood'; Stewart, 'Imperial Fortunes'.
21 For discussion of the 'messianic woes' in the Old Testament and Second Temple Judaism, see Gempf, 'The Imagery of Birth Pangs'; Dubis, *Messianic Woes in First Peter*, 5–36; Pitre, *Jesus the Tribulation, and the End of Exile*, 4–8, 29–30, 41–130.

beginning of the eschatological age. Syriac *Baruch*, an early second-century AD work, speaks of the 'sign' attending the last days in this way: 'When horror seizes the inhabitants of the earth, and they fall into many tribulations and further, they fall into great torments' (*2 Bar.* 25.1–3). In *2 Baruch* 27 the end time is divided into twelve parts. There are phenomena such as 'famine and withholding of rain' (*2 Bar.* 27.6), 'earthquakes and terrors' (27.7), 'a multitude of ghosts and appearances of demons' (27.9) and 'the fall of fire' (27.11).

The late first-century AD work *4 Ezra* catalogues the following end-time 'signs': the seizure of earth's inhabitants by terror (*4 Ezra* 5.1); the sun shining at night and the moon at day (5.4); the dripping of blood from wood (5.5); the birth of monsters from menstruous women (5.8). Further, people would convulse with terror as they heard the final trumpet (*4 Ezra* 6.23) and see friend pitted against friend in global war (6.24). In *4 Ezra* 9.1–14 the messianic woes are attended by 'earthquakes, tumult of peoples, intrigues of nations, wavering of leaders, confusion of princes' (9.3).

In the *Sibylline Oracles*, a work notoriously difficult to date, the same picture emerges.[22] The stars will 'appear in midday to all, with the two luminaries' (*Sib. Or.*, 2.184–185; cf. 2.35–36). Famine, pestilence, earthquakes, thunderballs, and lightning will also occur (*Sib. Or.*, 2.6–7, 23–25). In *Sibylline Oracles* 3 the appearance of a comet will signify to mortals the outbreak of the 'sword, famine and death, destruction of leaders and of great illustrious men' (*Sib. Or.*, 3.334–336). Further, earthquakes will cause damage (*Sib. Or.*, 3.457); swords will be seen at night in the starry heaven (3.798–799); the sun will suffer eclipse in a dust storm (3.800–803). Finally, in a cavalcade of the five kingdoms preceding the destruction of Jerusalem and the final judgement, the *Sibylline Oracles* again mention mid-day darkness, the disappearance of the sun and moon, and an earthquake (*Sib. Or.*, 4.57–59).

However, when we come to Josephus, a remarkable change occurs. Where apocalyptic literature associated portents with the future eschatological age, Josephus historicises his portents, grouping them around the fall of Jerusalem and the destruction of the temple by the Romans.[23] In *B.J.* 6.288–315, Josephus argues that the Jewish people had paid too much attention to messianic pretenders, and had ignored God-given warnings in the form of portents. He lists seven portents, which served as signs to show God's people the way of salvation: 1) a sword-shaped star and a comet stood over Jerusalem for a year; 2) during Passover a brilliant light shone round the altar and the sanctuary of the temple on the ninth hour of the night; 3) a sacrificial cow gave birth to a lamb in the temple court on Passover; 4) the bronze gate of the temple's inner court opened at the sixth hour of its own accord; 5) celestial armies, consisting of chariots and armed battalions, were seen in the air and clouds; 6) a voice in the inner court of the temple by night was heard saying, 'We are departing hence'; 7) the ominous words of Jesus, son of Ananias, who continually cried, 'Woe to Jerusalem' in spite of official punishments. Finally, rabbinic tradition also makes mention of the occurrence of portents some forty years before the destruction of the temple.[24]

1.2 Graeco-Roman Prodigies and Portents

In this section we will examine the Graeco-Roman understanding of prodigies and portents through the eyes of Livy (and his epitomiser, Julius Obsequens),[25] Dio, Tacitus, Suetonius, and

---

22 For dating, see Charlesworth (ed.), *The Old Testament Pseudepigrapha, Volume 1*.
23 See McCasland, 'Portents in Josephus', 325–26; Betz, 'Miracles in the Writings of Flavius Josephus', 231–33. See also Squires, *The Plan of God in Luke-Acts*, 84–89. In keeping with the theme of his book, Squires extends the 'omen' significance of 'portents' to 'signs and wonders', 'surprises and miracles', and 'divine providence'.
24 McCasland, 'Portents in Josephus', 326. See also cited there the references to portents accompanying the death of rabbis (all postdating AD 260).
25 See Franza and Pratesi, 'Julius Obsequens's Book, *Liber Prodigiorum*'.

Nigidius Figulus' *Almanac of Thunder*.[26] An examination of Plutarchan portents will be omitted, as there exists the fine discussion of the issue by Frederick Brenk.[27] David Engel's extensive examination of prodigies in the *Roman Antiquities* of Dionysius of Harlicarnassus also obviates the need for further investigation of the motif in what follows.[28] We will also confine the scope of our discussion of the sources to materials similar to the Lukan portents.

In looking at Livy's presentation of portents and prodigies, it is important to realise that Livy belonged to the Roman annalist tradition of historiography. The *Annales maximi* was a compilation of the early history of Rome into eighty books, undertaken about 115 BC. The information in the *Annales maximi* came from the *tabulae pontificum*. These white boards, which each year were fixed to the Regia's wall, recorded a variety of information: elections of magistrates, ambassadorial visits, military campaigns, as well as any eclipses and prodigies.[29] From this collection of religious detail Livy selected many examples of prodigies and portents for his history of Rome. For Livy and republican historiography, portents indicated the temper of the gods: ritual pacification of their wrath was the priority if national disaster were to be averted. According to Livy, the portents which accompanied the final critical moments of the Carthaginian war caused perturbation, precisely because 'men attributed to the gods the causes of everything fortunate and unfortunate'.[30] Livy's stated reason for including such material is revealing:

> I am not unaware that, as a result of the same disregard (*neglegentia*) that leads men generally to suppose nowadays that the gods foretell nothing, no portents at all are reported officially, or recorded in our histories. However, not only does my own mind, as I write of old-time matters, become in some way or other old fashioned (*antiquus*), but also a certain conscientious scruple keeps me from regarding what those very sagacious men of former times (*prudentissimi viri*) thought worthy of public concern as something unworthy to be reported in my history.[31]

As P. G. Walsh observes, Livy thought he was defending 'the older and better values'.[32] Fortunately for us, Julius Obsequens epitomised a book of prodigies from Livy, covering the years where we possess only the Oxyrhynchus summaries of Livy. A. H. McDonald has captured the significance of Julius Obsequens' collection thus: 'it represents the late heathen justification of the forms of the old faith'.[33]

In Livy, sky phenomena feature prominently as portents: showers of stones,[34] the heavens ablaze with fire,[35] eclipses,[36] meteors,[37] the appearance of phantom ships in the heavens,[38] and unusual occurrences associated with the sun or moon.[39] Stereotyped motifs of lightning,

---

26 For a translation of Nigidius' almanac, see Selling, 'The Brontoscopic Calendar of Nigidius Figulus'.
27 Brenk, 'Omens and Portents'; cf. Bosman, 'Signs and Narrative Design in Plutarch's *Alexander*'.
28 See Engels, 'Dionysius of Halicarnassus on Roman Religion'.
29 For the above information, see Walsh, *Livy*, 110–11.
30 Livy 28.10.1.
31 Livy, 43.13.
32 Walsh, *Livy*, 62. See also p.63 for Livy's more critical remarks concerning rash reporting of prodigies.
33 McDonald, 'Obsequens', 744.
34 Livy 1.31.1–2; 7.28.7; 21.42.5; 22.1.9; 26.23.5; 30.38.9; 35.8.4; 36.37.3; 39.22.3; 41.9.5.
35 Livy 3.5.14; 3.9.6; 22.1.12; 31.12.5; 32.8.3; 39.21.3; 43.13.3–4.
36 Livy 7.28.7.
37 Livy 29.13.3.
38 Livy 21.41.4.
39 Livy 21.1.9; 22.1.10; 28.11.3–4; 29.14.3.

pestilence, and earthquakes rate regular mention in Livy's account.[40] A variety of blood portents occur, as do sweating statues.[41]

Livy shows a particular interest in portents associated with temples. Inside the *cella* of the temple of Fors Fortuna at Rome, a 'small image on a garland fell off itself from the head of the statue into the hand'.[42] At Cumae the mice had gnawed the gold in the temple of Jupiter. Equally portentous was the flight of a vulture into the temple of Jupiter, and the case of two serpents gliding into its holy precincts.[43] Livy notes the appearance of wasps in the temple of Mars at Capua and a mighty noise heard at night in the temple of Juno Sospita.[44]

Finally, Livy continually underscores the fear which portents inspired in the minds of their observers: people were 'terror stricken', experienced 'universal anxiety', or reeled under the weight of 'superstitious fears'.[45] To offset the paralysing effect such portents had on the Roman psyche, the state instituted atonement on particular occasions, using full grown animal victims.[46] Such expiations—whether rites or sacrifice—could last up to nine days.[47] To sum up, portents filled Rome 'with forebodings of divine displeasure, and only the consultation of the Sibylline books would provide a correct unravelling of the gods' will'.[48]

The evidence of Julius Obsequens confirms the picture given above. Sky phenomena feature regularly: meteors, showers of stones, three suns, eclipses, fireballs, stars, shields, and weapons in the heavens.[49] Pestilences, earthquakes, and lightning portents also occur.[50] There is only one mention of famine, but several of rains of blood.[51] The same preoccupation with temple portents is apparent throughout Julius Obsequens.[52] Finally, Julius Obsequens links portents with the national fortunes of Rome: rebellions, civil wars, political crises, or military expeditions are occasions for prophetic signs. Three examples will suffice. The overthrow of the battlements of walls, with no indication of seismic activity, 'foretold civil strife'.[53] Flocks that ravaged their masters, and weeping dogs 'foretold disaster to their people'.[54] In 63 BC, according to Obsequens, a series of portents occurred. His conclusion, for readers with the 'portent mentality', would have been apt: 'With these portents the abominable conspiracy of Cataline began'.[55]

---

40 Lightning: Livy 1.31.8; 21.41.4; 22.1.9; 24.1.9; 24.10.9; 26.22.5; 27.11.2; 27.22.2–3; 28.11.2, 4; 29.14.3; 30.38.9; 32.8.2; 33.26.7; 35.9.3; 36.37.3; 37.3.2; 39.22.4; 40.44.3; 41.9.5–6. Pestilence: 1.31.5; 40.18.3. Earthquake: 3.9.6. See also Thucydides 1.23.4; Herodotus 6.98.
41 Blood portents: Livy 22.1.8; 27.22.5; 27.23.4; 39.46.5; 40.19.1–2. Statues which sweat or cry: 22.1.12; 40.19.1–2.
42 Livy 27.10.3.
43 Livy 27.22.2; 27.23.4.
44 Livy 35.9.4; 31.12.6.
45 Livy 3.5.14; 5.14.2; 29.13.2. See also 22.1.8.
46 Livy 24.10.13.
47 Livy 30.38.9. Interestingly, even prayer required a three-day session (Livy 3.5.14).
48 Livy 7.28.7. We will not examine Livy's tradition of animal *monstra*, human deformities, or hermaphrodites because it has no New Testament parallel. For discussion, see Krauss, *Interpretation of the Omens, Portents and Prodigies*, 199–232.
49 Julius Obsequens, *Liber Prodigiorum*, 1, 3, 11, 12, 14, 20, 23, 24, 27, 30, 32, 38, 41, 43, 45, 51, 52, 53, 54, 56, 56a, 61, 62, 68, 70, 71.
50 Pestilences: Julius Obsequens, *Liber Prodigiorum*, 10, 22. Earthquakes: 7, 46, 59, 68, 71. Lightning: 1, 3, 11, 20, 27b, 29, 36, 37, 41, 43, 46, 61, 68, 69.
51 Julius Obsequens, *Liber Prodigiorum*, 46. Rains of blood: 4, 6, 11, 12, 20, 25, 27, 27a, 44, 46, 49, 51, 53.
52 Julius Obsequens, *Liber Prodigiorum*, 1, 7, 8, 13, 16, 19, 27a, 28a, 39, 41, 42, 43, 46, 52, 55, 56b, 68.
53 Julius Obsequens, *Liber Prodigiorum*, 48.
54 Julius Obsequens, *Liber Prodigiorum*, 54.
55 Julius Obsequens, *Liber Prodigiorum*, 61.

Andrew Hadrill argues that by the time of Suetonius, portents no longer indicate 'the mood of the gods [...] but the inevitable course of the future'.[56] Suetonius employs portents as one of the biographer's stock tools-of-trade. The focus now centres on the great man, not the fortunes of state as in the earlier annalist tradition.[57] Birth portents chart for the reader the destiny of the great man (Augustus, Vespasian).[58] But, equally, portents can foreshadow the undoing of an emperor's career (Vitellius).[59] Suetonius heralds the deaths of emperors with prodigies and portents, enabling him to inject pathos into the event: the hubris of the great man cannot prevail over the predetermined pattern of events.[60] Further, portents can highlight a turning point in the narrative, such as Caesar's crossing of the Rubicon.[61] Occasionally, they can operate as a device for character revelation: whether it be Vespasian's witticisms or Augustus' belief in the infallibility of portents.[62]

Dio links portents to the various stages of the great man's career.[63] Nero's birth was heralded by rays of light, while a fiery sky accompanied the adoption of Nero by Claudius.[64] Vitellius' reign witnessed the appearance of comets, whereas the deaths of both Claudius and Vespasian were foretold by comets.[65] The deaths of Claudius, Nero, Vitellius, and Vespasian are preceded by a series of miraculous door openings.[66]

In the last five books of Tacitus' *Annals*, portents and prodigies appear for the first time.[67] Several of Tacitus' portents show the standard features of the annalist tradition, through their link with the consular year and military crises.[68] Tacitus captures the deteriorating state of public affairs by using traditional motifs: earthquakes, famine, heavenly fire, birds of omen, *monstra*, and hermaphrodites.[69] However Tacitus, like Suetonius, concentrates on the great man as well. For example, a comet provokes intense speculation as to who will be Nero's successor, while omens chart the course of Vespasian's rise to imperial power.[70] Overall, Tacitus is sceptical about the role of portents in traditional religion. The signs which predestined Vespasian for power are only accepted by Tacitus after the event.[71] Signs which herald national disaster are attributed to the gods' malevolence, rather than to their beneficence.[72] According to Tacitus, preoccupation with prodigies belongs to the 'barbarous ages'.[73] Further the interpretation of signs is arbitrary: in good

---

56 Hadrill, *Suetonius*, 191. Additionally, see Wardle, 'Suetonius on "Vespasianus Religious"' in AD 69-70'; Woods, 'Caligula, Asprenas, and the Bloodied Robe'.
57 Hadrill, *Suetonius*, 192.
58 Suetonius, *Aug.* 94; *Vesp.* 5.
59 Suetonius, *Vit*, 9, 18.
60 Suetonius, *Aug.* 97; *Tib.* 74; *Cai.* 57; *Claud.*, 45; *Nero* 36; *Galb.* 18.
61 Suetonius, *Jul.* 32.
62 Suetonius, *Vesp.* 23; *Aug.* 92.
63 On portents in Dio, see Satterfield, 'Livy, Cassius Dio, and Prodigies'; Kamezis, Bailey, and Poletti (eds.), *The Intellectual Climate of Cassius Dio*, 301–23.
64 Dio 61.1.2; 60.33.2.
65 Dio 65.8.1; 60.35.2; 66.17.2.
66 Dio 60.35.1; 65.8.2; 68.26.2; 66.17.2.
67 On Tacitus' use of portent and prodigy, see Syme, *Tacitus, Vol. 2*, 521–23. Additionally, see Morgan, 'Two Omens in Tacitus' "Histories"'; Morgan, 'Vespasian and the Omens in Tacitus'; Ginsberg, 'Allusive Prodigia'; Woods, 'Rewriting a Contentious Omen'.
68 Tacitus, *Ann.*, 12.43; 12.54.
69 Tacitus, *Ann.*, 12.43; 12.54.
70 Tacitus, *Ann.*, 14.22; *Hist.*, 2.78.
71 Tacitus, *Hist.*, 1.10.
72 Tacitus, *Hist.*, 1. 13.
73 Tacitus, *Hist.*, 1. 86.

times, a sign is labelled an act of chance or nature—in times of crisis, fate or the gods' wrath.[74] Certainly Tacitus concedes that truth is found in the common portent tradition. However, one suspects that behind Tacitus' disclaimer lies a critical spirit, intolerant of such 'fabulous tales' and 'fictitious stories'.[75]

Finally, there is the almanac of thunder portents compiled by the praetor and contemporary of Cicero, Nigidius Figulus.[76] The almanac places the interpretation of unsought signs (*auspicia oblativa*) in the hands of the non-specialist, who derives from the relevant calendar entry the significance of the thunder portent. Familiar themes reappear. There are threats of disease, pestilence, and plague.[77] A range of agricultural portents feature: food shortage, famine, crop failure, and drought.[78] A single reference to a comet exists: 'If it thunders, there will be a sign from Zeus and a comet'.[79] An atmosphere of crisis permeates Nigidius' pages, portending social dislocation and political uncertainty for the state. War constantly threatens, whilst the social fabric is torn by civil conflict, insurrection, or slave revolt.[80] Government fares no better: the people's counsel is divided, the prospect of tyranny looms, and the praiseworthy man falls.[81] There are, however, notes of hope: 'If it thunders, the evil dynast will fall by the will of god'.[82]

1.3 The Lukan Understanding of Eschatological Portents

Where does Luke fit into this wider spectrum of prodigy and portent, in both a Jewish apocalyptic and Graeco-Roman context? Several similarities and differences emerge.

a. The Lukan Jesus is clearly at home in using the language of Jewish apocalyptic: nation will rise against nation, kingdom against kingdom, in assorted wars and revolutions (Luke 21:9). The mention of cosmic catastrophes in Luke 21:10 (earthquakes, famines, pestilences) is also common apocalyptic fare, in conjunction with 'horrors' ($\phi\acute{o}\beta\eta\tau\rho\alpha$) and 'great signs from heaven' ($\dot{\alpha}\pi$' $o\dot{\upsilon}\rho\alpha\nuο\tilde{\upsilon}$ $\sigma\eta\mu\epsilon\tilde{\iota}\alpha$ $\mu\epsilon\gamma\acute{\alpha}\lambda\alpha$). But, like Josephus, the Lukan Jesus historicises these end-time portents, applying them to the time of tribulation for the first believers (Luke 21:12–19) and the destruction of Jerusalem (21:20–24).

In Acts, Luke gives glimpses of the presence of these apocalyptic $\sigma\eta\mu\epsilon\tilde{\iota}\alpha$—famines (Acts 11:28), earthquakes (16:26)—in the history of the primitive church of the earliest Christ-followers. But each of these apocalyptic $\sigma\eta\mu\epsilon\tilde{\iota}\alpha$ is differently conceived in comparison to their Graeco-Roman counterparts:

---

74 Tacitus, *Hist.*, 4. 26.
75 Tacitus, *Hist.*, 2. 50.
76 See now the collection of edited essays by Volk, ed., *Nigidius Figulus*.
77 There are 32 references to disease in Nigidius Figulus, 'An Almanac of Thunder'. Some representative examples are June 7, July 25, August 8, September 4, October 29, November 23, December 12, January 12, February 22, March 18, April 8, May 13. For pestilence, November 13, January 29, February 15, April 15. For plague, January 22, February 19.
78 For food shortage, see Nigidius Figulus, 'An Almanac of Thunder', July 11, 15, 26. For famine, September 12, 13, 18, 24, January 11, May 2. For crop failure, June 3, 14, 18. For drought, September 24, 29, March 9.
79 Nigidius Figulus, 'An Almanac of Thunder', May 27.
80 For war, see Nigidius Figulus, 'An Almanac of Thunder', June 16, July 16, August 14, September 3, October 14, November 8, December 18, January 7, February 25, March 23, April 1, May 29. For civil conflict, September 19; insurrection, December 30; slave revolt, January 15.
81 For divided counsel, see Nigidius Figulus, 'An Almanac of Thunder', February 16. For tyranny, October 1. For the fall of praiseworthy men, October 10.
82 Nigidius Figulus, 'An Almanac of Thunder', September 26.

- What does the 'famine' signify narratively in Acts? The famine in the time of Claudius substantiates that the outpoured Pentecost Spirit of Joel's prophecy was now powerfully operative in the prophecy of Agabus (Acts 11:28: cf. 2:17a,18b [προφεύσουσιν]), one of several Jerusalem prophets (προφῆται) who were visiting the church in Antioch (11:27–28). Furthermore, the occurrence of the Claudian era famine underscores the Spirit-inspired truthfulness of Agabus' prophecy. This prophetic intervention precipitated the sending of a relief collection from the Antioch church to Judaean believers through the agency of Barnabas and Saul (Acts 11:29–30). The significance of the famine is not revelatory in the manner of Graeco-Roman prodigies, but rather it demonstrates Spirit-orchestrated deeds of mercy and the Spirit-interconnectedness of the first believers in different locales.
- The earthquake at Philippi opens the opportunity for Paul, Silas, and fellow prisoners to escape from prison (Acts 16:25–26), a temptation which the apostle, his co-worker, and the other prisoners resist. A much greater need overrides their own: the prevention of the gaoler's suicide through the intervention of Paul and Silas (Acts 16:28) and his subsequent salvation, along with his family (16:29–34). In each case, the portents (famine, earthquake) move beyond their potential revelatory significance, however that might be conceived. The sign of Acts 11:28 functions as a prophetically guided opportunity for God's people to minister to those experiencing crisis, whereas the sign of Acts 16:26 leads to God's soteriological deliverance of the unsaved through the proclamation of the gospel. The sign also affirms Paul, the Jew, in Roman Philippi as God's emissary.

b. The eschatological signs in Luke 21:25–27 and 17:24 are paralleled in Jewish apocalyptic literature. But, in this case, Luke gives the eschaton a christological focus. Jesus, the glorious Son of Man, establishes the messianic reign and the end-time σημεῖα herald its inception.

c. Moreover, the end-time portents associated with Jesus' death (Luke 23.44–45) are given an unexpected eschatological twist by Luke. The death of Jesus on the cross inaugurates Joel's 'Day of the Lord' (Acts 2:18–19; Luke 23:44–45). This feature is underscored by Luke's telling addition of the eschatological phrase, ἐν ταῖς ἐσχάταις ἡμέραις ('in the last days'), to Joel's prophecy in Acts 2:17a,[83] though the context there is the outpoured Spirit-gift of Jesus (Acts 2:33). Thus, Jesus' 'messianic woes' at Golgotha establish the end of the age, out of which springs the new eschatological age, sealed through Jesus' resurrection, exaltation, and Pentecost outpouring of the Spirit (Acts 2:24–28,31–36).[84]

d. Furthermore, the τέρατα ἐν τῷ οὐρανῷ ἄνω (Acts 2:19) have also been fulfilled in the heavenly ascension of the risen Jesus (Luke 24:51–52; Acts 1:6–11),[85] a forerunner to his exaltation as the risen Messiah and Lord, now enthroned at God's right hand (Acts 2:33a), and his subsequent outpouring of the Spirit in tongues of fire (Acts 1:8; 2:1–4,18,33b). His ascension also presages his eschatological return to earth (Acts 1:11; cf. Luke 21:24–26,28) and unleashes his pneumatic endowment of his church for worldwide mission (Acts 1:8b). In sum, the portentous significance of the ascension is sweeping in its soteriological impact.

---

83 Luke replaces the LXX Joel 2:28 phrase, μετὰ ταῦτα ('after these things'), with ἐν ταῖς ἐσχάταις ἡμέραις ('in the last days'), 'making Pentecost part of an eschatological scenario' (Johnson, *The Acts of the Apostles*, 49). For full discussion, see Keener, *Acts, Volume 1*, 877–81.
84 See Allison, *The End of the Ages Has Come*, 38–39.
85 Schnabel, *Acts*, 138.

e. From a Graeco-Roman perspective, Luke's use of portents may have seemed somewhat restrained. There are no animal prodigies or *monstra*, no ominous variations of the human form (hermaphrodites). Given the Graeco-Roman interest in blood portents (nn.41, 51, supra), it is significant that Luke attached no explicit portentous significance to his mention of Jesus' blood-like sweat in Luke 22:44 (ὡσεὶ θρόμβοι αἵματος), unless there is a symbolic connection found in Joel's portent of the moon turning to blood (Acts 2:20 [LXX Joel 2:31a]).[86] That inter-textual possibility having been aired, the Luke 22:44 reference, in my opinion, more underscores Jesus' humanity and the difficulty of the trial to come rather than anything explicitly portentous.[87] Joel's 'blood moon' would have recalled in a very general way the preoccupation of the Graeco-Roman world with blood portents, but it is given no further application narratively in Acts. Further, apart from the destruction of Jerusalem, Luke does not link portents to affairs of state. Nor does Luke use portents to reveal the career path of the great man.[88] True, portents are associated with Jesus' death, but as noted above their real significance lies elsewhere. However, at the level of provoking the interest of his Graeco-Roman auditors, Luke is successful. We have seen from the evidence above that Luke's portents—cosmic catastrophes, national disturbances, lightning, great signs from heaven, eclipses, and temple omens (Luke 17:24; 21:9; 21:10; 23:44; 23:45)—were standard fare in the Graeco-Roman world.

We turn now to the central sign of the outpoured Spirit at Pentecost: the tongues of fire. How do these portents function in their Jewish and Graeco-Roman context?

---

86   Schnabel, *Acts*, 138, correctly observes that the 'blood moon' portent (Acts 2:20 [LXX Joel 2:31a]) is not 'easily [...] linked with Jesus' death, resurrection, or ascension'. In an extended discussion (pp.138–39), Schnabel dismisses purported connections with Jesus' shed blood (Luke 22:20) and the Pentecost supra-cephalic flames (Acts 2:3). For the former suggestions, see Witherington, *The Acts of the Apostles*, 143. Instead, Schnabel suggests that Acts 2:20 represents an allusion to the Sinai theophany at Pentecost and, much more likely, denotes the eschatological signs of the arrival of the 'Day of the Lord'. Similarly, see also Witherington, *The Acts of the Apostles*, 43. This eschatological perspective is also signalled by Luke's change of Joel's LXX phrase μετὰ ταῦτα (2:28a: 'after these things') to reflect a realised eschatology (ἐν ταῖς ἐσχάταις ἡμέραις, Acts 2:17a: 'in the last days') that finds its fulfilment in the Pentecost pneumatic outpouring. Notwithstanding, the strategic use of πρίν (Acts 2:20: 'before') prior to the Old Testament eschatological day of the Lord (Acts 2:20b) indicates that these cosmic signs *precede* the ultimate arrival of the eschaton. As Bock, *Acts*, 117, writes, 'Peter is saying that the eschatological clock is ticking'. Therefore, Luke's concern in Acts 2:20 is primarily *eschatological*, clarifying the end-time hope still to come, notwithstanding the powerful portents already associated with the Pentecost outpouring. In sum, Luke does not take up the opportunity of engaging cross-culturally with the widespread motif of blood portents in their Graeco-Roman context. Instead, Luke confines himself to three significant outworkings of Joel's prophecy in the expansion of the early church: (a) Jesus' ascension, (b) the Pentecost outpouring of supra-cephalic tongues of fire, and (c) the heated defence of the 'man-made' Artemis meteorite by the Ephesian town clerk.
87   On blood portents, note also the blood-coloured comets preceding the death of Augustus (Dio 56.29.3). For discussion, see Krauss, *Interpretation of the Omens, Portents and Prodigies*, 58–60, 92–95.
88   Regarding the emergence of the 'great man', it might be argued that the divinely imposed dumbness upon Zechariah functions narratively as a portent (Luke 1:22), mercifully unloosed by God later in Zechariah's revelation of John's name, resulting in his outburst of divine praise (1:44). But the so-called 'portent' is imposed because of Zechariah's unbelief regarding the angelic revelation of the future greatness of John the Baptist (Luke 1:18–20). This narrative sidelight is more about Zechariah's experience of God's punitive discipline and countervailing mercy than anything portentous. Moreover, the 'sign' of the Christ-child's birth, witnessed by the shepherds (Luke 2:8–20: cf. v.12, τὸ σημεῖον), is occasioned by angelic revelation rather than by portents. Last, the leaping of John in Elisabeth's womb upon the pregnant Mary's greeting (Luke 1:41,44) elicits a Spirit-inspired blessing of Mary and the 'fruit of her womb' (Luke 1:42, 45: εὐλογημένη, μακαρία), as opposed to espousing any portentous significance.

2. The Appearance of Supra-cephalic Flames as Portents: The Pentecost 'Tongues of Fire' in Their Jewish and Graeco-Roman Context

The outpouring of the Spirit was accompanied by several revelatory phenomena: wind, fire, and the speaking of tongues (Acts 2:1–4). Although the crucial word, τέρατα, signifying portents in Joel's prophecy (Acts 2:19: τέρατα ἐν τῷ οὐρανῷ ἄνω), is not employed here, the 'heavenly' origin of the phenomena is nonetheless emphasised (Acts 2:2: ἐκ τοῦ οὐρανοῦ). But an important difference emerges. In Joel's prophecy, the portents (τέρατα) reside in the heavens, whereas the 'wind' phenomena (Acts 2:2) and 'fire' portents (2:3) come from heaven (2:2). The difference in location is important and its interpretative meaning needs to be carefully considered. Significantly for our examination of the Pentecost portents, the supra-cephalic flame is prominent in Graeco-Roman literature and coinage as a sign of the divine presence.[89] Such portents chart the destiny of great men in epic and history, endowing them with the god's favour and providing omens of imminent events in their careers.[90]

In Virgil's *Aeneid* the tongue of flame is a sign of the future leadership of Anchises' line by his son Iulius: 'we behold a feathery tongue of flame luminously alight upon his head, licking the soft curls with fire that harmed them nil, and playing about his temples'.[91] Virgil also describes a shield, decorated with prophetic scenes from future Roman history. The central scene shows Augustus leading the Roman people into battle at Actium, divinely approved by two flames shooting from his helmet and by his father's star dawning over its crest.[92] In Homer's *Iliad* similar themes emerge. Homer describes the routing of the Trojans, whilst the goddess Athena kindled a flame above Achilles' head.[93]

Several authors ascribe portents to the Etruscan king of Rome, Servius Tullius.[94] According to Livy, the head of the child of Tullius burst into flames while he lay sleeping. In the view of Queen Tanaquil, the portent signified that Tullius would be 'a lamp to our dubious fortunes and a protector of the royal house in the day of distress'.[95] Later, upon his father's death, Tanaquil exhorted Tullius to follow the god's guidance, his future fame having been indicated by the divine fire.[96]

Fire portents also herald imminent events and, after the event, *miracula* show the god's approval of the outcome. The victorious Roman general Marcius had his victories over the Carthaginians in 212 BC acclaimed by a flame bursting from his head.[97] In Caesar's case, fire portents preceded the Ides of March.[98] Plutarch also cites Strabo, who mentions that on the very same day men on fire were seen rushing around, whilst a soldier's slave threw from his hand a copious flame.[99]

---

89 See van der Horst, 'Hellenistic Parallels', 49–50. For additional references, see Krauss, *Interpretation of the Omens, Portents and Prodigies*, 87–92.
90 The one exception to the rule that great men receive fire portents is the case of an unknown shepherd in Dio Cassius 48.33.2.
91 Virgil, *Aen.* 2.680–684.
92 Virgil, *Aen.* 8.680–681.
93 Homer, *Il.* 18.204–214.
94 In addition to the Livy texts cited below, see Ovid, *Fasti* 6.634–36; Pliny the Elder, *Nat.* 2.241; Apuleius, *De deo Socr.* 7.
95 Livy 1.39.1–4.
96 Livy 1.41.3.
97 Livy 25.39.16.
98 Plutarch, *Caes.* 63.1.
99 Plutarch, *Caes.* 63.2.

The only supra-cephalic flame appearing in a strictly prophetic context is found in Silius Italicus' description of the Numidian prince, Masinissa:

[S]uddenly a ruddy tongue of fire was seen to burn bright on the crown of his head; the harmless flame caught his curling locks and spread over his shaggy brow [...] but his aged mother recognised a divine omen and said: 'Be it so, you gods. Be propitious and ratify your portent. May the light shine on his head for centuries to come! And you my son, fear not such a favourable sign from heaven, and let not the sacred flame on your brow alarm you. The fire assures you of an alliance with the Roman people: this fire will bring you a kingdom wider than your fathers ever ruled and shall add your name to the history of Rome'. Thus spoke the prophetess.[100]

Finally, in terms of Graeco-Roman fire portents, there is the Augustan coin evidence of 18 BC. The coin issue shows the oak-wreathed head of Augustus on the obverse, but the reverse displays an eight-rayed comet with a fiery tail. There, across the field and between the rays, the legend DIVVS IVLIVS is displayed.[101] This comet, the *sidus Iulium*, had been observed shortly after Caesar's death in 44 BC, whilst Augustus had been celebrating the Victoria Caesaris (Pliny the Elder, *Nat.* 2.93; Dio Cassius, 45.7.1–2), pointing to Caesar's apotheosis.[102] Virgil, as we have seen, had linked two supra-cephalic flames issuing from Augustus' helmet with this same comet. In sum, fire portents were a potent motif in Graeco-Roman culture and some of Luke's audience, sensitive to the 'omen' mentality of a Nigidius Figulus or a Julius Obsequens, may well have interpreted Luke's supra-cephalic flame in the same way, at least upon their first public exposure to the text.[103]

The valid insights of 'reader reception theory' must be acknowledged here. But Luke's indebtedness to Second Temple Judaism, his commitment to the crucified, risen, and exalted Lord and Christ, and the first believers' experience of the Pentecost outpouring of the Spirit in the church, created a theological counterweight to the Julian apotheosis narrative, legitimised by its imperially-focused 'fire' and 'comet' portents. The Pentecost outpouring, as depicted by Luke, undermined the religious and social moorings of this narrative construct. What, then, was Luke's intention in introducing such a supra-cephalic flame at Pentecost? And how would Luke's auditors have responded to his portentous account?

Various Jewish backgrounds have been canvassed by scholars. Richard Longenecker and Darrell Bock, for example, opt for 'fire' as the Old Testament symbol of the divine presence (Acts 2:3: διαμεριζόμεναι γλῶσσαι ὡσεὶ πυρός): the burning bush (Exod. 3:2; cf. Acts 7:30), the wilderness pillars of fire (Exod. 13:21; cf. Deut. 4:33; 5:24–26; 18:16), the theophany at Mount Sinai (Exod. 19:18–19; cf. 24:17; Philo, *Decal.* 33, 46), the fire over the wilderness tabernacle (Exod. 40:38), and the fires associated with Elijah (1 Kgs 18:38) and Ezekiel (Ezek. 1:13–14,27).[104] The role of fire in relation to judgements and end-time judgements has been posited as well (Luke 3:16; 12:49–50; cf. Deut. 4:24; 9:3; *4 Ezra* 13:8–11).[105] While these allusions operate intertextually as echoes, nowhere

---

100 Silius Italicus, *Punica* 16.120–32.
101 Mattingly, *Coins of the Roman Empire, Vol. 1*, p.59. nos. 323–328; Grueber, *Coins of the Roman Republic, Vol 2*, p.29 no. 4416; pp.421–22, nos. 135–140.
102 See Scott, 'The Sidus Iulium and the Apotheosis of Caesar'.
103 For fire references in Julius Obsequens, 'An Almanac of Thunder': sky 'afire' (14, 15, 20, 28, 51, 61); comets (20, 68); blazing meteors (24, 41, 45); tongues of flame from the sky (52); fireballs (54); fire on soldiers' pikes (47); portents from fire damage (8, 25, 28, 41). In Nigidius Figulus' case, note the 'prophetic sign' of a 'rain of fire' (September 28); a comet (May 27).
104 See Longenecker, 'Acts', 270; Bock, *Acts*, 97–98; Conzelmann, *Acts of the Apostles*, 13.
105 Keener, *Acts, Volume 1*, 804; Schnabel, *Acts*, 114.

are they explicitly associated with the Pentecost outpouring of the Spirit in a textual citation, in sharp contrast to Luke's citation of Joel's prophecy in Acts 2:16–21. To cite another example, Enoch was carried up to God's heavenly court, which was 'surrounded by tongues of fire'.[106] But the Enochic context is one of an ecstatic visionary transportation to heaven: in contrast, the Pentecost outpouring of the Spirit is *from* heaven (Acts 2:2: ἐκ τοῦ οὐρανοῦ; 2:19: ἐν τῷ οὐρανῷ ἄνω). Moreover, the Pentecost experience does not involve ecstasy: the Spirit-filled disciples speak in known languages, praising God's deeds in a conscious state (Acts 2:4–13, cf. v.15) as opposed to being rapturously transported and speaking in unknown heavenly / angelic tongues (cf. 1 Cor. 14:13–17,23).[107] The Jewish backgrounds proposed for the 'tongues of fire' do not match with sufficient textual precision the features of the Pentecost narrative. Last, apart from Pieter W. van der Horst (*supra*, n.89), New Testament commentators overlook the Graeco-Roman background of the 'fire' portents. We must reckon, therefore, with Luke's authorial intention in this instance, as much as we can discern that by a consideration of *both* the Jewish and Graeco-Roman background, and not just make inferences from LXX intertestamental echoes alone.[108]

I propose that Luke chose 'fire' as a symbol of the divine presence at Pentecost for the transcultural possibilities offered and the christological focus effected theologically.

- First, the 'tongues of fire' image was familiar to the Graeco-Roman world and would have attracted the attention of eastern and western Mediterranean auditors. However, Luke's use of the motif allowed him to make some telling contrasts. The Lukan emphasis is on the universality of the experience: the tongues of fire rested on all the disciples, not just upon a select few (i.e. the great men of Graeco-Roman epic or history).[109]
- Second, the tongues of fire endowed all the disciples with the Spirit of prophecy and, as prophets (Acts 2:17a,18b), they exercised that ministry in speaking of God's mighty deeds (2:11; cf. προφεύσουσιν: 2:17,18; 11:28; 13:1; 15:32; 21:9–11).[110] This stands in direct contrast to the Graeco-Roman accounts. There the great man, heralded by tongues of fire, is totally dependent on others apart from himself to provide the prophetic understanding of the portent.
- Third, more importantly, the 'tongues of fire' motif allows Luke the opportunity to focus on Jesus, the Spirit-filled Messiah-Prophet. In Luke 3:16, John the Baptist prophesied that the coming Christ would baptise with 'Spirit' and 'fire'. Jesus as the risen and exalted Lord of the Spirit fulfilled exactly that role, outpouring his Father's promise of the Holy Spirit to his disciples (Acts 2:32–33).
- Fourth, the traditions of Second Temple Judaism knew nothing about a crucified man becoming the Lord of the Spirit (Acts 2:33; cf. vv.31–32,34–36). What created the impetus to bring such a strong eschatological emphasis to Joel's prophecy in Acts 2:17 (ἐν ταῖς ἐσχάταις ἡμέραις), signified by the addition of Luke to the LXX text? Apart from the Father's resurrection and exaltation of the crucified Christ, the answer must begin with

---

106 *1 En*. 14.8–25; cf. 71:5, cited by Longenecker, 'Acts', 270. Cf. 1Q29 1.3; 2:3: 'three tongues of fire,' cited by Fitzmyer, *The Acts of the Apostles*, 238.
107 Keener, *Acts, Volume 1*, 806–24, argues for genuine known diverse languages, as opposed to ecstatic phenomena, which function as one kind of prophetic speech (Acts 2:16–18) in cross-cultural mission.
108 See Hayes, *Echoes of Scripture in the Gospels*.
109 Note, too, the paradox in Luke's presentation: although the outpouring is corporate, the fiery tongues 'fork in such a way as to light on each Christian—and provide the visual evidence that the Spirit is given them as individuals' (Haenchen, *The Acts of the Apostles*, 168).
110 On the 'Spirit of prophecy', see Menzies, *The Development of Early Christian Pneumatology*, 205–44, esp. 214–29; Perry, *Eschatological Deliverance*, 12–169; Turner, 'The Spirit in Luke Acts'; Turner, *Power from on High*, 82–139.

the historical Jesus, who, as the herald of the Kingdom's advent, unleashed its pneumatic ministry focus and power as the Spirit-filled Messiah. The powerful historical and soteriological narrative inherited and articulated by Luke, transitioning from the earthly Spirit-filled Messiah in the Gospel of Luke to the current exalted and reigning heavenly Lord of the Spirit in the book of Acts, explains why the LXX intertestamental echoes of the 'fire portents' do not capture satisfactorily the full significance of what had happened at Pentecost. It also explains why the 'fire' portents do not now appear in heaven, as Joel's prophecy has proleptically anticipated: rather they issue from heaven to earth in soteriological fulfilment of Old Testament expectation of the outpoured Spirit.

How would Luke's auditors have responded to his presentation of the Spirit's portentous descent? Jewish auditors would probably have been genuinely surprised by Luke's bold presentation within the monotheistic confines of Second Temple Judaism, especially given Jesus' highly questionable status as a *crucified* 'Lord' and 'Messiah' (Acts 2:36b), provoking some to a derisive mockery of the tongue speaking involved (2:13; cf. Luke 9:7–9; Acts 17:32–34; 25:13–22).[111] In the case of Graeco-Roman auditors, the supra-cephalic fire portents would have occasioned cultural recognition, but such recognition was divorced from the increasingly imperial focus of portents in the early Roman Empire, and, more specifically, from their legitimation of Julian rule and the apotheosis of Caesar. The attribution of supra-cephalic fire portents to a Spirit-outpouring by a figure crucified by the prefect Pontius Pilate in a backwater of the Empire would have been very difficult to comprehend by Roman auditors.

3. An Alternative to Portents: Ephesian Artemis and the Lukan Paul

The Ephesian Artemis episode in Acts 19:23–41 is highly instructive. It documents the emerging conflict between the portent mentality of the ancient world and the Christian gospel. In his address to the crowd, the Ephesian city clerk said: 'the city of the Ephesians is temple keeper of the great Artemis, and of the sacred stone that fell from the sky (τοῦ διοπετοῦς)' (Acts 19:35).[112] The stone, probably a meteorite,[113] had been taken to be a heaven-sent image of the goddess.[114] In Euripides (*Iph. Taur.* 78–79, 977, 1384–1385; cf. *pace*, Pliny the Elder, *Nat.* 16.79.213–214) it is said that an image of Artemis of Tauris fell from heaven into her sanctuary, but there is no confirmatory evidence for the Acts' tradition of an Ephesian image.[115] Nor does the statue evidence of Artemis at Ephesus provide any hint in its iconography or shape of the meteorite tradition of Acts.[116]

However, there are clear parallels to this phenomenon of the *worship* of meteorite stones

---

111 Bruce, *The Acts of the Apostles*, 87, writes that 'In 1 Cor. xiv. 23 Paul points out that the glossolalia may be misunderstood for madness'.
112 On τοῦ διοπετοῦς ('fallen from Zeus', 'coming from the sky'), see Trebilco, 'Asia', 353.
113 Johnson, *The Acts of the Apostles*, 350, writes: 'It may have referred to a meteorite, or to the image of the goddess, or both'.
114 Williams, *Acts*, 335. Witherington, *The Acts of the Apostles*, 598, writes: '[I]t was not an unusual practice in this era to treat meteorites as cult objects (cf. Cicero, *Verr.* 2.5.187 for the same practice at Enna but in connection with the god Ceres, or at Emesa of El Gabal as mentioned in Herodian, *Hist.* 5.3, 5)'.
115 See also Fontenrose, *The Delphic Oracle*, 366, L.29.
116 See LiDonnici, 'The Images of Artemis'.

in other cults.[117] In isolating the substantial evidence for Greek meteor worship predating New Testament times, it is clear that this was a very widespread phenomenon, thereby lending credence to the Lukan report of meteorite worship in Acts 19:35.[118] First, the temple of Cybele at Pessinus had such a stone preserved within its precincts, which was later summoned by Rome in 205 BC for its own temple (Livy 29.3.10–11; Strabo, *Geogr.* 12.5.3; Herodian 1:11; Arnobius 7.49; Servius 7.188).[119] Second, a small stone of Kronos at Delphi was kept close to the tomb of Neoptelemus (the son of Achilles)— according to myth, a sacred object supposedly fed to King Kronos the god by his wife Rhea—and is not to be confused with Delphi's famous omphalos stone (Pausanias, *Descr.* 10.4.26). Third, at the town of Orchomenus in Boetia in the temple of the Charites, Pausanias mentions that the worshippers of Dionysius 'worship the stones, and say they fell for Eteocles out of heaven', the legendary king of Thebes (*Descr.* 9.38.1).[120] Fourth, there is mention of a stone of Apollo Karinos in the old gymnasium of Megara (Pausanias, *Descr.* 1.14.22), an Eros stone at Boetian Thespiae (Pausanias, *Descr.* 9.27.1), the Abydos stone worshipped in the gymnasium (Elder Pliny, *Nat.* 2.59), and the Cassandreia stone in the Chalcidice Peninsula (Elder Pliny, *Nat.* 2.59).[121]

The numismatic evidence also confirms the literary picture. A bronze coin, issued during Trajan's reign at Seleucia Pieria, shows on the reverse a sacred stone of Zeus Kasios. The stone rests within a shrine of four pillars, with a pyramidal roof surmounted by an eagle.[122] More important because of its contemporaneity with Acts, however, is the silver tetradrachm of Cyprus issued under the reign of Vespasian (RPC II 1803: AD 69–79), with the bust of the emperor on the obverse (legend: ΑΥΤΟΚΡΑΤΩΡ ΟΥΣΠΑΣΙΑΝΟΣ ΚΑΙΣΑΡ).[123] The reverse (legend: ΕΤΟΥΣ ΝΕΟΥ ΙΕΡΟΥ ['in the year of the new temple']) shows the temple of Aphrodite at Paphos, presumably from the legend either recently erected or restored. Two cross beams join the central columns, with two low-roofed wings present at the sides. The central space is dominated by a cone-shaped and flat-topped beatyl stone, sacred to the goddess and mentioned by Tacitus (*Hist.* 2.2 [AD 69]).[124] Once again, this contemporary visual evidence of meteorite worship in the imperial world of the Greek East confirms the overall accuracy of Luke's account, even if we have no confirmatory archaeological or numismatic evidence of an Ephesian stone.

Thus, when Paul preached that 'gods made with hands are not gods' (Acts 19:26: θεοὶ οἱ διὰ χειρῶν γινόμενοι),[125] a series of complex reactions probably took place within the minds of Ephesian Artemis worshippers (Acts 19:32). Some saw it as an attack on their trade as silversmiths (Acts 19:23,26–27). Others saw in it a denial of the missionary guidance Artemis gave her

---

117   For discussion, see Antoniadi, 'On Ancient Meteorites'; McBeath and Gheorghe, 'Meteorite Worship in the Ancient Greek and Roman Worlds'; Gheorghe and McBeath, 'Meteoric Portents from Livy and Julius Obsequens'; D'Orazio, 'Meteorite Records'. See Keener, *Acts, Volume 3*, 2930–32, for an extensive coverage of the literary evidence of images falling from heaven. By contrast, this essay focuses on the evidence for the worship of meteorites from heaven.
118   We omit from discussion the Phoenician evidence from Tyre and the late Roman evidence of the Emesa stone, associated with the life of the Roman emperor Elagabalus (AD 204–222). See D'Orazio, 'Meteorite Records', 220–21.
119   Williams, *Acts*, 335; D'Orazio, 'Meteorite Records', 219.
120   Johnson, *The Acts of the Apostles*, 350, observes that in Pausanias, *Descr.* 1.26.7 there is 'a similar legend concerning images of Athene that fell from heaven for the Athenians'.
121   I am indebted to D'Orazio, 'Meteorite Records', 218–21 for these references.
122   Plant, *Greek Coin Types and Their Identification*, coin 2034.
123   For four extra coins depicting baetyl stones postdating Vespasian, but not including the coin of Trajan noted above, see D'Orazio, 'Meteorite Records,' 219.
124   The canonical shape is often the result for comets that have survived the fiery passage through the atmosphere, a consistency in the shaping process that would have enhanced the impression of divine communication in the meteorite stone in antiquity.
125   Fitzmyer, *The Acts of the Apostles*, 658, notes: 'The Lucan formula echoes 17:24–25,29 and rings like a refrain. Cf. 7:48'.

worshippers through dream revelation.[126] Again, others would have heard a denial of Artemis' healing powers— the powers celebrated in the panelling of the Aetemiseion at Ephesus,[127] or a denial of her superior power over the machinations of the sorcerer's evil arts.[128] Some would have understood Paul's words as an assault on the veracity of heaven-sent portents. Such a stone was not 'manmade' precisely because it *did* come from heaven, possessing portentous significance as a gift from the goddess.[129] This seems to be the argument of the Ephesian town clerk who manages to calm down the crowds (Acts 19:26–27,35–41).[130] In this incident, then, we see something of the complex reactions which the gospel provoked and how its propagators could have been viewed as sacrilegious (ἱεροσύλους) and blasphemers (βλασφημοῦντας) (Acts 19:37).

But what would auditors and readers of the book of Acts have made of the episode? First, Luke's concentration on portents free from any imperial focus might have been important reminder for his first-century auditors that Romanisation, while a potent force throughout the Empire, had definite limits of influence.

Second, Luke recognised the abiding religious and social influence that indigenous deities continued to exercise in mainland Greece and Asia Minor. Luke was aware that the early believers regularly encountered powerful local deities and their worshippers in their missionary outreach, along with the associations connected to them (Acts 19:23–41)[131] and the various civic and religious officials (Acts 14:13; 19:30,35). These were just as important to the religious landscape as the adjudication of the Roman provincial procurator (cf. Acts 19:38).[132] Encounters of believers with the indigenous gods and their cults occurred because of (a) local opposition to the first Christ-followers (Acts 19:23–41), (b) the mistaken cultic veneration of Paul and Barnabas as miracle-workers (14:8–18), and (c) the presence of an inscription to the unknown god at Athens (17:16,22–23). Although the early believers boldly critiqued 'man-made' deities (Acts 14:15; 17:24–25; 19:26), Luke takes seriously the influence of indigenous gods and their portents in his narrative. Luke's non-believing auditors would have been faced with a personally challenging choice upon hearing his narrative: continue to worship the lifeless gods and be guided by their ambiguous portents or, through the Spirit, transfer their allegiance to the risen Lord of all, whose τέρατα and σημεῖα bring salvation from death to eternal life.

Third, for believing auditors, the Lukan Paul's curt dismissal of idols as being 'hand-made' pointed to the ultimate powerlessness of Artemis and all other indigenous deities. The Lukan Paul's polemic (Acts 19:26) recalled the many searing Old Testament denunciations of the lifeless idols (e.g. Ps. 97:7–9; 115:3–8; 135:15–18; Isa. 40:18–20; 43:8–13; 44:6–8,9–20; 45:18–21; 46:1–2,6–7; Hab 2:18–20), which as 'non-entities' could never be compared with the incomparable Yʜᴡʜ, the living God of all history.

---

126   Oster, 'The Ephesian Artemis as an Opponent of Early Christianity', 43.
127   Note Jayne, *The Healing Gods of Ancient Civilisations*, 313: '[T]he gold, silver and ivory models of limbs contained in the panelling of the Artemiseion at Ephesus testify to the gratitude of her suppliants'.
128   See Harrison, 'Artemis Triumphs', 39–49.
129   The way in which the clerk reports the charge probably reflects accurately his own formulation of Paul's message, as opposed to the (likely) LXX or pseudepigraphic distillation made by Paul or Luke, who would have drawn terminologically from their Jewish heritage: namely, χειροποίητος ('made by hand'): Lev. 26:1,30; Isa. 2:18; 10:11; 16:12; 19:1; 21:9; 31:7; 46:6; Dan. LXX [Daniel Old Greek] 5:4,23, 6:27(28); Da. TH. [Daniel Theodotion] Bel. 5; Jdt 8:18; Wis 14:8; *Sib. Or.* 3:606, 618, 722, 4.28A; cf. Mark 14:58; Acts 7:48; !7:24; Eph. 2:11; Heb. 9:11,24.
130   See the discussion of Bock, *Acts*, 612–13.
131   For the epigraphy of the Ephesian silversmith association, see IEph. 2.425, 2.547, 2.585, 2.586, 3.636, 6.2212, 6.2441.
132   See Yoder, *Representatives of Roman Rule*.

Why then does Luke seemingly pay so little attention narratively in Acts to τέρατα ἐν τῷ οὐρανῷ ἄνω ('portents in the heaven above'), in contrast to the miracle-working apostles (σημεῖα ἐπὶ τῆς γῆς κάτω) and their Lord in the Gospel of Luke? As noted above (n.86), the only τέρατα [...] ἄνω recorded in Acts are the ascension of Jesus, the supra-cephalic tongues of fire, and the meteoric image from heaven worshipped in the Artemis temple at Ephesus.[133] Moreover, we have argued that Jesus' ascension and the pneumatic supra-cephalic tongues of fire are pivotal eschatological events in the lives of the first believers, in the same way that the end-time portents associated with Jesus' death inaugurate Joel's 'Day of the Lord' in Luke's Gospel (23:44–45; Acts 2:18–19 [cf. v.17a: ἐν ταῖς ἐσχάταις ἡμέραις]). The geographical locus of the ascension and Pentecost outpouring was at Jerusalem, the centre of early first-century Judaism, whereas Paul's critique of the meteoric image of Artemis occurred in Ephesus, the capital of proconsular Asia from 27 BC onwards. Here we see the powerful impact of the gospel moving from Jerusalem to Samaria and then to the ends of the earth (Acts 1:8), expressed in this instance by the Spirit-orchestrated outworking of Joel's τέρατα in eschatological fulfilment and missionary outreach.

Having highlighted these eschatological and missionary emphases by means of the three narrative τέρατα outlined above, Luke chooses to concentrate heavily on σημεῖα ἐπὶ τῆς γῆς κάτω,[134] as well as upon the revelatory and hortative work of the Spirit of prophecy.[135] There was a compelling reason for Luke adopting such an approach. The ancients regarded the 'miraculous' as fundamentally embodied in divine revelatory portents, as opposed to the powerful deeds performed by miracle-workers, the oneiric visions of healing provided by Asclepius, and the so-called wonders of the ancient paradoxographers. The exceptionally few 'parallels' in antiquity to the wide-ranging extent of the miracles performed by the Spirit-filled Jesus, who as the Messiah actualised the presence of the Kingdom of God, underscores this precise point.[136] Luke inverts and re-orders the ancient understanding of the 'miraculous' by diminishing narratively the centrality of portents as the all-consuming indication of the divine will and operations in antiquity. Rather the prophetic, eschatological, christological, soteriological, and pneumatic dimensions of God's self-disclosure in history are the central focus of Luke's narrative.

Conclusion

This article has argued that Luke's addition of 'above' (ἄνω) to 'wonders in the heaven' (Acts 2:19; cf. LXX Joel 2:30) in his citation of Joel's prophecy in Acts 2:16–21 is not just a stylistic 'tidying up' of the Old Testament text. Rather, it points to the likelihood that the portents mentioned in the Gospel of Luke and in the Book of Acts have theological, eschatological, and apologetic significance. Significantly, Luke links τέρατα with σημεῖα in the Book of Acts, drawing upon the LXX Deuteronomic soteriological motifs which are identifiable contextually from their use in Acts.

The ancient portent mentality revealed in the early Jewish and Graeco-Roman literary evidence was then investigated. There are clear echoes of 'portent' motifs from that corpus (i.e. cosmic catastrophes, national disturbances, lightning, eclipses, temple omens, earthquakes) found in the

---

133 *Pace*, note the earthquake in Acts 16:25–26, but as argued above, this is accorded soteriological as opposed to portentous significance.
134 For miracles in Acts, punitive and soteriological, see 2:4; 3:1–10; 4:31; 5:1–11,17–21; 8:40; 9:1–19,32–35,36–41; 12:20–23; 13:6–11; 14:8–10; 16:25–27; 18:16–18; 20:7–12; 28:3–5; 28:8.
135 On the Sprit of prophecy, see Acts 2:17,18; 11:28; 13:1; 15:32; 21:9–11.
136 See Harvey, *Jesus and the Constraints of History*, 103–104.

Gospel of Luke (17:24; 21:9,10,11 [ἀπ' οὐρανοῦ σημεῖα]; 23:44,45) and in the book of Acts (11:28: famines; 16:26: earthquakes). It is significant that none of the Lukan portents cited above are designated τέρατα, underscoring Luke's LXX soteriological focus whenever the phrase τέρατα καὶ σημεῖα appears elsewhere in Luke's narrative.

While the occurrence of portents in the Lukan narrative are obvious enough, there are nonetheless distinctives differentiating Luke's approach from the portents found in Jewish and Graeco-Roman literature. Luke's portents are more restrained than many of their Graeco-Roman counterparts; nor is there any indication of the imperial focus of the first-century AD Graeco-Roman portents, focusing as they did on the various stages of the Roman ruler's birth, career, and death; portents bearing upon the rise of the great man and the affairs of the city-state are also of no interest to Luke. However, Luke's realised eschatology transforms his apocalyptic portents: the cross of Jesus inaugurates the 'Day of the Lord' (Luke 23:44–45; cf. Acts 2:17a: ἐν ταῖς ἐσχάταις ἡμέραις). The eschatological signs in Luke 21:25–27 and 17:24 are given a christological focus, whereas famine and earthquake portents (Acts 11:28; 16:26) garner interest not because of their revelatory potential but because of their ministry outcomes.

This article has argued that Luke employs three defining τέρατα ἐν τῷ οὐρανῷ ἄνω in the narrative of Acts. First, the heavenly ascension of the risen Jesus (Luke 24:51–52; Acts 1:6–11) proleptically presages his exaltation and enthronement, the outpouring of the Spirit at Pentecost, and his ultimate return at the eschaton.

Second, the supra-cephalic fire phenomena of Pentecost not only echoed various Old Testament theophanies, but they also recalled the supra-cephalic fire and comet prodigies commemorating the apotheosis of Julius Caesar. A cross-cultural engagement, it was argued, is occurring on Luke's part, but we should not infer, by way of an implicit comparison, the presence of an anti-Julian critique. Luke's interest in supra-cephalic portents is not motivated by the legitimation of the Julian regime, as per first-century prodigy conventions, or by a critique of imperial rule (*pace*, Luke 22:24–27).[137] Rather Luke's focus is pneumatic and christological. The crucified, risen, and exalted Messiah-Lord has received the promised Holy Spirit from his Father and has poured out this gift universally upon his dependants, as prophesied by Joel in the Old Testament. This pneumatic outpouring unleashed prophetic and oneiric guidance for the church, revelatory portents with ministry outcomes, miracles confirming the Gospel, and salvation for all those who cried out to God. The fire portents in Acts 2:3 heralded the beginning of this pneumatic process.

Third, Luke resisted the insistence of Romanisation that only imperial prodigies were worthy of note in the age of Augustus and his heirs. Luke knew the threat that the indigenous gods, their legitimating portents, and local supporters posed to the first believers. The portrayal of Paul's collision with the Ephesian silversmiths in Acts 19 graphically captures the problem that the early Christians faced in this regard. Paul's dismissal of the Ephesian meteorite statue from heaven as 'man-made' would have shocked Graeco-Roman auditors who knew perfectly well that the imperial cult did not supplant the indigenous deities: the traditional cultic worship and honours of the local gods had to be maintained at all costs.

James R. Harrison
Sydney College of Divinity
jimh@scd.edu.au

---

137 See Edelmann, *Das Römische Imperium*; Strait, *Hidden Criticism*.

Bibliography

Allison, Dale C. Jr	*The End of the Ages Has Come: An Early Interpretation of the Passion and Resurrection of Jesus* (Philadelphia, PA: Fortress, 1985).
Antoniadi, E. M.	'On Ancient Meteorites, and on the Origin of the Crescent and Star Emblem', *The Journal of the Royal Astronomical Society of Canada*, 33.5 (1939), 177–84.
Antoniou, Alex A.	'Athena Spits Blood at Rome, Victoria Flees from the Enemy: Portenta and Identity in the Early Principate', *Greece & Rome* 70.2 (2023), 175–96.
Barrett, A. A.	'Observations of Comets in Greek and Roman Sources Before A.D. 410', *Journal of the Royal Astronomical Society of Canada* 72.2 (1978), 81–106.
Berger, Klaus	'Hellenistich-heidnische Prodigien und die Vorzeichen in der judischen und christlichen Apocalyptic', *Aufstieg und Niedergang der romischen Welt*, 2.23.2 (1980), 1428–69.
Betz, Otto	'Miracles in the Writings of Flavius Josephus', in Louis H. Feldman and Gohei Hata (eds.), *Josephus, Judaism, and Christianity* (Detroit, IL: Wayne State University Press, 1987), 212–35.
Bloch, R.	*Les prodiges dans l'antiquité Classique (Grèce, Etrurie et Rome)* (Paris: Presses Universitaires de France, 1963).
Bock, Darrell	*Acts* (BECNT; Grand Rapids, MI: Baker Academic, 2007).
Bosman, P.	'Signs and Narrative Design in Plutarch's *Alexander*', *Akroterion* 56 (2011), 91–106.
Brenk, Frederick E.	'Omens and Portents', in L. R. Lanzilotta (ed.), *Frederick E. Brenk on Plutarch, Religious Thinker and Biographer* (Leiden/Boston: Brill, 2007), 96–102.
Bruce, F. F.	*The Acts of the Apostles: The Greek Text with Introduction and Commentary* (London: Tyndale, 1970).
Chalupa, Aleš.	'The Religio-Political Change in the Reign of Augustus: The Disappearance of Public Prodigies', *Graeco-Latina Brunensia* 17.2 (2012), 57–67.
Charlesworth, James H. (ed.)	*The Old Testament Pseudepigrapha. Volume 1: Apocalyptic Literature and Testaments* (New York, NY: Yale University Press, 1983).
Conzelmann, Hans	*Acts of the Apostles* (Hermeneia; Philadelphia, PA: Fortress, 1987).
Dick, Bernard F.	'The Technique of Prophecy in Lucan', *Transactions and Proceedings of the American Philological Association* 94 (1963), 37–49.
D'Orazio, M.	'Meteorite Records in the Ancient Greek and Latin Literature,' in L. Piccardi and W. B. Masse (eds.), *Myth and Geology* (Geological Society Special Publication 273; London: The Geological Society, 2007), 215–25.
Drews, Robert	'Pontiffs, Prodigies, and the Disappearance of the "Annales Maximi"', *Classical Philology* 83.4 (1988), 289–99.

Dubis, K.M.	*Messianic Woes in First Peter: Suffering and Eschatology in 1 Peter 4:12-19* (New York, NY: Peter Lang, 2002).
Edelmann, Jens-Arne	*Das Römische Imperium im Lukanischen Doppelwerk: Darstellung und Ertragspotenzial für christliche Leser des späten ersten Jahrhunderts* (WUNT 2.547; Tübingen: Mohr Siebeck, 2021).
Engels, David	'Dionysius of Halicarnassus on Roman Religion, Divination and Prodigies,' in C. Deroux (ed.), *Studies in Latin Literature and Roman History 16* (Collection Latomus 338; Bruxelles: Éditions Latomus, 2012), 151–75.
Fitzmyer, Joseph A.	*The Acts of the Apostles: A New Translation with Introduction and Commentary* (The Anchor Bible 31; New York, NY: Doubleday, 1997).
Flaceliere, Robert	*Greek Oracles* (London: HarperCollins, 1965).
Fontenrose, Joseph	*The Delphic Oracle: Its Responses and Operations With a Catalogue of Responses* (Berkeley, CA: University of California Press, 1978).
Franza, Annarita, and Giovanni Pratesi	'Julius Obsequens's Book, *Liber Prodigiorum*: A Roman Era Record of Meteorite Falls, Fireballs, and Other Celestial Phenomena', *Meteoritics & Planetary Science* 55.7 (2020), 1697–1708, doi: 10.1111/maps.13525, accessed 01.05.2024.
Frier, Bruce W.	*Libri Annales Pontificum Maximorum: The Origins of the Annalistic Tradition* (2nd edn; Ann Arbor, MI: University of Michigan Press, [1979], 1999).
Gempf, Conrad	'The Imagery of Birth Pangs in the New Testament', *Tyndale Bulletin* 45 (1994), 119–35.
Gheorghe, Andrei D. and Alistair McBeath	'Meteor Beliefs Project: Meteoric Portents from Livy and Julius Obsequens,' *WGN, Journal of the International Meteor Organization* 34.3 (2006), 94–100.
Ginsberg, Lauren D.	'Allusive Prodigia: Caesar's Comets in Neronian Rome (Tac. *Ann.* 15.47)', *Transactions of the American Philological Association* 150.1 (2020), 231–49.
Grueber, H. A.	*Coins of the Roman Republic in the British Museum, Vol 2* (Oxford: Trustees of the British Museum, 1970).
Hadrill, Andrew Wallace	*Suetonius: The Scholar and His Caesars* (New Haven, CT: Yale University Press, 1983).
Harvey, A. E.	*Jesus and the Constraints of History: The Bampton Lectures 1980* (London: Duckworth, 1982).
Haenchen, Ernst	*The Acts of the Apostles* (Oxford: Basil Blackwell, 1971).
Hammond, N. G. L.	'Portents, Prophecies, and Dreams in Diodorus Books 14–17', *Greek, Roman, and Byzantine Studies* 39 (1998), 407–28.
Harrison, James R.	'Artemis Triumphs Over a Sorcerer's Evil Art', in S. R. Llewelyn and James R. Harrison (eds.), *New Documents Illustrating Early Christianity Volume 10* (Grand Rapids, MI: Eerdmans, 2012), 39–49

Harrison, James R.	'Prophecy, Divination, and Oneirology in the Greek Magical Papyri: Situating Joel's Prophecy (Acts 2:16–21) in Its Graeco-Roman Revelatory Context', in Christina M. Kreinecker, John S. Kloppenborg, and James R. Harrison (eds.), *Everyday Life in Graeco-Roman Times: Documentary Papyri and the New Testament. Essays in Honour of Peter Arzt-Grabner* (Leiden: Brill, 2024), 99–124.
Hayes, Richard B.	*Echoes of Scripture in the Gospels* (Waco, TX: Baylor University Press, 2016).
Jayne, William A.	*The Healing Gods of Ancient Civilisations* (New York, NY: University Books, 1925, reprint 1962).
Johnson, Luke T.	*The Acts of the Apostles* (Sacrina Pagina 5; Collegeville, MN: Michael Glazier, 1992).
Judge, E. A.	'"Signs of the Times": The Role of the Portentous in Classical and Apostolic Narrative', in E. A. Judge, *The First Christians in the Roman World: Augustan and New Testament Essays* (James R. Harrison, ed.; WUNT 229; Tübingen: Mohr Siebeck, 2008), 416–23.
Keener, Craig S.	*Acts: An Exegetical Commentary. Volume 1: Introduction and 1:1—2:47* (Grand Rapids, MI: Baker Academic, 2012).
Keener, Craig S.	*Acts: An Exegetical Commentary. Volume 3: 15:1—23:35* (Grand Rapids, MI: Baker Academic, 2014).
Krauss, Franklin B.	'An Interpretation of the Omens, Portents and Prodigies Recorded by Livy, Tacitus, and Suetonius', (Ph.D. thesis., University of Pennsylvania, 1930).
Longenecker, Richard	'Acts', in Frank E. Gaebelein (ed.), *The Expositor's Bible Commentary*, Volume 9 (Grand Rapids, MI: Zondervan, 1981), 207–573.
Lorsch, Robin S.	'*Omnia imperii*: The Omens of Power Received by the Roman Emperors from Augustus to Domitian, Their Religious Interpretation and Political Influence', (Ph.D. diss., University of North Carolina, 1993).
Mattingly, Harold	*Coins of the Roman Empire in the British Museum Vol. 1 (Augustus to Vitellius)* (London: Trustees of the British Museum, 1965).
McBeath, Alistair and Andrei D. Gheorghe	'Meteor Beliefs Project: Meteorite Worship in the Ancient Greek and Roman Worlds,' *WGN, the Journal of the IMO*, 33.5 (2005), 133–44.
McCartney, Eugene S.	'Classical Lore of Thunder and Lightning,' *The Classical Weekly* 25.23 (1932), 183–92.
McCasland, S. V.	'Portents in Josephus and in the Gospels', *Journal of Biblical Literature* 55 (1932), 323–35.
McDonald, A. H.	'Obsequens', in N. G. L. Hammond and H. H. Scullard (eds.), *The Oxford Classical Dictionary* (Oxford: Oxford University Press, 1971), 744.

Menzies, R. P.	*The Development of Early Christian Pneumatology with Special Reference to Luke Acts* (JSNTS 54; Sheffield: Sheffield Academic, 1991).
Morgan, M. Gwyn	'Two Omens in Tacitus' "Histories" (2, 50, 2 and 1, 62, 2–3)', *Rheinisches Museum für Philologie*, 3/4.136 (1993), 321–29.
Morgan, M. Gwyn	'Vespasian and the Omens in Tacitus "Histories" 2.78', *Phoenix* 50.1 (1996), 41–55.
Oster, Richard	'The Ephesian Artemis as an Opponent of Early Christianity', *Jahrbuch für Antike und Christentum* 19 (1976), 22–44.
Perry, A.	'Eschatological Deliverance: The Spirit in Luke Acts' (Ph.D. thesis, University of Durham, 2008).
Pitre, Brant	*Jesus the Tribulation, and the End of Exile: Restoration Eschatology and the Origin of the Atonement* (Tübingen/Grand Rapids, MI: Mohr Siebeck/Baker Academic, 2005).
Plant, Richard	*Greek Coin Types and Their Identification* (London: Spink, 1979).
Rasmussen, S. W.	*Public Portents in Republican Rome* (Rome: L'Erma di Bretschneider, 2003).
Rawson, Elizabeth	'Prodigy Lists and the Use of the Annales Maximi,' *The Classical Quarterly*, 21.1 (1971), 158–69.
Rogers, Robert Samuel	'The Neronian Comets', *Transactions and Proceedings of the American Philological Association* 84 (1953), 237–49.
Santangelo, Federico	'Prodigies in the Early Principate?', in Lindsay G. Driediger-Murphy and Esther Eidinow (eds.), *Ancient Divination and Experience* (Oxford University Press, 2019), 154–77.
Satterfield, Susan	'Livy, Cassius Dio, and Prodigies in the Early Roman Empire', *Klio* 104.1 (2022), 253–76.
Satterfield, Susan	'The Prodigies of 17 B.C.E. and the "Ludi Saeculares"', *Transactions of the American Philological Association* 146.2 (2016), 325–48.
Satterfield, Susan	'Prodigies, the Pax Deum, and the Ira Deum', *Classical Journal* 110 (2015), 431–45.
Schnabel, E. J.	*Exegetical Commentary on the New Testament. Volume 5: Acts* (ECNT; Grand Rapids, MI: Zondervan, 2012).
Scott, Kenneth	'The Sidus Iulium and the Apotheosis of Caesar', *Classical Philology*, 36.3 (1941), 257–72.
Selling, Philippa	'The Brontoscopic Calendar of Nigidius Figulus—An Almanac of Thunder', *Ancient Society: Resources for Teachers*, 8.1 (1978), 47–64; 8.2 (1978), 123–34.
Squires, John T.	*The Plan of God in Luke-Acts* (SNTSMS 76; Cambridge: Cambridge University Press, 1993).

Stewart, Selina	'Imperial Fortunes: Portents, Prodigies and Dio's Astrology of the State', in Adam Kamezis, Colin Bailey, and Beatrice Poletti (eds.), *The Intellectual Climate of Cassius Dio: Greek and Roman Pasts* (Leiden: Brill, 2022), 301–23.
Strait, Drew J.	*Hidden Criticism of the Angry Tyrant in Early Judaism and the Acts of the Apostles* (Minneapolis, MN: Fortress, 2019).
Syme, Ronald	*Tacitus. Vol. 2* (Oxford: Oxford University Press, 1958).
Trebilco, Paul	'Asia', in David W. Gill and Conrad Gempf (eds.), *The Book of Acts in Its First Century Setting. Volume 2: Graeco-Roman Setting* (Grand Rapids, MI: Eerdmans, 1994) 291–362.
Turner, M. M. B.	*Power from on High: The Spirit in Israel's Restoration and Witness in Luke-Acts* (Sheffield: Sheffield Academic, 2000; Eugene, OR: Wipf & Stock, 2015).
Turner, M. M. B.	'The Spirit in Luke Acts: A Support or a Challenge to Classical Pentecostal Paradigms?', *Vox Evangelica* 27 (1997), 75–101.
Van der Horst, Pieter W.	'Hellenistic Parallels to the Acts of the Apostles (2:1-47)', *Journal for the Study of the New Testament* 25 (1985), 49–60.
Vette, Nathanael	'The Omens at Jesus's Death (Mark 15:33–39) and the Divine Abandonment of the Temple before Its Destruction in 70 CE,' *Journal of Biblical Literature* 142.4 (2023), 657–75.
Volk, Katharina (ed.)	*Nigidius Figulus: Roman Polymath Published* (Columbia Studies in the Classical Tradition 47; Leiden: Brill, 2024).
Walsh, P. G.	*Livy: His Historical Aims and Methods* (Cambridge: Cambridge University Press, 1970).
Wardle, D.	'Suetonius on "Vespasianus Religious" in AD 69–70: Signs and Times', *Hermes* 20.2 (2012), 184–201.
Whittaker, Molly	'"Signs and Wonders": The Pagan Background', in F. L. Goss (ed.), *Studia Evangelica*, Vol. 5 (Berlin, Akademie-Verlag, 1968), 155–58.
Williams, David J.	*Acts* (NIBC 5; Peabody, MA: Hendrickson, 1990).
Witherington, Ben III	*The Acts of the Apostles; A Socio-Rhetorical Commentary* (Grand Rapids, MI: Eerdmans, 1998).
Woods, David	'Rewriting a Contentious Omen: Tacitus, Caligula, and the Phoenix', *Mnemosyne* 76 (2023), 617–29.
Woods, David	'Caligula, Asprenas, and the Bloodied Robe,' *Mnemosyne* 71 (2018), 873–80.
Yoder, Joshua	*Representatives of Roman Rule: Roman Provincial Governors in Luke-Acts* (BZNW 209; Berlin: De Gruyter, 2014).

Human flourishing and the Paul of the book of Acts

CHRISTOPH STENSCHKE

Abstract

This essay explores the Book of Acts for its contribution to the wider discussions on 'human flourishing'. The focus is on Luke's portrait of Paul, especially as depicted through Paul's speeches to Jewish (13:16–41), non-Jewish (14:14–17; 17:22–32), and Christian (20:18–35) audiences, as well as his several defence speeches at the end of the Book, in order to discern clues pointing to his view of the essential ingredients to human flourishing. As with the Lukan beatitudes, human flourishing is found in being aligned with the salvific purposes of the living and faithful God who is revealed through his Son Jesus.

1. Introduction

Jonathan Pennington suggests that the idea or theme of human flourishing, broadly understood, is

> one meta-theme or meta-concept that appears with remarkable tenacity and consistency across times and worldviews. This concept has staying power and universal voice because it addresses what is most basic and innate to all of humanity, despite the diversity of race, culture, and values. It is a concept that proves to be the motivating force and end goal of all that humans do and think.[1]

This is the case because, as Pennington claims,

> Human flourishing alone is the idea that encompasses *all human activity and goals* because there is nothing so natural and inescapable as the desire to live, and *to live in peace, security, love, health, and happiness*. These are not merely cultural values or the desire of a certain people or time period. The desire for human flourishing motivates everything humans do ... All human behaviour, when analysed deeply enough, will be found to be motivated by the desire for life and flourishing, individually and corporately.[2]

---

1 'Theology', 1.
2 'Theology', 1–2, italics added.

In the past decade, Pennington and others have started to bring this concept to Christianity[3] and also read the Bible afresh from this perspective.[4] Some Christians might be reluctant to read the Bible as a source of guidance on human flourishing, perhaps due to the understandable unease with the widespread, much reduced, 'gospel' of health and wealth, or other emphases which developed in the history of doctrine.[5] However, to search in the Bible for examples of people who buoyantly lived their lives before God, and in alignment with his word and purposes, or for instructions for a blessed, God-pleasing life which at the same time ensures human flourishing, is a legitimate concern, although certainly not the only purpose of reading Scripture or the only valid perspective when one does so.

This study follows this quest and takes it to a biblical book which has been neglected in this regard. The following examination of one aspect of human flourishing according to the Book of Acts supplements Pennington's survey of biblical key terms for human flourishing[6] and takes Joel B. Green's study of happiness in Luke's Gospel further,[7] to add to the biblical explorations of the theme in the collection of essays edited by Brent A. Strawn.[8]

Before we embark, we need to ask what the 'thing' is we are looking for. Strawn rightly cautions against taking today's definitions of human flourishing, or the good life, or happiness as points of departure for approaching the Bible. Rather, efforts should be made

> to define biblical happiness, first, emically or inductively, from the Bible itself, utilizing the best tools of critical biblical scholarship, rather than by means of an over-, under-, or predetermined definition of 'happiness'. This 'Bible first' approach is crucial because, without careful investigation and definition, the 'happiness' that one finds generally available (whether in bookstores or on television) is often the polluted, flat kind, which will only go so far and which will typically not go nearly far enough—especially when the going gets rough.[9]

What people consider their own human flourishing and that of others depends on their personality, faith, value system, culture, and social and material circumstances, to name but a few of the factors involved.[10] Any assessment from our different perspectives must therefore remain tentative.[11]

Following these observations, we will start with gathering important clues from the text of Acts. In a second step, we will bring these clues into brief conversation with current understandings of human flourishing. One widespread definition is that used in the 2010 survey, 'Flourishing, Positive Mental Health and Wellbeing: How can they be increased?' of the *Mental Health Foundation of New Zealand*.[12] In this document, human flourishing is defined as

---

3   See, for instance, Volf, 'Flourishing', and Charry, *God*.
4   See the collection of essays edited by Strawn, *Bible*.
5   For an analysis, see Charry, *God*.
6   'Theology', 5–15.
7   'Celebrate', 233–47.
8   *Bible*.
9   *Bible*, 8–9.
10 For the cultural conditioning of what people might consider happiness / human flourishing, see the instructive studies discussed by Green, 'Celebrate', 234–35; for a fuller discussion, see Sahlins, *Natives*.
11 To guess how ancient people might have considered Paul's life, is difficult to assess. According to the New Testament evidence, Paul had a number of disciples and people around him who readily co-operated with him (some over longer periods of time), and must have found his life and calling (at least some aspects) persuasive and attractive, but he also faced critics and staunch adversaries who were irritated by his message and ministry. Whether and how they would have considered the 'quality' of Paul's life can hardly be known from the sources available to us.
12 Italics mine; the document refers to Fredrickson and Losada, 'Affect', see www.mentalhealth.org.nz/assets/Flourishing/Flourishing-and-Positive-Mental-Health-Dec-2010.pdf, accessed 01/07/2024.

a state where people experience positive emotions, positive psychological functioning and positive social functioning, most of the time. In more philosophical terms this means access to the pleasant life, the engaged or good life and the meaningful life [...] It requires the development of attributes and social and personal levels that exhibit character strengths and virtues that are commonly agreed on across different cultures.[13]

In their study *Human Flourishing: Scientific Insight and Spiritual Wisdom in Uncertain Times*, Andrew Briggs and Michael J. Reiss distinguish between the material, the relational, and the transcendent dimensions of human flourishing.[14] They argue that the concept of human flourishing 'provides a valuable framework within which to consider the importance of satisfying people's yearnings for material goods, successful relationships and the hope that we can achieve and experience things that give us a sense of something greater than ourselves—the transcendent'.[15] We will come back to both of these definitions.

Our endeavour is a bold undertaking as it raises a number of issues with regard to methodology. Obviously, the Lukan Paul cannot fill in a questionnaire (as those often used in social scientific studies) to assess the quality of his life. These and other tools are not available for assessing the measure of human flourishing for an ancient person.[16] While his letters offer clues on how Paul might have understood human flourishing (or what would, for him, have been essential ingredients for such a state), things become more complicated when we focus on Acts. We do not have Paul's own autobiography (which would give some indication of what was important to him about his life in retrospect), but only Luke's portrayal of Paul, shaped by what Luke (surely an admirer of Paul) chose to emphasise in his selective account. This limits all conclusions from our quest with regard to the historical Paul. All that we can do—with the necessary caution and restraint—is to draw from the Lukan Paul some conclusions with regard to *the good life according to the way in which Luke portrays Paul*.

A detailed description of Paul's 'good life' or portraying Paul's life as an example of human flourishing, readily to be imitated by all other believers, is *not* the main purpose of Luke-Acts. Rather, Luke briefly sketches Paul's pre-Christian past, his calling / conversion and ensuing faithful ministry over many years, including all the suffering it involved and how Paul set out 'to finish his course and the ministry that he received from the Lord Jesus, to testify to the gospel of the grace of God' (Acts 20:24). Luke did so to provide an apology for Paul's disputed ministry and to provide much-needed certainty to his readers, as he declares in the preface to Luke-Acts (Luke 1:4).

When thinking about human flourishing in the Bible, Paul may not be the first person who comes to mind. One might think of King Solomon in all his proverbial splendour (Luke 12:27), or turn to the Beatitudes of Jesus. Does he not describe (and prescribe at the same time) what such

---

13   Another definition is: 'For humans to flourish, it means we're on a path towards physical and mental wellbeing that's holistically good, both for individuals and communities. For us, human flourishing begins with self-determination and agency, scaffolded by strong social relationships. We flourish when we live with purpose; when we practice gratitude, forgiveness, and open-mindedness. We cultivate character strength and resilience to flourish in adversity, to lead with empathy and virtue. We flourish by maintaining a sense of wonder, curiosity, and humility about the world we all share and our place in it'.
From https://www.templetonworldcharity.org/our-priorities/launch/building-field-human-flourishing/what-is-human-flourishing (accessed 01/07/2024). Also see the more recent and more nuanced discussions in Cohen, *Religion*; McMahon, *History*; E. Mountbatten-O'Malley, *Flourishing*, and Zimmermann, *Flourishing*.
14   *Flourishing*, 5–10; described in detail on pp.23–107.
15   *Flourishing*, 4.
16   For a survey of ancient understandings of a / the good life, see Horn, *Lebenskunst*, 61–112, including a comparison of ancient and modern notions of happiness).

flourishing looks like in view of the kingdom of God? When thinking of Paul, the declaration in Acts 9:16, 'For I will show him how much he must suffer for the sake of my name', indicates an existence which, at first glance, is at odds with human flourishing as it is commonly understood. In addition, there is the impact of Paul's own long list of various sufferings in 2 Corinthians 11:23–33, which serves to authenticate his apostolic ministry (weakness as the characteristic of the true apostle), and other assertions of Paul regarding his own suffering and the suffering of Christ-followers in general.[17]

Indeed, the Book of Acts reports a number of instances of Paul's suffering.[18] Apparently, this suffering was in particular need of explanation. It is, however, less prominent in his biography when put into proper chronological perspective: although it is impossible to give precise dates, from Paul's conversion / calling to his imprisonment in Rome (Acts 28:31 can most probably be dated to the year AD 61 or 62), Acts covers, after all, about twenty-five to thirty years of his life and indicates that there was much more to his ministry than suffering. Our focus here is on Paul's speeches, as recorded in Acts, before different audiences, and on the clues which they provide to human flourishing.[19] We do so in order to comprehend how the author of Acts understood (or might have understood) the essential ingredients of such an existence. This quest can assist in seeing which aspects of human flourishing have been neglected, lead us beyond our culturally conditioned notions, or cast a different light on some of our notions of human flourishing.

2. Paul's Life and Human Flourishing

Before we look at Paul's speeches, we start with a brief survey of the portrayal of Paul's life in Acts from this perspective.[20]

In addition to Paul's faithful fulfilment of his calling, despite the hardships and suffering which this involved, Luke also offers other perspectives which suggest that Paul's life was a 'good life' from a spiritual perspective. Although initially an ardent persecutor of Christ and his followers (Acts 7:58—8:3; 9:1–2), Paul was not judged by God (as, for instance, King Herod was, see 12:23), but received grace, was forgiven and restored *by God / Jesus* (9:4–19). Paul was not only pardoned but also received the opportunity to serve the Christ he had persecuted (9:20–29; 11:26 to the end of Acts). During his ensuing ministry, Paul experienced the nearness, comfort, help, guidance, and affirmation of the Holy Spirit and of Jesus himself, amidst all turmoil (e.g. 18:10; 23:11; 27:23). In his ministry, Paul could see God at work to affirm his message and efforts through astonishing miracles (e.g. 13:11; 14:3,8–10), whether they were wrought by God or by Paul himself.

---

17 For recent studies on the indications for Paul's own view of the good life, see Shantz, 'Happiness', 187–202, and Smith, *Paul*.
18 It is impossible to ascertain whether Luke reports all instances of Paul's suffering during the ministry periods which Acts reports, and whether what is reported is indeed representative. For the motives of suffering and joy in Acts, see Cunningham, *Tribulations*.
19 Obviously, our focus on Paul's speeches determines the results. Focusing on the speeches of Peter in Acts, or all the missionary speeches or other aspects would lead to different results. Our examination of human flourishing in Acts has to be supplemented by other aspects, to secure a comprehensive picture and assess whether (and to what extent) our selection is representative of the entire book. For detailed treatments of the passages under consideration, see the commentaries by Schnabel, *Acts*, and Holladay, *Acts*.
20 For Acts and Paul, see Keener, *Acts*, 221–57. Prior to Paul coming on the scene of Acts, there are other instances of a good life / human flourishing. For instance, there are the descriptions of the earliest community in Acts 2 and 4, including its sharing of goods (often idealised), but also other aspects.

Also, on a human level, Paul's life contained several elements which many today would consider to be important aspects of human flourishing. Paul was accepted by the believers in Damascus (despite his problematic past), found Christian fellowship, and attracted adherents there who saved his life by helping him to escape (Acts 9:15–25). Barnabas was ready to trust him and introduce him to the community in Jerusalem (9:26–28). Paul's fellow believers cared for him, were concerned about his safety, and ushered him off when it was necessary to spare his life (9:29–39). There, and later on in Antioch, Paul experienced fellowship and co-operation with others (Barnabas) and was trusted by others (11:26–30). In his missionary enterprise, others joined Paul as his co-workers and travel companions (13:2—14:27; 15:41—18:5; 19:29; 20:4; 27:2). He received hospitality on many occasions (e.g. 9:19,27; 16:15; 18:7; 21:16; 28:7).

Although there were trials and set-backs, Paul's witness to Jesus was accepted eagerly by many people, Jews and non-Jews alike (e.g. Acts 13:42–44). Paul could see the fruits of his endeavours and start Christ-following congregations in major cities in the ancient Eastern Mediterranean world, which were to continue his mission in their vicinities. Other Christ-followers took an interest in what Paul was doing. He received some recognition for his achievements from the believers in Antioch and Jerusalem (14:27; 15:3–4; 21:17–20; although some Jewish Christ-followers remained suspicious of him). Paul had faithful friends during his long imprisonment who cared for him (24:23; 28:30), including on his journey to Rome as a prisoner (27:2; 28:14–15).[21] On several occasions, all kinds of people helped Paul when he was in need—from the Asiarchs of Ephesus, to relatives in Jerusalem, to friends in Sidon, to a Roman officer who wished to save his life, to the barbarous islanders on Malta who met Paul's physical needs (19:31; 23:16–22; 27:3,43; 28:2,10). While often hindered by circumstances (various forms of resistance) or other 'interference' (16:6–7; see also 27:9–11,21), and later on for several years as a Roman prisoner (from 22:33 onwards), Paul had the privilege of experiencing a certain measure of self-efficacy, often associated today with human flourishing.

In addition, Paul enjoyed many of the prerequisites of human flourishing. He had the privilege of receiving a comprehensive Jewish education (Acts 22:3–4; 23:6), including excellent knowledge of the Scriptures and early Jewish sources as well as familiarity with their interpretation, and also some knowledge of the Hellenistic cultural tradition (17:22–31). Paul knew how to use these assets in his ministry (see the many quotations) and for receiving guidance as to his own course of action. He could communicate in at least two languages (Greek and Aramaic, 22:2; and he had knowledge of ancient Hebrew). Paul had skills with which he could earn a living whenever it became necessary (18:2–3). It also seems that he was not poor, but had access to considerable financial means (21:24–26). Since his birth Paul was a Roman citizen (16:37; 22:26–29; 23:28; 25:10–12, and a citizen of Tarsus, 21:39), with all the privileges which this implied and which he knew to employ wisely (16:37–40; 22:24–29; 25:10–12). In his personality, Paul displayed zeal and determination and was not one to be discouraged or dismayed easily. Last but not least, he must have had a fairly robust physical condition to be able to minister in the way he did.

How does this survey relate to the first definition quoted above? It defined human flourishing

---

21 We do not know what Paul (and Luke) made of the (from our perspective!) fascinating opportunities which this particular calling provided to Paul, such as the chance to travel, seeing significant parts and places of the ancient Mediterranean world, and cross-cultural boundaries. Could and did Paul appreciate these aspects of his ministry as opportunities for human flourishing, or were they more of a burden to him? Some of these opportunities, what they entailed and what might have excited others (for the widespread ancient appreciation of travelling, see Casson, *Travelling*), seems to have irritated him (Acts 17:16). Due to the circumstances of his travels (far from comfortable!) it seems to have been a burden, if only due to the frequency and dangers involved (see 2 Cor. 11:23–33).

as 'a state where people experience positive emotions, positive psychological functioning and positive social functioning, most of the time'. Although it is impossible to tell how Paul may have responded emotionally to the circumstances in which he found himself, one can argue that in Luke's portrayal, there were, at least, some occasions and periods of time in Paul's life where he, in our assessment, could have had and probably actually had some positive emotions and found himself in conditions where he could function psychologically and socially in a positive way. Following the proposal by Briggs and Reiss of material, relational, and transcendent dimensions and preconditions of human flourishing,[22] one could argue that, at least for some of the periods of his life which are narrated in some detail in Acts, Luke's portrayal suggests that Paul had the material, relational, and transcendental prerequisites for such a life.[23]

After these reflections on the portrayal of Paul's life, we now survey his speeches in Acts to find clues to human flourishing.[24] How do they reflect on human existence in general, and on the life of Christ-followers? What clues do they provide to human flourishing? Unsurprisingly, these speeches focus on human flourishing in relation to God and in and through lives lived before him.[25]

3. Paul's Speeches and Human Flourishing

3.1 Addressing Jewish Audiences

Acts contains one major speech of Paul to his fellow non-Christ-believing Jews, and a number of summary reports of his message and ministry in Jewish contexts (preaching Jesus as God's Messiah in fulfilment of Scripture in various synagogues). Here the focus is on this speech, reported in Acts 13:16–41. Paul begins with a summary of the history of Israel and focuses on God's faithfulness. God chose, multiplied, and liberated Israel (v.17), patiently put up with this people in the wilderness (v.18), and gave them the land of Canaan as an inheritance (v.19). Later, God provided leaders (v.20, the judges, the prophet Samuel, King Saul), removed Saul and elevated David (v.22). From David's offspring God brought to Israel as saviour Jesus, as he had promised (v.23). Through the ministry of John, the Baptist, God prepared the people for this saviour (vv.24–25). God sent this message of salvation to his people (v.26). Although the people rejected Jesus, God raised him from the dead, affirmed him, and instituted witnesses to this key event (vv.27–31). In all of this, God fulfilled his promises (vv.32–35). Through the risen Jesus, forgiveness is possible and proclaimed (v.38); liberation is available to all: 'By him, everyone who believes is freed from everything from which you could not be freed by the law of Moses' (v.39). In all of this, God is doing the marvellous work of fulfilling his promises in the present time (see Luke 1:1), which must be recognised, not rejected (41).[26]

While far from a treatise on human flourishing, there are several clues as to what such flourishing might have looked like for the Lukan Paul: owing to God's faithfulness to his promises,

---

22 *Flourishing.*
23 For the material dimension see Blanton and Pickett, *Paul.*
24 Obviously, these speeches are also part of the Lukan portrayal of Paul. For a detailed assessment of the speeches of Acts, see Keener, *Acts,* 258–319.
25 This focus needs to be kept in mind. It is one major aspect of a good life, but not the only one to consider.
26 Later on, the missionaries indicate that the word of God had to be spoken first to the Jews, respecting the salvation-historical priority of Israel. In their mission, Paul and Barnabas see the command in Isa. 49:6, of being a light to the non-Jews, fulfilled (Acts 13:46–48). They are called to bring salvation to the ends of the earth. A good life lies in fulfilling this call, and in offering God's salvation to others.

humans can flourish. Being able to rely on these promises and God's provision will give them security and space to live in. Human flourishing depends on God's manifold gracious provisions. He is the one who can undo human mistakes. God's salvation—that is, forgiveness of sins and liberation—is crucial for human flourishing. Life is good because God's reliable promises of old have been fulfilled in Jesus, the Christ. The privilege of living in the age of the fulfilment of divine promises, and the ability and opportunity for recognising and acknowledging what God is doing in the present time and living accordingly, are crucial ingredients for human flourishing.

3.2 Addressing Non-Jews

Acts contains only two relatively short speeches of Paul before non-Jewish audiences (Acts 14:14–17; 17:22–32).[27] What clues to human flourishing do they provide?

Before the crowds of Lystra, ready to venerate Paul and Barnabas after their impressive healing miracle, the missionaries insist that they bring the good news, that these polytheists should turn from their vain idols and deities, towards the living God, 'who made the heaven and the earth and the sea and all that is in them' (Acts 14:15). While in the past he allowed the nations to walk in their own ways (14:16), God nevertheless did not leave himself without witness to his existence and nature. He did so through his charitable acts of giving rain from heaven and fruitful seasons. It was this gracious, faithful, living creator God who, in this way, satisfied their hearts with food and gladness (14:17). The nature of God, his grace, patience, and friendliness, become apparent in that God provides faithfully even for those who ascribe his gifts to their own idols and venerate them.

Human flourishing is intimately related to existing in harmony with the living God. This means knowing and worshipping the creator and true provider of all things. God's revelation in his creation is to be recognised and appreciated, and he is to be acknowledged accordingly. Human flourishing is dependent on divine care and the provision of sustenance for the body and, in this way also, gladness of heart (14:15–17).

In Athens, Paul proclaims the God unknown to the audience (Acts 17:23). This creator God does not live in temples or need anything humans could provide him with. He is the one who gives life and breath and everything (v.25). The people he created are to seek him, perhaps feel their way toward him and find him. God is actually not far from every person (v.27). In God, all people live and have their being (v.28). Despite their massive idolatry (as evident in a plethora of idols in Athens, v.16), God patiently and graciously overlooked the past times of ignorance, and now calls on all people everywhere to repent (v.30): the opportunity and call to repentance, rather than judgement, is God's response to human ignorance and failure. On the appointed day, God will judge the world in righteousness. Of this he has provided assurance through the resurrection of Jesus (v.31).

This speech indicates that, for the Paul of Acts, a crucial ingredient of human flourishing is being attuned to what is and can be known about God. It is a life which recognises that God is the one who gives this life and everything else which people need, a life characterised by seeking God and in appreciation of his nearness, a life lived with God and in dependence on him, a life defined by the knowledge of God and in response to his prompting to turn to him, a life oriented towards God's righteousness and, finally, a life under the promise of the sure resurrection from the dead, as God has demonstrated in raising Jesus from the dead. In contrast to much human experience, divine judgement will be just, and lead to the establishment of God's righteousness. While the divine ability and power to resurrect the dead is cited with reference to Jesus (referring back to the

---

27 For a detailed treatment see Stenschke, *Portrait*, 185–90, 210–21.

earlier misunderstanding of Paul's initial proclamation in Athens, 17:17–20), the prospect of being resurrected one day also contributes to human flourishing in the present.

When people live in harmony with the way things are because of God's creation and generous provisions even for those who do not honour him, and because of his gracious interventions in history in fulfilment of his promises, they will *experience positive emotions* as they worship God and align themselves with his purposes and live and serve in fellowship with his people. As they do so, they will, like Paul, probably also *experience positive psychological functioning and positive social functioning*.

3.3 Addressing Christ-followers

Acts contains only one major speech by Paul to a Christian audience. His farewell speech to the elders of Ephesus consists of a statement of account for his past ministry, and his charge to the elders on how they are to conduct themselves as leaders and continue Paul's ministry (Acts 20:18–35).

In the report of his past ministry (Acts 20:18–27,33–35), Paul recounts how he served with all humility, tears, and trials (v.19). He declared in public and private all that was profitable, 'testifying both to Jews and Greeks repentance toward God and faith in our Lord Jesus Christ' (vv.20–21; see also v.27). Paul now travels to Jerusalem, 'constrained by the Holy Spirit' (vv.22–23), awaiting imprisonment and afflictions. Paul's determined goal is to finish ('I do not account my life of any value nor as precious to myself') his course and the ministry he received from the Lord Jesus, that is, to testify to the gospel of the grace of God (v.24). Paul testifies to his faithful fulfilment of this commission. For three years, Paul did not cease night or day to admonish everyone with tears (v.31). Later, he emphasises that the purpose of his ministry was not to enrich himself materially. Rather than coveting what belongs to others (fellow Christ-followers), Paul provided for himself and others around him. He did so to demonstrate that 'by working hard in this way we must help the weak and remember the words of the Lord Jesus, how he himself said: "It is more blessed to give than to receive"' (vv.33–35).

In the charge to the elders, Paul emphasises that they must look after each other and the entire congregation. Having been called by the Holy Spirit to their ministry, they must carefully and responsibly care for the Church of God, which he obtained with the blood of his own [Son Jesus] (v.28). They must be careful as there will be threats from outside and temptations from within (vv.29–30). In all this, they have Paul's example of faithful ministry to follow (v.31), and divine provisions: God and the word of his grace (the Gospel of Christ Jesus), which is able to build them up and sustain them in their ministry and the prospect of an inheritance, a heavenly reward, among all those who are sanctified (v.32, recalling 14:22: 'through many tribulations we must enter the kingdom of God').

What clues for human flourishing does this speech provide? Paul's summary of his own ministry indicates that, for him, a good life is characterised as a life of humility, faithful service to God and people, and passing on to others what one was entrusted with by God. A good life is attuned to the promptings of the Holy Spirit, and is one of experiencing and passing on the grace of God. Human flourishing is closely connected to fulfilling the will of God, despite (or in) all adversity. A good life is a life devoted to others and their well-being, including all the emotions which this might involve. Human flourishing does not come from enriching oneself at the expense of others, but from taking responsibility for one's own material needs, and providing for others. Human flourishing is built on remembering and following the words of Jesus. It increases when people understand and practise that it is more blessed to give than to receive (time, material means, concern, interest). Paul and Jesus represent the insight expressed by Pennington as 'our flourishing is tied to the flourishing of others'.[28] Paul's Miletus speech is an antidote to the loss of solidarity, rightly identified and bemoaned by Pennington and others as a recent development.[29]

Paul's charge to the elders suggests that human flourishing needs some binding fellowship and relations ('Pay attention to yourselves', each individually but also among the group of elders), the willingness to take responsibility for others, and the clear acknowledgement of limits (the church is and remains the flock of God, not the possession of the elders to be exploited by them at their will). A good life means refraining from lording it over others and misusing them to serve our interests as if those people belonged to us, but respecting that they belong to (the flock of) God. Human flourishing thrives when people respect this, and treat others accordingly. Foresight and care are needed to prevent dangers and avoid temptations. Human flourishing needs good human examples to follow (people who live transparently for others, to observe and emulate them) and, above all, the example and teaching of Jesus. Human flourishing depends on divine provisions: God and his word, with all the benefits it offers ('Man shall not live by bread alone', Matt. 4:4), such as building up and providing orientation. Human flourishing is closely tied to the prospect of a divine inheritance, that is, his approval and reward for faithful service in this life. While pursued (and to be pursued) in the present, human flourishing needs this future reference point: a life that will win God's approval and ensure this inheritance, both now and in the future, will also be a 'good' life in the present. This life is not an end in itself, but a means of serving God and others. Without this orientation towards God, human flourishing is limited.

3.4 Defence Speeches before Jewish and Non-Jewish Audiences

We cannot offer a detailed analysis of the several defence speeches Paul gave in Jerusalem, Caesarea, and Rome, before Jewish and non-Jewish audiences.[30] In these apologies Paul explains his pre-Christian past and his rather unexpected encounter with the risen Jesus on the road to Damascus. Its implication was his calling to be an apostle to the non-Jews, kings, and his fellow Jews (Acts 26:16–18), his deep loyalty to the Jewish people,[31] his initial reluctance to accept this calling and ministry to non-Jews, and how he had fulfilled this commission to the present day: 'Therefore, O King Agrippa, I was not disobedient to the heavenly vision, but declared first to those in Damascus, then in Jerusalem and throughout all Judea, and also to the Gentiles, that they should repent and turn to God, performing deeds in keeping with their repentance' (26:19). As a statement of account, Paul assures: 'To this day I have had the help that comes from God, and so I stand here testifying both to small and great, saying nothing but what the prophets and Moses said would come to pass: that the Christ must suffer and that, by being the first to rise from the dead, he would proclaim light both to our people and to the Gentiles' (vv.22–23).

Paul also defends in some detail his motives for coming to Jerusalem and his behaviour since he arrived there at the end of the third missionary phase (for instance, in Acts 24:11–21). He is not guilty of profaning the temple, as some of his opponents had claimed, but came to Jerusalem and its temple as a devout Jew with pious and fully legitimate intentions. He did nothing which would warrant an arrest; he is not guilty of the charges levelled against him.

---

28 'Theology', 3.
29 'Theology', 3.
30 For detailed examination see Omerzu, *Prozess*. By analogy with the missionary speeches earlier in Acts, there are also shorter summaries of Paul's defences before various officials (e.g. Acts 25:8,10–11).
31 For the distinctly Jewish portrayal of Paul in Acts, see Stenschke, 'Emissary', and 'Jude'.

These speeches suggest that human flourishing is linked to loyalty to ancestral traditions ('a Pharisee, a son of Pharisees', Acts 23:6; 'and to present offerings', 24:17–18) and to the Jewish people ('I came to bring alms to my nation', 24:17), the worship of God (24:14), faith in divine revelation (the Law and the prophets, 24:14), a hope in God with regard to the resurrection (24:15)—all essential ingredients of revelation-based Jewish identity. In addition, there is the faithful fulfilment of a divine commission, despite adversities of various kinds, and a life conducted in view of the resurrection of Jesus and the dead in general (23:6; 'So I always take pains to have a clear conscience toward both God and man', 24:16,21: 'It is with respect to the resurrection of the dead that I am on trial today'), and behaviour characterised by a clear conscience (24:16).

Green concludes that, according to Luke's Gospel, 'Luke sees happiness not as the goal of living but as the outcome or by-product of *living in harmony with the way things are*' (italics mine).[32] The narrative articulation of the larger context within which human flourishing is possible is 'defined by God's eschatological intervention to bring salvation in all its fullness to all and, then, by the invitation to persons to order their lives accordingly'.[33] According to Paul's defence speeches, the Lukan Paul claims to have done precisely that: with all of his existence, he fully aligned himself throughout his ministry with the way things are now in view of God's salvific intervention in Jesus the Christ, for Jews and non-Jews alike. He also associated himself with the role he had been given by the risen and exalted Jesus to play in testifying to these events before Jewish audiences, and in being a light for the non-Jews and, in this way, bringing God's salvation to the ends of the earth (Acts 13:47). In Luke's portrayal, such existence and ministry in harmony 'with the way things are' suggests a good life, and provided the conditions for human flourishing despite the adversities and suffering which Paul also had to face.

Again, we ask how this survey of Paul's speeches in Acts relates to the recent definition quoted above which defined human flourishing as 'a state where people experience positive emotions, positive psychological functioning and positive social functioning, most of the time'.

The wise restriction in the definition 'most of the time' also applies to these speeches. The occasion for some of them is the Lukan Paul's need to give an account of his message or to defend himself before various audiences. In these speeches, Paul speaks as a prisoner. At the same time, he is portrayed as somebody who is content with his life and who wishes others to share it—however, with one exception: 'I would to God that not only you but also all who hear me this day might become such as I am, except for these chains' (26:29). Whether and how these circumstances affected Paul is hard to tell. Although not explicitly noted, for Luke, Paul probably experienced what was promised by Jesus, i.e. that when the disciples are brought before the rulers and the authorities, they need not be anxious about how they should defend themselves or what they should say, 'for the Holy Spirit will teach you in that very hour what you ought to say' (Luke 12:11–12). There is a self-confident, perhaps even triumphant note in these defences. Paul affirms that he is innocent before God and humans and has no regrets with regard to the life which he lived in obedience to the divine commission he received ('Therefore ... I was not disobedient to the heavenly vision', 26:19): 'But I do not account my life of any value nor as precious to myself, if only I may finish my course and the ministry that I received from the Lord Jesus, to testify to the gospel of the grace of God' (20:24). With this purpose and determination in mind (finishing the course

---

32 'Celebrate', 247, italics mine. On p.234, Green notes: 'With the Stoics and against the Epicureans, Luke sees happiness as the effect or by-product of living in harmony with the way things are ... Luke has a particular perspective on "the way things are", and thus what it might mean to live, as the Stoics might put it, in harmony with the natural order of things'.

33 Green, 'Celebrate', 247.

and ministry), Paul is portrayed as experiencing human flourishing despite the hardships and suffering which this life also entailed.

Relating the picture of Paul's speeches in Acts to the proposal by Briggs and Reiss of material, relational, and transcendent dimensions and preconditions of human flourishing,[34] one could argue that God provides the material prerequisites for all people (Acts 14:17) and for Paul, in particular, some means to fulfil his own religious duties (21:26) and assist his people (21:26; 24:17). Paul's missionary speeches before Jewish and non-Jewish audiences, but also his statements of account in his defences, indicate that God's gracious interventions and human alignment with his purposes play crucial roles in the relational and transcendent dimensions and preconditions of human flourishing.

4. Summary and Implications

The Book of Acts combines a selective portrayal of large periods of Paul's life and ministry, and summaries of some of his speeches to different audiences. Although Paul suffered considerably as Christ's emissary to Jews and non-Jews, the Lukan portrayal also indicates several factors that are or, at least can be, conducive to human flourishing. As we have seen, Paul was blessed and affirmed by God in many ways, surrounded by people who provided fellowship, followed and assisted him in many ways, and he also had many assets associated with human flourishing on his side.

Despite these factors present in the narrative, we cannot know whether Paul, as portrayed by Luke, was 'happy', as we might understand this ambivalent term. What Green observes with regard to the apostles—that is, 'rejoicing that they were counted worthy to suffer dishonour for the name' (Acts 5:41)[35]—perhaps also apply to Paul. The happiness which he experienced 'was a by-product of their faithful service'. This portrayal in Acts has to be compared with Paul's own assertions in his extant letters regarding his own life and the believers' existence in general.[36] Although there are different nuances, there is much which agrees with the portrayal in Acts.

In his speeches to Jews, non-Jews, and Christ-followers, and his various defences, Paul calls people to align themselves a) with God the creator and worship him appropriately, b) with, in particular, his recent salvific activities in Jesus of Nazareth, crucified, resurrected, and exalted, and believe in him, and c) with the church of God, which he obtained with his own blood (Acts 20:28). People are to live readily and joyfully according to these realities: 'With Jesus's advent, death, and exaltation the times have changed; those who orient their lives to the divine purpose disclosed in Jesus will experience the pleasure and meaningfulness associated with human flourishing within this eschatologically determined world'.[37] According to Green,

> Luke's contribution lies particularly in the context within which happiness thus understood might be cultivated, modulated, and experienced. This context is defined by God's eschatological intervention to bring salvation in all its fullness to all and, then, by the invitation to persons to order their lives accordingly. ... [This] does not mean that Luke's narrative is bereft of interest in what we might call the psychological and relational aspects of happiness. It is, rather, that with the advent, death, and exaltation of the Messiah the times have changed,

---

34 *Flourishing*.
35 'Celebrate', 234.
36 Shantz, 'Happiness'.
37 Green, 'Celebrate', 247.

and that humans who orient their lives to the divine purpose disclosed in the Messiah will experience the pleasure and meaningfulness associated with human flourishing within this eschatologically determined world.[38]

This new orientation to God's salvific purposes is what Paul himself experienced dramatically on the road to Damascus and in the ensuing divine commissions, so meticulously described in Acts 9:3–19; 22:3–21; and 26:4–23. This fulfilment of the promises and purposes of God is *the way things are now*; this is the new reality Paul came to understand, accept, and align himself with, and in which he came to flourish as Christ's emissary.

Our examination of the portrayal of human flourishing in the 'Paul-chapters' of Acts affirms Green's analysis of the Lukan beatitudes: 'God describes as happy those who fully align themselves with God's royal rule revealed in the mission and message of Jesus'.[39] Human flourishing is closely linked to discipleship and to faithful fulfilment of one's calling, empowered and guided by the Spirit, in fellowship with others and with the prospect of divine reward. Living faithfully and joyfully in harmony with this reality is essential for human flourishing. Far from being a fatalistic acceptance of one's circumstances, it is a God-centred, joyous acceptance of how God brought about salvation in fulfilment of his promises.[40] The picture in Acts affirms Pennington's short summary of Volf's analysis[41] that, according to Augustine (and much of the Christian tradition), 'human happiness and flourishing come about through the harmonious fellowship of enjoying God and others'.[42] Luke (and Paul) would perhaps have added *serving* and *obeying* to *enjoying* God and *serving* others.

What we have pondered on human flourishing with regard to Paul according to Acts presents a much-needed challenge and correction to many developments in our day and age, as summarised by Pennington.[43] In the end, human flourishing is impossible apart from the faithful God and his salvific purposes, and a genuine concern for the flourishing of other people.

Christoph Stenschke
Department of New Testament and Related Literature,
Faculty of Theology and Religion,
University of Pretoria, South Africa
CStenschke@t-online.de

38 'Celebrate', 235.
39 'Celebrate', 247.
40 For the Lukan motif of joy, see Wenkel, *Joy*.
41 'Flourishing'.
42 'Theology', 3.
43 'Theology', 3–4.

Bibliography

Blanton, T. R. and R. Pickett (eds.) *Paul and Economics: A Handbook* (Minneapolis, MN: Fortress, 2017).

Briggs, A. and M. J. Reiss *Human Flourishing: Scientific Insight and Spiritual Wisdom in Uncertain Times* (Oxford: Oxford University Press, 2017).

Casson, L. *Travel in the Ancient World* (Baltimore, MD: Johns Hopkins University Press, 1994).

Charry, E. T. *God and the Art of Happiness: An Offering of Pastoral Doctrinal Theology* (Grand Rapids, MI: Eerdmans, 2010).

Cohen, A. B. (ed.) *Religion and Human Flourishing* (Waco, TX: Baylor University Press, 2020).

Cunningham, S. *'Through Many Tribulations': The Theology of Persecution in Luke-Acts* (JSNT.SS 142; Sheffield: Sheffield Academic Press, 1997).

Fredrickson B. L. and M. F. Losada 'Positive Affect and the Complex Dynamics of Human Flourishing', *American Psychologist* 60 (2005), 678–86 (https://www.ncbi.nlm.nih.gov/pmc/articles/PMC3126111/pdf/nihms305179.pdf) (accessed 07.07.2024).

Green, J. B. '"We had to Celebrate and Rejoice": Happiness in the Topsy-Turvy World of Luke-Acts', in J. B. Green, *Luke as a Narrative Theologian: Texts and Topics* (WUNT 446; Tübingen: Mohr Siebeck, 2020), 233–47 (here used; also in Strawn, *Bible*, 169–85).

Holladay, C. R. *Acts: A Commentary* (The New Testament Library; Louisville, KT: Westminster John Knox, 2016).

Horn, C. *Antike Lebenskunst: Glück und Moral von Sokrates bis zu den Neuplatonikern* (Beck paperback; Munich: C. H. Beck, 2014).

Keener, C. S. *Acts: An Exegetical Commentary: Introduction and 1:1—2:47* (Grand Rapids, MI: Baker Academic, 2012).

McMahon, D. M. (ed.) *History and Human Flourishing* (The Humanities and Human Flourishing; Oxford: Oxford University Press, 2022).

Mental Health Foundation of New Zealand (2010) *Flourishing, Positive Mental Health and Wellbeing: How can they be increased?* (https://www.mentalhealth.org.nz/assets/Flourishing/ Flourishing-and-Positive-Mental-Health-Dec2010.pdf, accessed 09.07.2024).

Mountbatten-O'Malley, E. *Human Flourishing: A Conceptual Analysis* (London: Bloomsbury, 2024).

Omerzu, H. *Der Prozess des Paulus: Eine exegetische und rechtshistorische Untersuchung der Apostelgeschichte* (BZNW 115; Berlin: de Gruyter, 2002).

Pennington, J. T.	'A Biblical Theology of Human Flourishing' (Tysons, VA: Institute for Faith, Works, and Economics, 2015), 1–22; https://tifwe.org/resource/a-biblical-theology-of-human-flourishing-2 (accessed 08.07.2024).
Sahlins, M.	*How 'Natives' Think: About Captain Cook, for Example* (Chicago, IL: University of Chicago Press, 1995).
Schnabel, E. J.	*Acts* (ECNT; Grand Rapids, MI: Zondervan, 2012).
Shantz, C.	'"I Have Learned to Be Content": Happiness according to St. Paul', in Strawn, *Bible*, 187–202.
Smith, J. C. H.	*Paul and the Good Life: Transformation and Citizenship in the Commonwealth of God* (Waco, TX: Baylor, 2020).
Strawn, B. A. (ed.)	*The Bible and the Pursuit of Happiness: What the Old and New Testaments Teach Us about the Good Life* (Oxford: Oxford University Press, 2012).
Stenschke, C. W.	'Der Jude Paulus in der Apostelgeschichte des Lukas: Beobachtungen zur Akzentuierung und Bedeutung der lukanischen Paulusdarstellung', *Estudios Bíblicos* 82 (2024), 93–119.
Stenschke, C. W.	'Emissary to Jews in the Diaspora and to Some Non-Jews, Champion of Jewish Monotheism and Circumspect of Diaspora Judaism: Paul of Tarsus in the Book of Acts', *New Testament Studies* 70 (2024), 72–87.
Stenschke, C. W.	*Luke's Portrait of Gentiles Prior to Their Coming to Faith* (WUNT II.108; Tübingen: Mohr Siebeck, 1999).
Volf, M.	'Human Flourishing', in R. Lints (ed.), *Renewing the Evangelical Mission* (Grand Rapids, MI: Eerdmans, 2013), 13–30.
Wenkel, D. H.	*Joy in Luke-Acts* (Paternoster Biblical Monographs; Milton Keynes: Authentic Media, 2015).
Zimmermann, J. (ed.)	*Human Flourishing in a Technological World: A Theological Perspective* (Oxford: Oxford University Press, 2023).

Herod Agrippa II
The embodiment or extinction of Israel's hope?

ANDREW STEWART

Abstract

This article examines the significance of Paul's defence before Herod Agrippa II (Acts 26) in the narrative of Luke-Acts. Agrippa II is the last of a series of ten Herodians found in the Lukan narrative. Recent scholarship has sought to hold together two themes in tension, one is the idea of Herod as a composite character representing hostility to God while the other is the distinctive significance of individual Herodians. The essay will argue that Agrippa II continues the Herodian trajectory as king and representative of the covenant nation of Israel but displays an openness to Paul's gospel not found in previous Herodians. This sets the scene for Paul's gospel proclamation in Acts 26 where he demonstrates his enduring commitment to preaching the gospel to Jewish people in the hope that God will fulfil his promise of salvation to Israel.

Introduction

Luke's account of Paul's testimony before Herod Agrippa II in Acts 26 is a dramatic highlight in the book of Acts. The grand setting in the Roman governor's audience hall in Caesarea and the illustrious audience before whom Paul speaks (25:23) capture the reader's imagination. In this setting Luke gives a third account of Paul's conversion, and Paul delivers the last of his five defence speeches.[1] This passage has also been described as the climax of the book of Acts.[2] While that honour properly belongs to Acts 28:23–31,[3] Paul's testimony before the Jewish King in Caesarea serves to establish in the reader's mind the message which Paul will present to the Jewish community (28:23) and 'all who came to him' (28:31) in Rome.

This essay will examine the role played by Herod Agrippa II in the narrative of Acts 26. One obvious role which Agrippa II plays is that of an expert who can explain Jewish customs to Festus,

---

1   Soards, *Speeches in Acts*, 111–26.
2   Gaventa, *Darkness to Light*, 129, 'Paul's final defence speech is the climax of the second half of Acts, with the trip to Rome and events there forming the denouement of that story'. Schubert, 'Final Cycle', is more guarded, describing Acts 21–28 as an 'ascending climax' to Luke's two-volume work (10); Acts 26 as 'the literary climax' of the three accounts of the Damascus vision (7,15); while Acts 28:23–31 is 'the final climax' which summarises Luke's theology (9,10).
3   Marshall, *Acts*, 441–42, identifies Acts 28:14–31 as the climax of Acts as 'the missionary programme of Acts 1:8 is now brought to a decisive point'; see also Bauer, *Acts as Story*, 242.

the Roman governor, as he struggles to understand the charges of the Jewish leaders against Paul (25:14–21,24–27). In 26:2–3 Paul affirms Agrippa II's familiarity with 'all the customs and controversies of the Jews'.

It has been argued that Agrippa II's familiarity with Jewish customs highlights other aspects of Luke's presentation of Paul. Richard I. Pervo argues that the presence of 'an expert on Judaica' lends weight to the declaration of Paul's innocence in 26:32, which in turn presents him as a heroic figure whose reputation is enhanced as he emerges from a series of trials.[4] Craig S. Keener claims that Agrippa II's significance for Luke is apologetic rather than dramatic, in that he 'provides a significant Jewish verdict, by which he can counter as bias and misunderstanding the Jewish objections to Paul that his narrative records'.[5]

Granted that Agrippa II's expertise in Jewish law and custom makes him an ideal person to assess (and dismiss) the charges against Paul, this alone does not satisfactorily explain the length, content, and form of Luke's narrative. It is Paul who does most of the talking in this passage. How Paul addresses Agrippa II, both in his defence speech (26:2–23) and the ensuing dialogue (26:24–29), suggests that Paul had more on his mind than the charges against him. His concern was the salvation of Agrippa II and the nation of which he was the titular head.

Herodians in Luke-Acts

A fuller understanding of this chapter may be gained by reading it against the background of Luke's wider interest in the Herodian family. The Herodians served the Roman empire as client kings over territories in the eastern Mediterranean from the time of Herod the Great (37–4 BC) until the death of Agrippa II in AD 100.[6] Not only do they set the scene for Luke's narrative (as in Luke 1:5; 3:1), but several leading Herodians also appear as antagonists in the narrative of Luke-Acts. At least ten Herodians are mentioned—most by name—in Luke-Acts.

- Herod the Great. He is briefly mentioned in Luke 1:5, and alluded to in the reference to Herod's praetorium in Acts 23:35.
- Herod Archelaus. The Ethnarch of Judea, Samaria, and Idumea from his father's death in 4 BC until he was removed in AD 6. Although not mentioned by name in Luke-Acts, he is named in Matthew 2:22 and is referred to indirectly as the nobleman in the parable of the ten minas in Luke 19:11–27.
- Herod Antipas. The ruler of Galilee from 4 BC to AD 39, he is referred to thirteen times in Luke-Acts (Luke 3:1,19; 8:3; 9:7,9; 13:31; 23:6,7,8,11,12,15; Acts 4:27).
- Herod Philip. The son of Herod the Great, he is referred to as Philip the Tetrarch (Luke 3:1) or Herod Philip II. He ruled Ituraea and Trachonitis from 4 BC to AD 34.
- Herodias. The wife of Philip (Luke 3:1), who left him to marry Herod Antipas (Luke 3:19).
- Lysanias. Sometimes referred to as Lysanias the younger;[7] he was Tetrarch of Abilene (Luke 3:1).
- Herod Agrippa I. The King of Judaea between AD 41–44 (Acts 12).

---

4 Pervo, *Profit with Delight*, 46.
5 Keener, *Acts*, 4.3490.
6 Kokkinos, *Herodian Dynasty*, 338, 396–99, supports the traditional date, in the third year of Trajan, as advocated by Photius of Constantinople. Schwartz, 'Agrippa II's Death,' 272–74, argues that more recently discovered evidence from inscriptions and coins support Photius' date. However, Jacobson, *Agrippa II*, 133–34, suggests AD 94–95.
7 Kokkinos, *Herodian Dynasty*, 280.

- Drusilla. The Daughter of Agrippa I, who married Antonius Felix, Governor of Judaea (Acts 24:24).
- Herod Agrippa II. He was the son of Herod Agrippa I, who enters the narrative of Acts in chapters 25 and 26. In AD 48 he was appointed to rule the Kingdom of Chalcis, and in AD 53 he was given the Tetrarchy of Herod Philip. Later other territories in Galilee and beyond were given to him.
- Bernice. A daughter of Agrippa I and sister of Agrippa II (Acts 25:13,23; 26:30).

In Luke-Acts only three members of the Herodian family play a significant role: Herod Antipas, Herod Agrippa I, and Herod Agrippa II. Narrative criticism has focused on their role within the Lukan narrative.

In his 1998 monograph, *Herod the Fox: Audience Criticism and Lucan Characterisation*, John Darr surveys Luke's presentation of Herod Antipas as an example of character formation in Luke-Acts. In the narrative of Luke-Acts, Herod Antipas is said to serve four purposes: he *connects* the different phases of the Lukan narrative; he is a *foil* for two of the main protagonists, John and Jesus; he *focalises* issues by asking the important question, such as 'who is Jesus?'; and he is a *negative paradigm* of recognition and response. That is, he heard John but did not understand him; he saw Jesus but did not recognise who he was.[8]

In Luke-Acts Herod Antipas is certainly an example of hostility against John and Jesus. When John the Baptist reproved him for taking his brother's wife and 'other evil things that Herod had done' (Luke 3:19), Herod Antipas had John imprisoned (Luke 3:20) and beheaded (Luke 9:7–8). However, by this stage Herod's interest has moved to Jesus. The Pharisees tell Jesus that Herod wants to kill him (Luke 13:31–32). Jesus dismisses their warning as 'that fox' can only touch him in Galilee. Jesus knows that he will die in Jerusalem (Luke 13:33).[9]

In Jerusalem Jesus does appear before Herod (Luke 23:6–12). At last Herod saw Jesus, but Jesus performed no miracle, nor did he say anything. Herod's response was scorn and mockery (23:11). One thing, however, is clear. Jesus was innocent of the charge of sedition brought against him. On that Herod and Pilate agreed (23:15). However, the apostolic prayer in Acts 4:27–28 presents their agreement in a more sinister light. By agreeing to put this innocent man to death they followed the pattern described in Psalm 2:1, where Gentiles rage and people plot against the Lord and his Messiah. The LXX of Psalm 2:1 (ἔθνη καὶ λαοί), suggests that this hostility comes from Gentiles and Jews who formed an unholy alliance against the Messiah. Luke presents the pact between Pilate and Herod Antipas as emblematic of that alliance.

Nevertheless, Luke tells us that Herod Antipas was *curious*. He wanted to see Jesus (Luke 9:9; 23:8). Luke also tells us that some from within his household were supportive of the ministry of Jesus and the mission of the early Church (Luke 8:2–3; Acts 13:1). These references are often examined for evidence that Luke had a Herodian source of information. If Luke had such a source, the information which came to him suggests that there was a range of responses to the ministry of Jesus (some of them positive) within Herodian circles.[10]

The next major Herodian figure in Luke-Acts is Herod Agrippa I in Acts 12:1–23. He is called

---

8 Darr, *Herod the Fox*, 211–12.
9 Verrall, 'Christ', 352–53.
10 Tyson, 'Herod Antipas', suggests that 'the recognition that Jesus was making inroads into royal circles' may have fuelled Herod Antipas' resolve 'to hunt out Jesus'. The texts in Luke and Acts do not suggest that the presence of disciples of Jesus in Antipas' household was met with hostility. They do, however, suggest that the Herodian 'movement' was not monolithic.

'Herod the King' in Acts 12:1, a designation which recalls the reference to Herod the Great in Luke 1:5 as 'Herod, king of Judea'.[11] The violent hostility of Herod Agrippa I against the apostles in Jerusalem was designed to please the Jews (Acts 12:3). Yet the Lord intervened to prevent his hostility from silencing the witness of the gospel (Acts 12:11). Not only were his plans foiled (Acts 12:19), but Herod Agrippa I himself came to a terrible end as is described in Acts 12:20–23.

The significance of this episode in the narrative of Luke-Acts is examined in O. Wesley Allen's 1997 monograph, *The Death of Herod: The Narrative and Theological Function of Retribution in Luke-Acts*. He compares Acts 12:20–23 with the death-of-a-tyrant type scene in classical and Hellenistic literature.[12] By means of this type scene Allen argues that Luke conveys his theology of retribution. Acts 12:20–23 concludes a narrative of persecution which began at 12:1. The theological message of this passage has significant points of contact with the wider Lukan narrative. However, unlike Darr, Allen does not see Herod Agrippa I as an archetypal Herod, that is, a figure who continues the narrative of Herodian hostility against Jesus and his disciples.[13]

In his 2014 study, *Herod as a Composite Character in Luke-Acts*, Frank Dicken argues that major Herodian figures form a narrative trajectory running through Luke-Acts. More than that, he argues that the figure of 'Herod' is a composite character in Luke-Acts. Blended into this composite character are the historical figures of Herod the Great (or perhaps Herod Archelaus) in Luke 1:5; Herod Antipas in Luke-Acts; and Herod Agrippa I in Acts 12. The defining characteristics of this composite figure are set out in Acts 4 where 'Herod' is seen to embody Satanic hostility against the main protagonists in the gospel narrative of Luke-Acts, Jesus and his apostles. This 'Herod' is climactically defeated in the death of Herod scene of Acts 12:20–23. Thereafter the gospel advances mightily, as Luke describes in Acts 12:24.[14]

Dicken argues that the 'death of Herod' in Acts 12 has important implications for Luke's presentation of Agrippa II. He acknowledges the existence of certain parallels between the composite 'Herod' and Agrippa II. One of these is the similarity between Jesus' appearance before 'Herod' in Luke 23:6–13 and Paul's appearance before Agrippa II in Acts 26.[15] This sets an 'ominous tone' for the narrative of Acts 25–26.[16] However, by the time the reader reaches Acts 25–26, the 'death of Herod' in Acts 12 has changed the dynamic of the narrative by indicating that kings and rulers are powerless to prevent the spread of the gospel.[17] Satan has been defeated and 'Herod' is dead. Thus, Luke never refers to Herod Agrippa I as 'King Agrippa'; nor does he describe Herod Agrippa II as a Herod.[18]

---

11   Keener, *Acts*, 2.1868, claims that this allows the possibility that less informed readers might confuse the two figures. Luke would hardly have been unaware that readers might make this connection and it might be argued that he intended it, as Herod Agrippa I continued an established pattern of hostility against Christ and his people.
12   Allen, *Death of Herod*, 74, 'Acts 12:19b–24 is clearly a Death of Tyrant type scene'. Thus, it plays a different role in Acts from its narrative function in Josephus.
13   Thompson, 'Thwarting the Enemies of God,' 96, seeks to correct this reading 'by extending the literary and political approaches to include the larger narrative conflict between Herod and Jesus in Luke-Acts and the political force of Luke's Christology'.
14   Dicken, *Composite Character*, 106, 133. See also 164–65, 'So while this characterisation of Agrippa often recalls his characterisation of "Herod," the difference in their respective portrayals highlights the Lucan theme [...] that political opposition cannot hinder the proclamation of the good news to the end of the earth'.
15   Dicken, *Composite Character*, 158.
16   Dicken, *Composite Character*, 6.
17   Dicken, *Composite Character*, 162.
18   Dicken, *Composite Character*, 6. A similar point is made by Thompson, 'Thwarting the Enemies of God', 97, who notes that 'Agrippa II, despite being a Herodian, is never called Herod in the narrative of Acts. Rather, the use of "Herod" as an appellation links all three Herodian kings (Herod the Great, Antipas, and Agrippa I) into a single character that is constantly opposing God, who subsequently disappears from the narrative after his death in Acts 12'.

The aim of this article is to argue that, while Dicken's assertion regarding the death of Herod in Acts 12 is insightful and advances our understanding of the narrative structure of Acts, more can be said about the relationship between Agrippa I and Agrippa II in the Lukan narrative. Luke highlights both similarities and differences between these two Herodian figures. The Herodian trajectory continues into Acts 25–26, but it takes a surprising turn.

Agrippa II and Herodian Hostility

Marcus Julius Agrippa II[19] enters the narrative of Acts at 25:13. Along with his sister Bernice, who acted as his consort, he came to Caesarea to pay his respects to the newly-appointed Roman governor, Porcius Festus. Festus told him about the curious case of Paul, the prisoner who had appealed to Caesar. Festus had granted Paul's appeal (25:12) even though he was unsure how to summarise the charges against Paul (25:20). When Agrippa II heard about Paul, he was curious (25:22a,24–26). Paul eagerly grasped the opportunity to defend his ministry and the gospel he preached (26:2–23). When Festus rudely interrupted Paul's defence (26:24–25), Paul virtually ignored the governor and directed his response to the Jewish king (26:26–29). After a brief but pointed exchange Agrippa, Festus, and the governor's advisers agree that Paul could have been released had he not appealed to Caesar (26:30–32).

Three features of the narrative in Acts 25—26 recall the history of Herodian hostility directed against Jesus and his followers in Luke-Acts.

i. The *location* in which Paul spoke was the audience hall (τὸ ἀκροατήριον) of the Governor's residence in Caesarea (25:23). This is the place where Agrippa I—the Herod of Acts 12—had appeared to receive the people of Tyre and Sidon.[20] In Acts 12:19 Luke tells us that Agrippa I went down to Caesarea, and describes his public address in 12:21 as follows: 'On an appointed day Herod put on his royal robes, took his seat upon the throne, and delivered an oration to them'. He delivered a public address (ἐδημηγόρει πρὸς αὐτούς) from the seat of judgement (καθίσας ἐπὶ τοῦ βήματος). The most plausible setting for such an oration is the audience hall of the Herodian palace in Caesarea.[21]

The audience hall in Caesarea was part of the suite of buildings where Paul was imprisoned while in Caesarea (23:35). Its description in Acts 23:35 as 'Herod's praetorium' is unusual, in fact, almost a contradiction in terms. A praetorium was the headquarters of a Roman governor[22] rather than the palace of a Jewish king. Though this structure had been built as a palace by Herod the Great, it was now the praetorium of the Roman governor of Judaea. Thus, the Herodian history is not forgotten. Indeed, it brought to the fore by Luke's description of the centre of Roman rule in Judaea as 'Herod's praetorium' in 23:35. Looking forward, Luke sets the scene for Paul's appearance before another Herodian king in 25:23f.

ii. Luke describes the *grandeur* of Agrippa's appearance in 25:23. Both Agrippa and Bernice 'came with great pomp (μετὰ πολλῆς φαντασίας) and [...] with the military tribunes and prominent men of the city'. This splendid setting recalls the radiance of Agrippa I's appearance in Acts 12:21:

---

19 Rajak, 'Marcus Julius Agrippa II', gives his full name.
20 Alexander, Acts, 348, notes that this palace was where Agrippa I died a protracted and painful death.
21 However, Josephus locates Agrippa's address in the theatre, see *AJ* 19.344.
22 BDAG, 859, 'the word came to designate the governor's official residence'. Jesus was tried in Pilate's praetorium in Jerusalem, see Matthew 27:27; Mark 15:16; John 18:28,33; 19:9. Keener, *Acts*, 3.3346, notes that in Acts 23:35 Luke *omits* the opportunity to draw a parallel between the trial of Jesus and the trial of Paul.

'On an appointed day Herod put on his royal robes, took his seat upon the throne'.[23] Josephus' description of Agrippa I's appearance is even more sumptuous, for he was 'clad in a garment woven completely of silver so that its texture was indeed wondrous'.[24] If Luke was aware of the writings of Josephus, or the tradition he reports, he may well have seen a parallel between the grandeur of the elder Agrippa in Acts 12 and his son in Acts 25.

iii. The *parallels* between Jesus' appearance before Herod Antipas in Luke 23:6–15 and Paul's appearance before Agrippa II in Acts 25—26 are pronounced. These parallels have been well documented. Robert O'Toole lists twelve similarities between the two episodes.[25] Some of these parallels are based on literary judgements which will not be compelling to every reader, but the basic point is widely accepted. Particularly compelling are the parallels between Luke 23 and Acts 25—26 which are corroborated by other episodes in Luke-Acts involving members of the Herodian family.

Three such parallels between the trial of Jesus in Luke 23 and Paul's appearance before Agrippa II in Acts 25—26 may be noted. First of all, Luke describes *the friendly relations* forged between a Herodian ruler and a Roman governor. Luke 23:8 tells us that Herod Antipas and Pilate became friends with each other on the very day that Jesus appeared before them; while Acts 25:13–15 begins the Agrippa II narrative with a courtesy visit to Festus, one which established a solid working relationship. This theme of Herodian–Roman solidarity is described in the prayer of the apostles in Acts 4:27 as one of the driving forces behind official opposition of the Jewish leaders to the gospel of Jesus.

A second parallel is *the hostility of the Jewish leaders* who press charges against both Jesus and Paul. In Luke 23:13–14 Pilate calls 'the chief priests and the rulers of the people' to tell them that neither he nor Herod has found Jesus guilty as charged. Nevertheless, because of their hostility Pilate ordered Jesus to be punished (23:16). Likewise, in Acts 25:15 Festus tells Agrippa II that 'the chief priests and the elders of the Jews' in Jerusalem laid charges against Paul which caused Festus some bewilderment (25:17–18). This theme of Jewish hostility can also be found in Acts 12:1–2 where Agrippa I 'laid violent hands on some belonging to the church'. When he saw that his execution of James 'pleased the Jews' Agrippa I ordered Peter's arrest (12:3).

A third parallel is that in both cases the Herodian king acted in *a judicial (or quasi-judicial) capacity*. In Luke 23:7 Pilate sent Jesus to Herod because 'he belonged to Herod's jurisdiction', while in Acts 25:25 Festus tells Agrippa II that his task is to help him prepare a legal statement to send to the emperor. This appearance of legality is also found in Acts 12:4 where we are told that Agrippa I intended to bring Peter out to the people (ἀναγαγεῖν αὐτὸν τῷ λαῷ) after the Passover. Ben Witherington III claims that this phrase 'suggests the Roman practice of public trial'.[26]

A fourth parallel is the *curiosity of a Herodian king*. In Luke 23:8 Herod Antipas was glad when Jesus was sent to appear before him for 'he had long desired to see him, because he had heard about him, and he was hoping to see some sign done by him'. Likewise in Acts 25:22 Agrippa II responds eagerly to Festus' request for help with the curious case of Paul, 'Then Agrippa said to Festus, "I would like to hear the man myself"'. These examples of Herodian curiosity are not

---

23 Blaiklock, *Acts*, 184, notes the points of comparison between Acts 12:21 and 25:23 and comments, 'The taste for showmanship had obviously passed to the son'.
24 Josephus, *Jewish Antiquities*, 19.344.
25 O'Toole, *Christological Climax*, 22–24. Both episodes are structured as hearings; both involve four main characters; both are held at the instigation of a Roman procurator; both Jesus and Paul are 'led'; in both cases the accused is judged to be innocent; both defendants are accused by Jewish leaders; Herodians want to see Jesus; a Herodian happens to be in Jerusalem; both are Lukan creations; the accused could have been freed; both draw upon the suffering servant motif; both narratives possess illogical elements; both appear inserted into their literary position.
26 Witherington, *Acts*, 385.

limited to the two trial narratives, for Herod Antipas had long harboured a desire to see Jesus, going back to the early days of Jesus' Galilean ministry. 'Now when Herod the tetrarch heard about all that was happening, and he was perplexed [...] he sought to see him' (Luke 9:7,9).

These four parallels between the Herodians in trial narratives of Luke 23 and Acts 26, as well as the location of the hearing and the grandeur of Agrippa II's appearance in Acts 25—26, suggest that a narrative trajectory runs through Luke-Acts which connects Agrippa II with other members of his dynasty. This trajectory is, however, not simply one of Machiavellian hostility. It is true that the hostility of the Jewish leaders is the dark backcloth to this narrative. However, Luke locates Agrippa II theologically as well as socially. As a Herodian king he is more than simply a member of the Jewish ruling elite. As a king in Israel he represents the corporate identity of the covenant nation, and is called to 'kiss the Son, lest he be angry, and you perish in the way' (Ps. 2:12).

The curiosity of the Herodians in Luke-Acts keeps alive a flicker of hope that such a leader in Israel will embrace the Messiah of Israel and lead his people into the paths of peace (Luke 1:79; 19:42). The curiosity which sought a sign from Jesus (Luke 23:8) was not limited to the Herodians. Others in Israel also sought signs from Jesus (Luke 11:16,29–30; 21:7). Although Jesus' response was guarded, he did not dismiss their desire. He responded to his disciples' request in Luke 21:7 by describing the future of the Temple in 21:8f; and he responded to the request of 'this generation' in Luke 11:30 by pointing forward to his resurrection. Might Agrippa II be the Herodian who seeks the Lord and finds salvation? That is a hope which animates the Lukan Paul.

King Agrippa—A Sympathetic Listener?

Notwithstanding these reminders of Herodian hostility and curiosity in Luke-Acts, Agrippa II is presented in a comparatively favourable light. Richard Rackham states that of all the Herodians in Luke-Acts 'Agrippa II comes out the best. [...] It is true that Agrippa somewhat cynically warded off Paul's advances, but had he been as morally worthless as the other Herods, we feel sure that the apostle would have adopted a different tone'.[27] Robert F. O'Toole pictures Agrippa II as 'a good man'.[28] David F. Jacobson's biography of Agrippa II states that he gets 'a favourable press from his contemporaries—including Acts'.[29]

It would be possible to go further and argue that Luke's account of Paul's encounter with Agrippa II presents the Jewish king as a responsive hearer of Paul. Moreover, Paul sees an opportunity to preach the gospel to the civil head of the Jewish nation and grasps it with alacrity. At least seven aspects of the Lukan narrative support this conclusion:

i. Paul responded eagerly to Agrippa's invitation to Paul to defend himself (26:1a). Even before Paul spoke, his actions reveal an eagerness to take up Agrippa II's invitation. 'Then Paul stretched out his hand (ἐκτείνας τὴν χεῖρα) and made his defence' (Acts 26:1b).

ii. Paul's *captatio benevolentiae* in Acts 26:2–3 shows his eagerness to discuss the gospel with Agrippa II. 'I consider myself fortunate that it is before you, King Agrippa, I am going to make my defence today against all the accusations of the Jews, especially because you are familiar with all the customs and controversies of the Jews'. The sincerity of Paul's words in these verses has been

---

27   Rackham, *Acts*, 458. This may be a naïve assessment of Agrippa's moral standing, but it is an accurate assessment of Luke's presentation of Agrippa in comparison to other Herodians.
28   O'Toole, *Acts 26*, 25.
29   Jacobson, *Agrippa II*, 143.

questioned. David Jacobson claims that they are laced with sarcasm.[30] Steve Mason argues that they are tantamount to mockery, because Josephus presents a very different picture of Agrippa II in *AJ* 20.141–143 (which reports rumours scandalous conduct in his family); and *AJ* 20.145 (which reports rumours of an incestuous affair between Agrippa and Bernice).[31]

However, the assumption that Luke (or Paul) was aware of rumours about an incestuous relationship between Agrippa II and Bernice rests on shaky foundations. The earliest evidence of such rumours is late (late-First and early-Second Century) and limited to Roman gossip.[32] Daniel Schwartz has argued that Josephus included his negative presentation of Agrippa II in *AJ* 20 on the basis of an anti-Herodian source circulating in Rome in the 90s.[33]

That Luke was not influenced by this negative view of Agrippa II and his family is suggested by his statement in 24:22 that Felix had 'a rather accurate knowledge of the Way', with the implication that this was derived from his Jewish wife, Drusilla (24:24), a sister of Agrippa II.[34] Together, Felix and Drusilla 'sent for Paul and heard him speak about faith in Jesus Christ'. This suggests that when Paul speaks of Agrippa II's 'familiarity with all the customs and controversies of the Jews' he meant what he said. Thus, John J. Kilgallen rightly states: 'Herod Agrippa, then, is a listener welcome both to Festus and Paul'.[35] Moreover, the contrast between Paul's eager acceptance of Agrippa II's invitation to defend himself and the silence of Jesus in Luke 23:9b is striking. If Jesus was silent before a man whose curiosity was evidently insincere, what does Paul's enthusiasm to speak to Agrippa II suggest?

iii. The thrust of Paul's defence speech was not to defend himself against Jewish claims that he had caused unrest in Jerusalem.[36] Instead Paul argued that the real reason for Jewish hostility against him was his belief in the resurrection of the dead. Paul made this claim in Acts 23:6; 24:21; and 25:19, and returns to it in 26:6–8. Paul's resurrection hope was based on God's promise to Israel (26:6); it was the hope of the twelve tribes of Israel (26:7a); and it was an eschatological hope, now realised in the resurrection of Jesus (26:22–23).[37] Thus, Paul viewed his message as a matter of common interest to any Jew who believed the Scriptures (26:27). His question in 26:8 was addressed to those who looked for the salvation of Israel. In the eyes of the Lukan Paul, that clearly included Agrippa II.[38]

iv. Paul's description of his apostolic commission in 26:16–18 echoes Jesus' words to Ananias in Acts 9:15, 'he is a chosen instrument of mine to carry my name before *Gentiles and kings and*

---

30 Jacobson, *Agrippa II*, 140.
31 Mason, *Josephus*, 164.
32 Macurdy, 'Berenice', 249–50, identifies only two sources, Juvenal, *Satires* 6.155ff.; and Josephus, *AJ* 20.145-46.
33 See Schwartz, 'Josephus' Source'. Macurdy, 'Berenice', 248, states that Josephus makes no mention of these rumours in his earlier works, *Life* and *Jewish War*, thus reserving the malicious tone for *AJ* 20.
34 Spencer, *Journeying Through Acts*, 230–31; though Keener, *Acts*, 4.3422, suggests that his role as an administrator would have brought the Nazarenes to his attention more directly.
35 Kilgallen, 'Paul Before Agrippa', 171.
36 O'Toole, *Acts 26*, 39, commenting on 26:2, 'one by one the various political and religious charges are taken up, eliminated, or modified; so in our speech Luke's readers are ready to move smoothly from all the charges against Paul to that which Luke sees as the real charge, Paul's hope in the resurrection'. By contrast Kilgallen, 'Paul before Agrippa', 171, says of v.2, 'This formulation indicates that the accusations are plural in number and are still being urged against Paul. So much are they still present to Paul that one can expect them to form the matrix out of which Paul's discourse will emerge as a response'. However, the absence of Jewish accusers and the contents of Paul's apologia favour O'Toole's reading.
37 Crowe, *Hope of Israel*, 78–82, discusses the significance and meaning of the resurrection of Jesus in Paul's defence before Agrippa.
38 *Pace* Kilgallen, 'Paul before Agrippa', 176, 'In this way, Paul challenges both Sadducee and pagan to review their convictions about the resurrection of the dead'. Yet the thrust of Paul's rhetoric presumes Agrippa's assent, rather than his dissent.

the children of Israel'. This is the moment for which Paul has been waiting since his calling on the Damascus road to preach the gospel to Jews, Gentiles, and their rulers. In Paul's account of his apostolic calling in 26:16–18 he states that he was called to preach Christ to Jews as well as Gentiles. Jesus told him, 'I have appeared to you for this purpose [...] delivering you from your people and from the Gentiles—*to whom* (εἰς οὕς) I am sending you to open their eyes so that they may turn from darkness to light'. The masculine form of the relative pronoun (οὕς) refers specifically to the people of Israel.[39] Now, with the civic head of the nation of Israel and the guardian of the temple before him, Paul grasps his opportunity to hold out the promise of salvation in Christ Jesus to Agrippa II, a king who represented the people of Israel. Paul goes so far as to claim that through him Christ was proclaiming light 'both to *our people* and the Gentiles' (26:23).

v. When Festus interrupted Paul in 26:24–5 Paul refused to be diverted from his aim of preaching the gospel to Agrippa II.[40] Throughout his defence speech he directly addresses Agrippa II four times; twice calling him, 'King Agrippa' (26:2, 19) and twice saying, 'O King' (26:7, 13). In the dialogue which follows Festus' interruption Paul quickly refocused his efforts on probing the conscience of King Agrippa in 26:26–27.

vi. Agrippa II's response to Paul's probing question in v.28 is defensive. 'And Agrippa said to Paul, "In a short time would you persuade me to be a Christian?"' C. K. Barrett describes Agrippa II's words to Paul as 'perhaps the most disputed, as regards to their construction and meaning, in Acts'.[41] The ambiguity of Agrippa II's response is reflected in the various readings found in the textual witnesses to this verse.[42] The phrase ἐν ὀλίγῳ has been taken to mean in a short time,[43] with such little argument,[44] with matters of such little importance,[45] or to a small degree.[46] The infinitive ποιῆσαι has been translated to mean either to make me a Christian[47] or to induce me to play at being a Christian.[48] The designation of a follower of Jesus as a Christian had Gentile origins (Acts 11:26) and may suggest a measure of scorn for the new sect.[49] Nevertheless, it is clear that Agrippa was deeply affected by Paul's forthright presentation of Christ's call to repentance and faith. Agrippa II may not have been converted to Christianity, but he was challenged. F. Scott Spencer states, 'in some sense Paul has obviously struck a nerve with the king'.[50]

vii. While Agrippa II's response is ambiguous, Paul's desire for his salvation is unambiguous. Paul stated this desire in 26:29: 'And Paul said, "Whether short or long, I would to God that not only you but also all who hear me this day might become such as I am—except for these chains"'. Paul's prayer (εὐξαίμην ἂν[51]) was that Agrippa II would embrace God's promise to Israel

---

39 Keener, *Acts*, 4.3519, argues that if Paul had been referring to Gentiles he would have used the neuter form.
40 It is a matter of debate whether Paul was interrupted or had come to the conclusion of his defence. Smith, 'Interrupted Speech in Luke-Acts', 179, 190, argues that Festus' interruption is an example of a literary device in Luke-Acts. However, Williams, *Acts*, states that Paul's apology reached its climax in v.23 and had said 'what was most important for him to say'.
41 Barrett, *Acts*, 2.1169.
42 Metzger, *Textual Commentary*, 439.
43 Haenchen, *Acts*, 689, '"in short" = soon'; Marshall, *Acts*, 420.
44 Johnson, *Acts*, 439–40.
45 Harlé, 'Private-Joke'.
46 Alexander, *Commentary*, 429, 'somewhat'.
47 Marshall, *Acts*, 420.
48 Haenchen, *Acts*, 689; see also Nairne, 'ΕΝ ΟΛΙΓΩ'; Harrell, 'Almost Persuaded', states that a sincere response is out of the question.
49 Alexander, *Commentary*, 429, describes it as a 'heathenish and disrespectful designation'.
50 Spencer, *Journeying through Acts*, 239.
51 Haenchen, *Acts*, 689, the rare potential optative 'is formulated as a wish capable of fulfilment'.

by believing in Jesus as the Messiah of Israel. His final defence speech was devoted to achieving that goal. Thus Luke does not present King Agrippa as an enemy hardened beyond hope, but an *opportunity* for gospel proclamation. Paul's prayer for Agrippa was also his prayer for the nation of Israel. He desired that his fellow countrymen would embrace in Jesus the hope of Israel.

Conclusion: Paul's Missionary Strategy in Caesarea and Rome

This is significant because the Agrippa narrative serves another purpose in the narrative of Luke-Acts. It marks the transition from Luke's narrative of Paul's trials in Jerusalem and Caesarea to his final ministry in Rome. In 26:30–31 Agrippa, Festus, and those sitting with them conclude that Paul had done nothing deserving of death or imprisonment (26:31). Agrippa reinforces this conclusion in 26:32, 'This man could have been set free if he had not appealed to Caesar'. However, Paul has appealed to Caesar and to Caesar he must go.

Luke makes no mention of a trial before Caesar in Acts 28. Instead, he describes Paul's defence before the Jewish community in Rome (28:17–28). Paul spoke to this Jewish audience, 'testifying to the kingdom of God and trying to convince them about Jesus both from the Law of Moses and from the Prophets' (28:23). His message in Rome echoes his defence speech before Agrippa in Acts 26. Preaching the gospel of Jesus to Jewish people remained his priority, for the hope of Israel has not been extinguished.

The response to Paul's preaching among the Jews of Rome was mixed (28:24). Consequently, Paul turned to the Gentiles in 28:28. This is the third occasion in Acts when Paul turned from Jews to Gentiles. He declared his intention to direct his evangelistic energies towards Gentiles in Pisidian Antioch (13:46) and Corinth (18:6). The scope of these turnings was clearly limited to those local situations, as he pointedly made the synagogue his first place for ministry when he arrived in Ephesus (18:19,26; 19:8). Paul was called to preach the gospel of Jesus to both Jews and Gentiles, and he remained faithful to that calling. His turning from the Jews in Pisidian Antioch and Corinth was not a final rejection of the people of Israel. Nor was his turning from the Jewish community in Rome.

That is demonstrated by the way Paul conducted his two-year ministry in Rome (28:30–31). He preached the kingdom of God, which was a message of God's promises to Israel fulfilled in Jesus (cf. Acts 1:3,6; 28:23). He welcomed all who came to him, Jews and Gentiles alike.[52] Central to Paul's message about the kingdom of God was his hope for the fulfilment of God's promise of salvation to Israel. This is a theme which he developed at greater length in his letter to the Roman church, particularly in Romans 9—11.[53]

One argument which supports this understanding of Paul's missionary vision in Luke-Acts is the surprising twist in the trajectory of Herodian hostility in Luke-Acts. The death of Herod in Acts 12 was indeed an act of divine judgement on Israel's hostility against Jesus and his disciples. However, the death of Herod did not extinguish the hope of salvation for Israel. Paul's preaching

---

52 Troftgruben, *Conclusion Unhindered*, 139: 'And since the ending refers to both Jews (28:17) and Gentiles (28:28), "all" in 28:30 encompasses both'.
53 Voorwinde, 'One Story', 25, argues that Luke-Acts conveys a message about the ingrafting of the Gentiles and the cutting-off of Israel which is in essence that of Romans 9—11. I would argue that both Paul and Luke have a more optimistic outlook for the salvation of Israel. Alexander, 'Back to Front', 442, suggests that Luke-Acts invites the reader 'to do some theological reflection of the kind Paul undertakes in Romans 9—11'.

before Agrippa II demonstrated that this hope remains alive and well. The risen Christ sent Paul to turn Israel and the nations from darkness to light (26:18). Through Paul Christ proclaimed light to both the people of Israel and the Gentiles (26:23). Paul proclaimed that hope not only in Herod's praetorium in Caesarea but also in Rome and to the ends of the earth.

Andrew Stewart
Reformed Theological College, Melbourne
andrewstewart7@bigpond.com

Bibliography

Alexander, Joseph A. — *A Commentary on the Acts of the Apostles* (London: The Banner of Truth Trust, 1963 [1857]).

Alexander, Loveday C. A. — 'Reading Luke-Acts from Back to Front', in J. Verheyden (ed.), *The Unity of Luke-Acts* (Louvain: University of Louvain Press, 1999), 419–45.

Allen, O. Wesley — *The Death of Herod: The Narrative and Theological Function of Retribution in Luke-Acts* (SBL Dissertation Series 158; Atlanta, GA: Scholars Press, 1997).

Barrett, C. K. — *A Critical and Exegetical Commentary on The Acts of the Apostles* (ICC; J. A. Emerton, C. E. B. Cranfield, and G. N. Stanton, eds.; 2 vols.; Edinburgh: T & T Clark, 1994–98).

Bauer, David R. — *The Book of Acts as Story: A Narrative-Critical Study* (Grand Rapids, MI: Baker Academic, 2021).

Blaiklock, E. M. — *The Acts of the Apostles: A Historical Commentary* (TNTC; London: Tyndale Press, 1959).

Crowe, Brandon D. — *The Hope of Israel: The Resurrection of Christ in the Acts of the Apostles* (Grand Rapids, MI: Baker Academic, 2020).

Darr, John — *Herod the Fox: Audience Criticism and Lucan Characterisation* (LNTS; Sheffield: Sheffield Academic Press, 1998).

Dicken, Frank — *Herod as a Composite Character in Luke-Acts* (WUNT 2.375; Tübingen: Mohr Siebeck, 2014).

Gaventa, Beverly R. — *From Darkness to Light—Aspects of Conversion in the New Testament* (Philadelphia, PA: Fortress Press, 1986).

Haenchen, Ernst — *The Acts of the Apostles* (Bernard Noble and Gerard Shinn, trans.; Oxford: Blackwell, 1971).

Harlé, Paul — 'Un "Private–Joke" de Paul dans le Livre des Actes (XXVI.28–29)', *NTS* 24 (1977–78), 527–33.

Harrell, Pat, — ' "Almost Persuaded" Now to Believe? Acts 26:28', *Restoration Quarterly* 4 (1960), 252–54.

Jacobson, David M. — *Agrippa II: The Last of the Herods* (Routledge Ancient Biographies; London and New York, NY: Routledge, 2019).

Johnson, Luke T. — *The Acts of the Apostles* (Sacra Pagina; Collegeville, MN: The Liturgical Press, 1992).

Josephus — *Jewish Antiquities* (LCL; Louis H. Feldman, trans.; Cambridge: Harvard University Press, 1965).

Keener, Craig S. — *Acts: An Exegetical Commentary* (4 vols.; Grand Rapids, MI: Baker Academic, 2012–15).

Kilgallen, John J.	'Paul Before Agrippa (Acts 26,2–23), Some Considerations', *Biblica* 69 (1988), 170–95.
Kokkinos, Nikos	*The Herodian Dynasty: Origins, Role in Society and Eclipse* (London: Spink, 2010).
Macurdy, Grace H.	'Julia Berenice', *American Journal of Philology* 56 (1935), 246–53.
Marshall, I. Howard	*Acts—An Introduction and Commentary* (TNTC; Nottingham: Inter-Varsity Press, 1980).
Mason, Steve	*Josephus and the New Testament* (2nd edn; Grand Rapids, MI: Baker Academic, 2013).
Metzger, Bruce M.	*A Textual Commentary on the Greek New Testament: A Companion Volume to the United Bible Societies' Greek New Testament (Fourth Revised Edition)* (2nd edn; Stuttgart: Deutsche Bibelgesellschaft, 1994).
Nairne, A.	'ΈΝ ΟΛΙΓΩ ΜΕ ΠΕΙΘΕΙΣ ΧΡΙΣΤΙΑΝΟΝ ΠΟΙΗΣΑΙ—Acts xxvi 28', *JTS* 21 (1920), 171–72.
O'Toole, Robert F.	*Acts 26: The Christological Climax of Paul's Defence* (Rome: Biblical Institute Press, 1978).
Pervo, Richard I.	*Profit with Delight: The Literary Genre of the Acts of the Apostles* (Philadelphia, PA: Fortress, 1987).
Rackham, Richard B.	*The Acts of the Apostles: An Exposition* (London: Methuen, 1901).
Rajak, Tessa	'Marcus Iulius Agrippa II', *The Oxford Classical Dictonary* (Simon Hornblower and Anthony Spawforth, eds.; Oxford: Oxford University Press, 2012), 756.
Schubert, Paul	'The Final Cycle of Speeches in the Book of Acts', *JBL* 87 (1968), 1–16.
Schwartz, Daniel R.	'Kata Touton Ton Kairon: Josephus' Source on Agrippa II', *JQR* 72.4 (1982), 241–68.
Schwartz, Daniel R.	'Texts, Coins, Fashions and Dates: Josephus' *Vita* and Agrippa II's Death', in *Studies in the Jewish Background of Christianity* (Tubingen: J. C. B. Mohr, 1992), 243–82.
Smith, Daniel L.	'Interrupted Speech in Luke-Acts', *JBL* 134 (2015), 177–91.
Soards, Marion L.	*The Speeches in Acts: Their Content, Context and Concerns* (Louisville, KY: Westminster/John Knox, 1994).
Spencer, F. Scott	*Journeying Through Acts: A Literary-Cultural Reading* (Grand Rapids, MI: Baker Academic, 2004).
Thompson, Alexander P.	'Thwarting the Enemies of God: Contrasting the Death of Herod and the Resurrection of Jesus in Luke-Acts', in John A. Dunne and Dan Batovici (eds.), *Reactions to Empire: Sacred Texts in their Socio-Political Contexts* (Tübingen: Mohr Siebeck, 2014), 93–110.

Troftgruben, Troy M.	*A Conclusion Unhindered: A Study of the Ending of Acts within its Literary Environment* (Tübingen: Mohr Siebeck, 2010).
Tyson, Joseph B.	'Jesus and Herod Antipas', *JBL* 79 (1960), 239–46.
Verrall, A. W.	'Christ Before Herod', *JTS* 10 (1909), 321–53.
Voorwinde, Stephen	'Luke-Acts: One Story in Two Parts', *VR* 75 (2010), 4–32.
Williams, David J.	*Acts* (NIBC; Peabody, MA: Hendrickson, 1985).
Witherington, Ben III	*The Acts of the Apostles: A Socio-Rhetorical Commentary* (Grand Rapids, MI: Eerdmans, 1998).

Book reviews

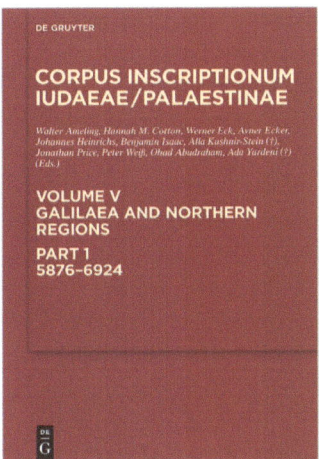

Walter Ameling, Hannah M. Cotton, Werner Eck et al. (eds.). *Corpus Inscriptionum Iudaeae / Palaestinae: Volume V. Galilea and Northern Regions Part One: 5876–6924. Corpus Inscriptionum Iudaeae / Palaestinae:* **A Multi-lingual Corpus of Inscriptions from Alexander to Muhammad V.** Berlin, Boston: De Gruyter, 2023. Xliv + 1041 pp.175 €

The first part of the fifth volume of inscriptions from ancient Judea/Palestine contains 1048 inscriptions of different length and content and in different languages (Greek, Aramaic, Latin). Volume 1 of this project covered inscriptions from Jerusalem, volume 2 from Caesarea and the Middle Coast, volume 3 the South Coast and volume 4 Judea/Idumea (for the project see https://www.degruyter.com/serial/ciip-b/html?lang=de).

The present volume covers the region from ancient Galilea to the entire north of present-day Israel from the Mediterranean Coast in the west to the eastern shore of the Sea of Galilee during the time period under consideration. The inscriptions are arranged from north to south. For each inscription and graffito on stone, amphorae, in mosaics and other material, the editors provide a succinct title and a more detailed description, the approximate date, a photograph or drawing, the findspot, the text in the original language, an English translation, a brief commentary, and up-to-date bibliography. For the places, the editors also provide the extant literary sources in the original languages and English translation. Of particular interest for New Testament studies are the inscriptions from Chorazin (6225–6226, pp. 399–401), from Capernaum (6239–6418, pp. 422–520; for example, donors' inscriptions from the sixth century AD Synagogue), Tiberias (6650–6706, pp. 701–782, detailed description of the town on pp. 701–709) and Sepphoris (6783–6880, pp. 857–981, detailed description of the town, 857–864), though (due to their mostly late date) they add relatively little to our understanding of first century Northern Judea. The volume is also, and much more so, of great interest for the study of the history, culture and spirituality of Judaism (or even Judaisms) in Judea before and after the two Jewish wars, of early and late ancient Christianity or of the non-Jewish/non-Christian presence and religiosity in Roman Judaea. A good number of the sources gathered here attest both to a vibrant Jewish life and a strong Christian presence in the area in the first six centuries CE.

The remaining inscriptions from the area (including Nazareth) will be covered by part two of volume five (2023). It is most convenient to have these epigraphic sources gathered in one volume with translations, brief commentaries, and up-to-date bibliographies.

Christoph Stenschke
University of Pretoria, South Africa

Folker Siegert, Johann Maier, Frieder Lötzsch (eds.). *Rechtsgeschichtlicher Kommentar zum Neuen Testament Band I: Einleitung, Arbeitsmittel und Voraussetzungen.* Rechtsgeschichtlicher Kommentar zum Neuen Testament 1. Berlin, Boston: De Gruyter, 2023. Xiii + 734 Seiten. Gebunden. ISBN 978-3-11-065606-0.

This is volume one of a projected seven volume series of commentaries on legal-historical issues in about 250 passages of the New Testament (*RKNT*; see https://www.folker-siegert.de/). The first volume provides an introduction, the methods to be employed, a survey of the nature or the relevant sources and treatment of some legal themes. It is of interest to *JGAR*, as the major emphases of the following volumes will be on the trials of Jesus in the Gospel and the legal actions taken against Paul, narrated in detail in the final quarter of the Book of Acts.

In *part one*, Folker Siegert begins with six chapters which describe the purpose of this commentary (3–14, pp. 85–122 on studies in preparation for this commentary and on its structure, 119–122) and define the notion of law/jurisprudence (the relationship between legislation and ethics, morale and religion, 15–51). Chapter three summarises the characteristics of the Roman legal system and of Roman legislation (53–76). Siegert also relates the quest of this commentary to the legal tradition of the European baroque period in the 17th and 18th century with scholars like Hugo Grotius and Samuel Pufendorf and the heyday of Lutheran natural law (Christian Wolff, 77–84); for an astute survey see John Witte, Rafael Domingo (eds.), *The Oxford Handbook of Christianity and Law* (Oxford: Oxford University Press, 2023).

Part two offers a detailed survey of the legal presuppositions for the New Testament. Johann Maier (1934–2019) sketches the constitutional history of Judea from the Old Testament kings to the patriarchy of the House of Hillel (125–173) and provides a detailed introduction to the sources of Jewish law and legislation and a survey of them (175–234). Folker Siegert offers a list of the papyri from the Judean desert (235–238) and a glossary of the most important legal technical terms (253–267, not in alphabetical order, an odd selection of terms). Martin Schermaier surveys the sources of Roman legislation (239–252).

Part three consists of four longer essays on major legal issues: Boaz Cohen (1899–1968) writes on the relationship between letter and spirit in Jewish and Roman law (271–286; German translation of "Letter and Spirit in the New Testament" of 1954! Has nothing else been written on this subject since then?). Johann Maier examines the legislation of early Judaism regarding swearing oaths (287–309, bibliography, terminology, sources, gestures and symbolic actions, and the various occasions for swearing oaths; Maier well illuminates the backdrop to Matt 5:33–34; 23:16; 26:72; Mark 6:23; Luke 1:76). Ulrich Kellermann studies the legal parameters for widows and orphans in early Judaism and early Christianity (311–339). His examinations of Mark 12,40–44, Luke 18:2–5; Acts 6:1–6 and 1Tim 5:3–16 against this backdrop (on pp. 322–339) indicate what the following volumes seek to offer.

Folker Siegert follows with a detailed examination of the relationship between Bible and legislation/the legal tradition from the Decalogue to the present (341–465). While interesting and no doubt erudite, this is not what one would expect in a project entitled *Rechtsgeschichtlicher Kommentar zum Neuen Testament*. This observation also applies to the more than two hundred pages of additional essays by Folker Siegert which address a wide range of issues (467–626) and indicate Siegert's broad interests in legal issues over years, rather than contribute to the focus of this introductory volume. These texts should have been published separately in a collection of essays. The volume closes with detailed bibliographies and also an instructive list of legal themes and issues in the New Testament (699–720) which gives an indication of what will be covered in the following volumes.

The volume thus leaves the present reader with mixed feelings. While there is much to commend (up-do-date surveys of the legal issues in the "background" of the New Testament), one wonders about other aspects and the, at times, slightly idiosyncratic approach. Why is the legislation concerning swearing and widows and orphans treated, but legislation concerning other issues such as marriage, the status of women, property issues or slavery not addressed? Why is so much material included which is not directly related to the quest of this project? The following volumes will indicate whether and in what way this endeavour will succeed in shedding fresh light on the issues related to law and legislation in the New Testament beyond what is found in the detailed commentaries (such as C. S. Keener on Acts with his emphasis on ancient sources) or in the various substantial monographs on the trial and crucifixion of Jesus (see, for instance, D. Chapman, E. J. Schnabel, *The Trial and Crucifixion of Jesus: Ancient Texts and Modern Commentary: Texts and Commentary*; Peabody: Hendrickson, 2019, 867 pp.).

The projected volume II will cover legal issues in Q and in the Gospel of Mark; volume III the *Sondergut* in Luke's and Matthew's Gospel and volume IV the Gospel of John and the Book of Acts. Volume V and VI are devoted to the letters of the New Testament and the Book of Revelation (see the preview on pp. 689–697). Whether these volumes will ever appear will also depend on whether a younger generation of German and international scholars will be included and willing to contribute to this project.

Christoph Stenschke
University of Pretoria, South Africa

BOOK REVIEWS

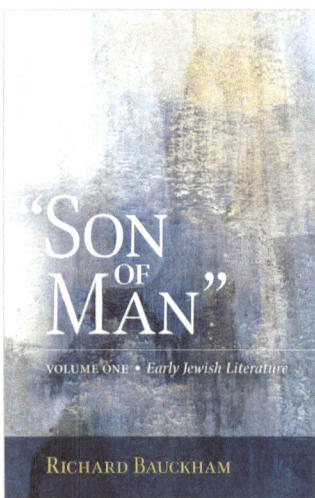

Richard Bauckham. *"Son of Man," Volume 1: Early Jewish Literature.* Grand Rapids, MI: Eerdmans, 2023. xiii + 433 pp. ISBN 9780802883261 (hardcover). $US44.95.

The meaning of the expression, 'the Son of Man', has been studied extensively, but rarely as meticulously and with such erudition as in this study by Richard Bauckham, professor emeritus at the University of St Andrews and senior scholar at Ridley Hall, University of Cambridge. The current volume is the first of two on 'the Son of Man', divided into two parts—the first on the Parables (or Similitudes) of Enoch and the second on interpretations of Daniel 7 in Jewish literature of the Second Temple period. Volume 2 will be devoted to the Gospels and Jesus. When someone of Bauckham's learning in the literature of the Second Temple period produces a work of such scope on a topic as contentious as 'the Son of Man', students of the Gospels and Acts cannot afford to ignore it.

In a brief introduction, Bauckham explains the scope of his broader project and outlines reasons for focusing this first volume on the Parables of Enoch and Jewish interpretation of the figure referred to in Dan. 7:13 as 'one like a son of man'. Bauckham considers that his discussion of the Parables of Enoch constitutes the most comprehensive study to date of messianic figures in that text and that his discussion of Jewish interpretations of Dan. 7:13 leads to his most novel interpretative conclusions.

After an opening chapter that introduces readers to the Parables of Enoch within the context of other parts of the apocalyptic text known as 1 Enoch, Bauckham narrows his focus to the messianic figure introduced in the Parables as 'the Chosen/Anointed One' or 'that Son of Man'. In chapter 1.2 he surveys recent developments in Enoch studies, especially with respect to comprehending the status of the Enochic Son of Man, on which he signals a change of mind from earlier publications. He then sets about showing that the three messianic designations within the Parables—Chosen or Elect One, (that) Son of Man, and Anointed One—occur in discrete sections of the Parables, probably corresponding to biblical sources drawn upon in those respective passages. For Bauckham, 'the Messianic Figure is this author's novel contribution to the Enoch tradition, and for sources he has turned to biblical prophecies' (27), namely, Isa. 11:2–5; 42:1–7; 49:1–7; Dan. 7:9–27; and Psalms 2 and 72. The principal role of this Enochic messianic figure is eschatological judgment of those who oppress the chosen people of God.

In chapter 1.3 Bauckham focuses on those sections of the Parables that feature Enoch's end-time visions, within which he finds narrative sequences of future events in 1 Enoch 39:3–41, 45:1–51:5, and 61:6–63:12. Key stages in the sequence of eschatological events are: (1) Enoch's pre-judgment vision of One with a head of days and a humanlike figure; (2) prayers of righteous people and angels answered when the 'Head of Days' sits on his throne for judgment; (3) the summoning of 'that Son of Man' into the presence of the 'Head of Days'; (4) the appearance of the messianic figure in God's presence; and (5) the sitting of the messianic figure on his throne (distinct from God's throne) to judge kings and other powerful persons. In chapter 1.4 Bauckham discusses a series of textual clues within the Parables that, in his view, prepare readers for the identification of 'that Son of Man' with Enoch in 1 Enoch 71:14 (echoing 46:2–3). He also considers why the author of the Parables identified Daniel's 'one like a son of man' and Isaiah's 'chosen one' with Enoch.

Chapter 1.5 presents Bauckham's own summary of key conclusions reached in preceding chapters. First, 'son of man' is neither a title nor a conventional expression or technical term but simply means 'human'. 'As applied to the Messianic Figure, it is almost always accompanied by a demonstrative ("that son of man" or "this son of man") or other qualifying expression ("the son of man who…")' (109). Nor, second, is there a concept of 'the son of man' in the Parables (or 4 Ezra). Third, the expression, 'throne of glory', merely means 'glorious throne', whether God's heavenly throne, the Messiah's throne, or thrones of earthly kings. Fourth, the messianic figure is not divine, nor did he exist before creation. Fifth, 'the Messianic Figure is Enoch' (111). And sixth, the Parables differentiate between obeisance and cultic worship, with the latter reserved for God alone.

Chapters 1.6 and 1.7 address the date and provenance of the Parables. Bauckham leans toward a post-70 CE dating of the Parables, a topic to which he returns in chapter 2.7, and he is noncommittal regarding provenance.

Part 2 begins with a brief introduction to the Jewish interpretation of Daniel 7 in Jewish literature of the late Second Temple period (and shortly thereafter). Bauckham eschews historical-critical exegesis of Daniel 7 itself, focusing instead on Jewish interpretations of this text. Chapter 2.2 composes a wide-ranging treatment of the two Greek versions of Daniel 7 (Old Greek and Theodotion), but the burden of Bauckham's discussion is to contest the view that ancient Greek translations of Dan. 7:13–14 support the notion that what is said about 'one like a son of man' points to his divine status.

Discussing 4Q246 (4Q Aramaic Apocalypse) in chapter 2.3, Bauckham argues toward the conclusion that this text construes the 'one like a son of man' in Dan. 7:13–14 as a future Davidic messiah, influenced by the promise to David articulated in 2 Samuel 7 and texts such as Isaiah 11 and Micah 5. For Bauckham, 'This is why there is no Son of Man figure in early Judaism, a kind of eschatological savior from heaven conceived as an alternative to the Davidic ruler of earthly origin' (191), although his own research reveals that not all anticipated saviour figures were understood to stand in the Davidic line. For example, regarding oracles about the advent of a saviour figure from the celestial sphere in Book 5 of the Sibylline Oracles, Bauckham contends (in chapter 2.4) that they identify the 'one like a son of man' in Dan. 7:13 with Joshua, remembered for his role in routing Israel's enemies.

As one would expect, Bauckham attends to the interpretation of Daniel 7 in the related apocalyptic texts known as 4 Ezra and 2 Baruch. A chapter is devoted to each of these works but not in immediate succession. Chapter 2.5 is devoted to a detailed discussion of 4 Ezra, focusing on the role of Daniel 7 in the argument of the book, as well as on the progressive unveiling of the messianic figure across several of the seven episodes that comprise this apocalypse. According to Bauckham, 'A crucial point of interpretation is that the figure in Daniel 7:13 is understood to be a man, a descendant of David, who lived on earth in the past, was exalted to heaven without dying, and has been preserved by God until the time when he is "revealed" and performs his eschatological role' (253).

> A future Davidic messiah, influenced by the promise to David.

Before turning to 2 Baruch in chapter 2.8, Bauckham interposes two chapters. The first of these, chapter 2.6, seeks to show that the conception of the messianic figure in 4 Ezra was not a bolt from the blue by briefly addressing several rabbinic traditions in which a past descendant of David is envisaged to play an eschatological role as God's messianic agent. Then in chapter 2.7 Bauckham returns to the topic of dating the Parables of Enoch to the late-first or early-second century CE. His reason for doing so is to argue for the literary dependence of the Parables on 4 Ezra to explain messianic parallels distinctive to these two texts. He also proposes a common sociohistorical context for these works. In Bauckham's view, 'A context in the late first century (or the very early second century) explains … the literary relationship between the Parables and 4 Ezra and the fact that they agree in not calling their Messianic Figure a king' (275).

Regarding the interpretation of Daniel 7 in 2 Baruch, Bauckham acknowledges that this apocalypse contains no explicit reference or allusion to Dan. 7:13–14. Since 2 Baruch reflects familiarity with other features of Daniel 7, however, Bauckham contends that 2 Baruch equates the Messiah with the humanlike figure of Dan. 7:13–14. Although possible, perhaps the following conclusion should have been articulated more tentatively: 'There is no allusion to Daniel 7:13, but an identification of the Messiah as the humanlike figure of Daniel's vision is evidently presupposed' (305).

In the penultimate chapter of the body of this book, Bauckham briefly considers rabbinic traditions associated with Rabbi Aqiva in which the plural thrones of Dan. 7:9 are construed as two, one for the Ancient of Days and one for the humanlike figure of Dan. 7:13–14, understood as David. Then in a lengthy discussion (chapter 2.10) of the studied avoidance of Daniel 7 in the historical works of Josephus, Bauckham argues for the likelihood that Josephus anticipated a messiah comparable to the interpretation of Dan. 7:13–14 found in 4 Ezra 13.

In a concluding chapter, Bauckham reiterates key points about 'the son of man', as interpreted in Jewish literature roughly contemporaneous with the canonical Gospels and Acts: that 'son of man' and 'man' are synonymous; that 'one like a son of man' is a human figure from the biblical past preserved by God to exercise end-time messianic functions, in much the same vein as eschatological expectations associated with Elijah; and that the humanlike figure of Dan. 7:13–14 was not envisaged as a messianic figure significantly different from those associated with other messianic hopes, whether Davidic or non-Davidic. Presaging what is to follow in volume 2 of *"Son of Man,"* Bauckham writes: 'In the interpretations of Daniel 7 we have studied, the Messiah has been born on earth and will come in the future from heaven. This is remarkably close to the way early Christians read Daniel 7, a comparison that will be explored in part 3 of this work' (375).

This review is unable to convey an adequate sense of the wealth of information and insight contained in this volume. Quite apart from Bauckham's investigations into various nuances of 'the Son of Man' in early Jewish literature, one also learns much about this body of literature itself. As for Bauckham's main interpretative conclusions, I suspect that, even if this or that detail is contested, many scholars will be forced to reconsider previously held views. Interpreting certain 'Son of Man' sayings in the Gospels, I have appealed to a Jewish 'Son of Man' mythical tradition evidenced in the Parables of Enoch and 4 Ezra, a tradition that Bauckham might well have demonstrated to be a scholarly construct without sufficient textual support. What impact this may have on my reading of the Gospels remains to be seen, but I look forward to finding out when volume 2 of *"Son of Man"* is published.

David Neville
St Mark's National Theological Centre
Charles Sturt University, Canberra

BOOK REVIEWS

Udo Schnelle, Manfred Lang (Hrsg.). *Texte zum Matthäusevangelium Teilband 2: Matthäus 11–28. Neuer Wettstein: Texte zum Neuen Testament aus Griechentum und Hellenismus Band I/1.2.* Berlin, Boston: De Gruyter, 2023. Vi + S., Leinen, gebunden. ISBN 210 Euro. ISBN 978-3-11-024744-2.

Like the previous volumes of this new and expanded version of Johann Jacob Wettstein's collection of parallels to the New Testament text, the present second volume contains some 2000 Greek texts which relate to Matthew 11–28 more or less closely and in one way or another and some 440 cross-references to texts already covered in other volumes of the revised version (1986ff; see https://www.theologie.uni-halle.de/nt/corpus-hellenisticum/226905_226953/nw/). All of Wettstein's texts have been thoroughly checked against the most recent critical editions and assessed afresh. In addition, some 550 parallels from Philo (gathered in the *Corpus Hellenisticum* project) have also been included as well as other early Jewish sources in Greek and Latin and some texts from the papyri which have been discovered and edited since Wettstein's first edition (1751/52). The first volume (Matthew 1–10) appeared in 2013. With regard to the focus of this revision project, the editors note 'Das *Corpus Hellenisticum* analysiert die hellenistische Umwelt, um so die Lebens- und Gedankenwelt des Neuen Testaments zu erheben. Es ist damit mehr ein Beitrag zur antiken Kultur- und Rezeptionsgeschichte als ein literargenetischer. Wie (Strack/)Billerbeck so will auch der Neue Wettstein ein Lesebuch sein, um zur weiteren Lektüre des entsprechenden Materials anzuregen und so selbst das eigene Verstehen zu fördern' (https://www.theologie.uni-halle.de/nt/corpus-hellenisticum/226905_226910/).

For each 'parallel', the editors offer Matthew's text in Greek, the exact reference of the 'parallel', the Greek text under consideration with a brief introduction to its nature and context and a German translation. With longer texts, the relevant Greek words, expressions or sentences appear interspersed in the German text. Footnotes offer some comments and mainly identify the translations which are quoted. The volume closes with an index of all the references to ancient authors, of names and subjects and of the passages from Matthew for which 'parallels' have been adduced, including the references to the ancient Greek texts. Students of New Testament lexicography and semantics will appreciate having these Greek and Latin parallels according to the latest critical editions all available in one volume. Exegetes will appreciate having at their hand most of the Greek and Roman texts which are referred to or discussed regularly in the scholarly commentaries on the biblical text.

For parallels from Rabbinic literature scholars still have to depend on the dated and problematic collection of H. L. Strack and P. Billerbeck (*Kommentar zum Neuen Testament aus Talmud und Midrasch*) which awaits a thorough revision. The papyri are covered more extensively by the *Papyrologische Kommentare zum Neuen Testament* series (see https://www.plus.ac.at/bibelwissenschaft-und-kirchengeschichte/forschung/publikationen/pknt/). Volumes are available on 1 and 2 Corinthians, 2 Thessalonians and Philemon.

Christoph Stenschke
University of Pretoria, South Africa

BOOK REVIEWS

Nathan C. Johnson, *The Suffering Son of David in Matthew's Passion Narrative.* SNTSMS 183. Cambridge: Cambridge University Press, 2023. 263pp. ISBN 978-1-00-926165-4. €101.76. $110.00.

Johnson begins his work by emphasising that the Graeco-Roman world perceived crucifixion as humiliating and horrific. He suggests that a crucified, Davidic messiah could have posed many problems for Matthew. In the first chapter, Johnson briefly explains how others have approached Matthew's messianism beginning with Wrede. Within these studies, Johnson identifies a methodological focus on the *Davidssohnfrage* and explicit references to David. As a result, many have argued for a disappearance of the Davidic emphasis after the *Davidssohnfrage* and a dichotomy between the son of God and the son of David. Johnson removes this dichotomy by appealing mainly to 2 Samuel 7 and Psalm 2, in which the son of David and the son of God are closely associated. Johnson then introduces his methodology for the study of David in Matthew's passion narrative (26:30–27:56). He proceeds primarily by identifying intertexts and then explaining how these intertexts function within Matthew.

The second, fourth, and fifth chapters follow three stages of Jesus' passion narrative: the arrest, the trial, and the crucifixion. In the second chapter Johnson identifies an intertextual link between the arrest narrative and the Absalom revolt against David (2 Sam. 15–19). For example, he identifies that for both narratives the Mount of Olives is significant, there is a traitor, and the traitor hangs themself (Matt. 27:5 and 2 Sam. 17:23). Furthermore, Johnson observes that the intertexts correspond sequentially. In order to show the significance of these intertexts for Matthew's readers, Johnson identifies two forms of messianic expectations possible within the first century: one in which God wages war on behalf of the Messiah and another where the Messiah is himself expected to enact eschatological violence. In contrast to these contemporary expectations, Matthew presents a Davidic messiah who suffers.

In the third chapter Johnson offers a brief but robust investigation into the relationship between David and the Psalms in antiquity. By investigating the development of the superscriptions and historical ascriptions to the Psalms, Johnson is able to challenge those who would attribute the Psalms to an anonymous 'psalmist'. Such an attribution, he notes, is anachronistic for the first century. Instead, he argues, it is more fitting to attribute the Psalms to David. By emphasising the strong Davidic character of the book, in subsequent chapters he is able to move beyond intertextual identification and display how Matthew's allusions to the Psalms fits within his Davidic messianism.

In Chapter four, Johnson investigates the references to the Psalms throughout Matthew's trial narrative. In particular, he notes that within the trial narrative, a particular use of lament psalms within chapters 26—39. For example, Johnson identifies an intertext between 'from afar' in Matthew 26:58 and 27:55 to Psalm 37:12 LXX (with a Davidic ascription). In this psalm, David laments that his friends have abandoned him.

In chapter 5, Johnson examines Matthew's use of the Psalms in the crucifixion narrative.

He focuses primarily on the many allusions to Psalm 69 and Psalm 22. He observes that previous identifications of these intertexts tend to focus on Matthew's use of scripture. Instead, Johnson relates these intertexts to Matthew's characterization of David. For instance, in Matthew 28:10, Johnson identifies Jesus' unusual description of the disciples as 'my brothers' as a reference to the latter half of Psalm 21:23 LXX (Ps. 22 MT). He observes that the small Greek phrase is significant (it occurs in the Old Greek exclusively in the Psalms) and finds support from Justin Martyr and Eusebius. He adds that this intertext would support a reading of the cry of dereliction (from Ps. 21 LXX) which recalls the psalm in its entirety.

In the final section of chapter 5, Johnson discusses the implications of Matthew's use of the intertexts he has identified in chapters two, four, and five. He identifies three primary ways Matthew's use of the Psalms describe the passion narrative in terms of David's suffering: the description of Jesus' persecution, Jesus' followers, and Jesus' own actions and reactions.

After providing a summary of his argument, in chapter 6, the final chapter, Johnson relates his study back to the problems explored in the first chapter. He reaffirms that Matthew's fulfilment passages of 26:54 and 26:56 should be understood in light of the passion narrative. Thus, the fulfilment referred to in Matthew 26 concerns the Absalom revolt and the Psalms as they relate to the identified intertexts of the passion narrative. Thus, Matthew reframes Jesus' suffering in terms of David's suffering to show that someone greater than David has come.

Overall, Johnson's work is a joy to read. Johnson provides a host of fresh intertexts in the passion narrative and situates those readings within Matthew's Davidic framework. At the end of each relevant section, Johnson provides tables of the intertexts he has identified. These tables can be found on page 60 (Absalom revolt and Arrest narrative), page 145 (the trial narrative and the Psalms), and page 192 (the crucifixion and the Psalms). Although one may not agree with all of the intertexts Johnson has identified, one is more willing to defer to the Davidic character of more faint allusion when they are read together with intertexts that seem more convincing.

Throughout his study, Johnson often refers to the reception history and relevant Rabbinic and Christian texts. This is especially effective when discussing more faint echoes. Although this material postdates Matthew, Johnson seems very careful in maintaining this distinction. Johnson's strongest contribution is not primarily in collating and adding to the intertextual connections of the passion narrative to the Absalom revolt and the Psalms, but in maintaining the Davidic character of these allusion and demonstrating how they relate to the Matthean portrayal of Jesus as the suffering Davidic messiah.

Eric Espinoza
Gateway Seminary
ericespinoza@gs.edu

Gene L. Green. *Vox Petri: A Theology of Peter.* Eugene: Cascade Books, 2020. pp. 485. ISBN: 9781532683107.

It has long been argued that any conception of a 'Petrine theology' is not possible. Anyone sympathetic to the possibility see it, at best, as a pipedream. The more critical might suggest that any such attempt would present little more than a warmed-over Pauline theology with little, if anything unique to contribute to Christian theology. In *Vox Petri*, Gene Green argues that a Petrine theology can, in fact, be pursued successfully.

The book spans 9 chapters beginning with a critical assessment of available sources for a Petrine theology and the value of 'testimony' as a source for reasonable belief (ch. 1–2). From there Green considers the testimony and theology of Peter in Mark's Gospel (ch. 3–4); the testimony and theology of Peter in Acts (ch. 5–6); the testimony and theology of Peter in 1 Peter (ch. 7–8); and finally, Peter's theological contribution to the church (ch. 9).

Chapter 1 provides a review of the scholarly discussion that swirls around possible Petrine sources and the question of whether they might be fit for purpose. The discussion takes the reader from Lapham's scepticism to the borderline naivety of David Gill (p. 10). Cullmann offers a more moderate position (pp. 11–12) while works by the likes of Foakes-Jackson, Pesch, Gnilka, Perkins, Wiarda, and Bockmuehl offer varying degrees of scepticism and hopefulness with regard to the reliability of Petrine testimony. Green's conviction is that the NT provides Peter's *ipsissima vox* though not his *ipsissima verba* (p. 18).

Chapter 2 invites the reader to consider the value of testimony as an epistemological category in modern and ancient contexts (p. 20). Drawing on the work of C. A. J. Coady, Green notes that even theoretical domains including the physical sciences 'rely on the testimony of groups and individuals' (p. 21), but that this has been rather ignored since the renaissance. A discussion on the definition of testimony unfolds from which some important points should be noted:

1. Definitions need not take the truthfulness of testimony into account.
2. Epistemologically, testimony is neither good nor bad, therefore the *presumption* that testimony is bad not unjustified (p. 25)
3. Testimony as historical knowledge may still be subject to interrogation with regards to the intent, coherence, and competence of the one who bears witness (p. 27).

From this platform, Green assesses the possible sources for a Petrine theology and finds good reason to proceed with the Gospel of Mark, Peter's speeches in Acts, and the letter of 1 Peter providing the framework for his ensuring discussion (2 Peter is left aside due to the hotly disputed nature of its authenticity, or lack thereof).

Chapters 3–4 open Green's investigation proper with the Gospel of Mark as a source for testimony and theology of Peter. In chapter 3, Green takes as his starting point the testimony of the Church Father's dating back to Papias' now infamous statement found in Eusebius regarding Mark as the 'interpreter of Peter' (p. 104). Green remarks how surprising it is that that scepticism should prevail given the consistency of testimony regarding

Mark's authorship (p. 104). For Green, Mark represents 'a redaction of Peter's gospel story', but this doesn't mean Mark is not active in shaping the form and character of the narrative (p. 105). Specifically, 'Mark takes Peter's testimony and interprets it in translation for his audience' (p. 107).

Green places Peter and Mark in Rome and writing for the Roman church (p. 109), made up of predominantly gentiles who need Jewish customs to be unpacked for them (p. 113). Peter's message conveyed in Mark is aimed at both believers and non-believers with a focus on Jesus and the nature of discipleship including a theology of suffering (p. 122).

Chapter 4 spans more than 100pp so here we must be selective. Green highlights Mark's theological framework as God's 'new exodus' (pp. 128–48). For Green, 'Mark is the story about the struggle with a colonial power, and the perseverance of traditional hopes and outlooks' (p. 136). He posits further that while the audience is gentile, the Gospel's foundation is thoroughly Jewish, reflecting the Palestinian roots of both Peter and Mark (p. 231). The fundamental message of the gospel is true to its origins and is simultaneously contextualised for its Roman audience.

Chapters 5–6 guide the reader through Peter's speeches in Acts. In chapter 5, Green acknowledges that the speeches certainly convey Luke's own point of view, yet at the same time he considers the speeches to be a recognisable rendering of Peter's thought (p. 234). Green notes that Peter's primacy is evident throughout the gospels and that Luke/Acts is no exception (pp. 236–38). For Luke, Green argues, Peter is the main player in unifying the Jewish and gentile church (p 238), while Paul comes only after Peter has laid the necessary foundation (p. 239) and provided its theological direction (p. 241).

Again, Peter's 'new exodus' motif is prominent for Green. He critiques David Pao for his omission of Peter's contribution to this theme in Acts (pp. 248–50), noting that Peter is at the forefront of the gospel's progression from Jerusalem (Acts 2) all the way through to Cornelius and the gentiles (Acts 10) (pp. 249–50). Green ties this progression to the message of the restoration of David's kingdom, the Word of God as active agent, and the recognition of Yahweh as Lord of the nations (pp. 250–51). The rest of the chapter picks up on major themes in Petrine speeches including the Gospel of the kingdom, the fulfillment of God's plan, Jesus as suffering servant, and the Lordship of the Messiah, among others. One outworking of Jesus' lordship is that he is God's 'exclusive agent of salvation' and yet the invitation is open to all 'without distinction'. (p. 287). For Green, Peter's speeches present him as 'a theological innovator who was responsible for the primitive church's theology about Jesus' person and work' (p. 299).

> **Peter's 'new exodus' motif is prominent for Green.**

Chapter 7 would not be out of place in most commentary introductions on 1 Peter. Here Green covers questions of authorship, the community to whom he writes, the ethnicity of the recipients (predominantly gentile, p. 309), and the circumstances and social status of the recipients. Chapter 8 then spends some +80pp. on the theology of 1 Peter. Once again, as earlier in chapter 4, we must be selective in what to cover here. Green covers topics of eschatology; consecutive sections on the character of God, the person and work of Jesus, and the Holy Spirit, present something of a Trinitarian angle within 1 Peter. The chapter concludes with musings on 1 Peter's ecclesiology, and the ethics of discipleship. Green does well in acknowledging the tension that Anatolian believers lived with as they sought to live out their newfound faith among their people. They are to:

> promote social harmony, loving one another, forgiving one another. But they also had to negotiate the hostility they faced in society … They are to avoid

retaliation and live by the highest norms in their communities. Yet, at the same time, Peter problematizes their relationship with extant social structures by counselling behaviour governed by higher norms set by God and Christ (p. 399).

The book concludes with a summary, considering Peter's theological contribution to the church. For Green, Peter is one who provides the church a 'sweeping view of God's overarching plan' for the world (p. 405); a theological framework grounded in Isaiah's New Exodus (p. 406); a consistent and robust Christology (pp. 407–11), the Holy Spirit as one who 'leads and empowers Christian mission' (p. 411); and what it means to live in the world in an honourable way (pp. 415–417). If one finds agreement with Green's case, it would not be a stretch to suggest that the Scriptures may well be read from a Petrine perspective (p. 418).

Green's book makes a compelling case. Some will certainly quibble with his taking the early Church Fathers at face value, but as he observes, they provide consistent testimony upon which one may build. Green does so with aplomb. Indeed, the content of chapter 2 on the epistemological value of testimony and the scholarship surrounding it is significant for the field of biblical studies and well worth the price of the book.

> Peter ... [provides] a 'sweeping view of God's overarching plan' for the world.

That said, coming, as I do, as a 1 Peter scholar, I have questions about how up to date some of Green's research is. While the bibliography is perfectly substantial, Green cites a PhD thesis by Patrick Egan completed in 2011, yet the thesis was formally published in 2016 some 4 years before Green's work being reviewed here (published 2020). Why not cite the book? Other 1 Peter monographs left on the sidelines include those authored by Andrew Mbuvi, *Temple, Exile, and Identity in 1 Peter* (2007); Abson Joseph, *A Narratological Reading of 1 Peter* (2012); Paul Himes, *Foreknowledge and Social Identity in 1 Peter*, and Travis Williams, *Good Works in 1 Peter* (both 2014); and Shively Smith, *Strangers to Family* (2016). Though not necessarily essential to Green's case, it's hard to imagine they couldn't have contributed in a more nuanced and specific way over and above the use of standard commentaries.

These minor quibbles notwithstanding, I commend Green's work wholeheartedly. Those interested in Markan studies, the book of Acts, and the Petrine correspondence, not to mention the New Testament more broadly would do well to consult Green's work. Indeed, guided by Green's able scholarship, one finds that far from being a warmed-over Pauline theology, Peter's theological contributions to the church are far more substantial and foundational than he is given credit for.

David M. Shaw
North-West University—Potchefstroom, South Africa

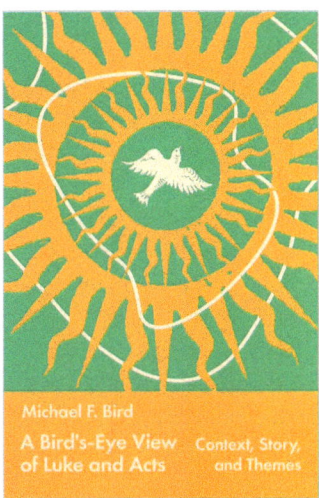

Michael F. Bird. *A Bird's-Eye View of Luke and Acts: Context, Story, and Themes.*
Downers Grove: IVP Academic, 2023. xi + 328 pp. ISBN 978-1-5140-0809-6.

Michael F. Bird's *A Bird's-Eye View of Luke and Acts: Context, Story, and Themes* aims to fill a significant gap in the library of books on Lucan studies – a textbook for the classroom and a survey for the general reader. It succeeds in providing an accessible and engaging introduction to the main themes of Lucan scholarship.

Naturally, Bird makes his own contributions to the topic which often land on a mediating position. Thus, for example, he presents Luke as a second generation, post-Pauline Christian writer who was also a co-worker with Paul and who wrote what Paul described as 'my gospel'. Moreover, Luke was probably a gentile but one who was well-versed in Jewish Scripture and history and held an optimistic outlook for the salvation of Israel.

On the question of whether the Lucan corpus is best described as Luke and Acts or Luke-Acts, Bird acknowledges that Luke's writings form a distinct corpus within the New Testament (chapter 1). They are, however, 'different texts' which tell 'united albeit distinguishable stories' (chapter 2). They tell the story of Jesus and his Church, but Luke and Acts 'function in different ways'. Their functionality is summarised in Bird's discussion of their genre, which describes Luke as a 'kerygmatic biography', and Acts as historiography which is not only 'influenced by Israel's Scriptures', but 'a new piece of "biblical history"'.

While acknowledging that Luke and Acts fall into differing generic categories Bird discerns a common purpose or combination of purposes (chapter 3). He begins with the stated purpose in the prologue addressed to Theophilus (Luke 1:1-4), which he applies to Acts as well as Luke. After examining the unstated purposes which emerge from a close reading of Luke-Acts, Bird identifies several utilities (or purposes for which Luke-Acts was used) which may or may not have been in the author's mind as he wrote. Wisely, Bird acknowledges that Luke has a wide range of purposes as he wrote Luke-Acts but describes telling the story of salvation as one of Luke's main aims. Alongside this evangelistic purpose, Bird also discerns apologetic, polemical, and legitimising aims.

In chapter 4 the question of whether Luke is a historian, a theologian, or both is discussed. Bird poses the question whether Luke is more like William Ramsay (sifting evidence) or C. S. Lewis (telling stories). He considers passages which have been central to this debate (the census of Luke 2:1f., the speeches in Acts, and the Lucan portrait of Paul) before concluding that Luke was as accurate as his methods and sources permitted and arguing that Luke's interest was not in 'cataloguing facts' but in recording 'God's revelation in Christ and the Church'. This leads into a discussion of the theological message embedded in Luke's version of history.

> A textbook for the classroom and a survey for the general reader.

Subsequent chapters develop in more detail Luke's theology and its implications. These include discussions of Christology (chapter 5), salvation (chapter 6), the Old Testament and

BOOK REVIEWS

the heritage of Israel (chapter 7), discipleship (chapter 8), women in the Lucan narrative and feminism (chapter 9), social issues and socialism (chapter 10), the Holy Spirit and the question as to whether Luke might be described as the first Pentecostal theologian (chapter 11), Jews, gentiles and the hope of Israel (chapter 12), empire and imperialism (chapter 13), and finally, eschatology (chapter 14).

Readers may find Bird's conclusions regarding these topics more compelling than others. For example, I found the discussion of Luke's alleged 'delay of the parousia' particularly insightful but would argue that the author's characterisation of Lucan salvation as 'holistic' blurs the distinction between metaphor and reality – that is, salvation's essence and salvation's implications. Nevertheless, each chapter models a helpful way of approaching the topics of Luke's theology.

> **A helpful way of approaching the topics of Luke's theology.**

Bird's approach to these topics is to collate and summarise the relevant data from the narratives of Luke-Acts. Thus, the primary focus of each chapter is an analysis of the primary sources. Scholarly debates are briefly summarised in each chapter and representative quotations are regularly highlighted in breakout boxes. This means that the student or general reader approaching Lucan studies for the first time will not be overwhelmed by debates with which they may be unfamiliar. Each chapter concludes with a brief list of recent and relevant literature on the topic in hand.

In keeping with the intended readership of this Bird's Eye View the style is accessible and engaging. Topics about which much has been written in highly technical language are well summarised in memorable phrases. For instance, the vexed question of what constitutes genre is summarised as 'the reality, rules and reception of a text' (p.23). A certain rhetorical flair can be heard in the description of Luke's message of salvation through entering the kingdom as 'a mixture of destination, deliverance and discipleship' (p.35).

The author's rhetorical style also has its downside. In places (for example p.105) it was possible to detect a sharpness in the swipes taken at certain types of evangelicalism. In the opinion of this reviewer some of these characterisations were unfair and would be more at home in a denominational magazine than a textbook on Lucan studies. Moreover, at points the author seems to get carried away. In a reconstruction of popular Messianism the author suggests that some of Jesus' followers might have expected not only a military victory over the Roman Legions, but also 'bawdy banquets in the Herodian fortress in celebration'. The image of bawdy messianic banquets certainly captures the imagination, but it must be asked whether it was a feature of first century political Jewish Messianism.

Notwithstanding these reservations this *Bird's Eye View of Luke and Acts* is comprehensive in its scope, deft in summarising scholarly debates, and accessible in its presentation. It will be welcomed by those who teach Lucan studies and students seeking a general introduction.

Andrew Stewart
Reformed Theological College, Melbourne.

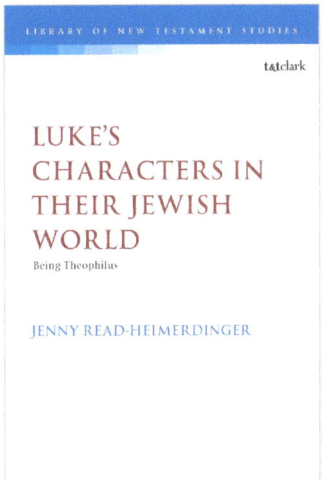

Jenny Read-Heimerdinger. *Luke in His Own Words: A Study of the Language of Luke-Acts in Greek.* LNTS 672. London/New York: Bloomsbury T&T Clark, 2022. 248pp. ISBN 978-0-567-69298-6. £77. $83.

This volume is a collection of previously published essays by Jenny Read-Heimerdinger with several short additions to bring cohesion to the studies. Those who know Read-Heimerdinger's work will be familiar with her emphasis on discourse analysis of individual manuscripts—Bezae, Sinaiticus, and Vaticanus in this case—rather than an eclectic text such as the NA[28].

The introduction provides background on the studies and includes, among other issues, an outline of methodological considerations, an explanation of the author's conception of discourse analysis, and the choice of manuscripts. Chapter two examines the use of the article before proper names. Her conclusion is that Luke normally uses the article with a person or place name and omits it when he wishes to mark that name as salient.

Connecting words and asyndeton are the subject of chapter three, with expected (and therefore meager) results. In chapter four, Read-Heimerdinger tackles the highly debatable matter of word order. Obviously, she is unable to study every possible variation in word order, so she limits the investigation to variation in noun phrases and the use of adjectives in noun phrases. One interesting, and important, conclusion she draws on variation within adjective-noun phrases in the Bezan text of Acts 'underlines the Jewish significance of the subject matter' but 'does not reproduce the typical Hebraic word order of noun-adjective' (120); that is, the text draws attention to Jewish settings, but does so in keeping with Greek language conventions.

Chapter five looks at expressions for the Holy Spirit, long-recognized as one of Luke's distinctive emphases, concluding that the different expressions (e.g., arthrous or anarthrous, and adjective-noun versus noun-adjective) 'distinguish among the various operations and manifestations of the Spirit' (157). The topic of chapter six is the use of the third person pronoun to track participants in the narrative after their initial introduction. Read-Heimerdinger sums up the data with five rules (two of which have two parts) for Luke's default/unmarked use of the pronoun.

In chapter seven, the author examines Luke's precise usage of alternate words and phrases to distinguish between: 1) introducing the addressee of direct speech with either the dative or πρός + accusative; 2) introducing a character's name with ὀνόματι, καλέω, a dative article (ἧ, ᾧ), and combinations of them; and 3) making comparisons with ὡς or ὡσεί. Read-Heimerdinger pulls together a lot of data in this chapter, but she admits that with the exception of Luke's use of ὡς or ὡσεί (ὡς is used to introduce a clause and to highlight the *nature* of the entities being compared, whereas ὡσεί is used to highlight the fact of comparison) firm conclusions will require further work.

In chapter eight, Read-Heimerdinger seeks to ascertain structural elements in

> **Read-Heimerdinger's data collection is meticulous, her analysis is thorough, and her conclusions are judicious.**

Luke-Acts using discourse analysis. The study helps confirm some widely held conclusions concerning the structure of Luke-Acts (e.g., its geographical orientation). Read-Heimerdinger also profitably applies principles of marking narrative divisions in Greek literature such as connectives and word order at the beginning of sentences to draw helpful conclusions about both the micro- and macro-structure of the Lukan *Doppelwerk*. Chapter nine is a summative conclusion with suggestions for avenues of further research.

While the title of this collection promises attention to the Greek text of Luke and Acts, the overwhelming majority of the work is dedicated to the Book of Acts. Read-Heimerdinger's examination of Acts does, however, provide methodological parameters for others to use in similar studies of the third canonical gospel. This small quibble aside, Read-Heimerdinger's data collection is meticulous, her analysis is thorough, and her conclusions are judicious. Though scholars and researchers will already be familiar with the information contained in these essays, this single-volume collection will be a useful reference work to those conducting research on the Greek text of Acts, and to those who wish to employ discourse analysis to the Gospel of Luke. Advanced students in graduate schools and seminaries will benefit from Read-Heimerdinger's example of methodological precision and clear presentation of her findings in these essays. The essays contained in this volume are wide-ranging and therefore, a brief review such as this can only touch on the topics covered in each chapter. Those who are interested and have not read the essays in other publications will do well to carefully consult this work which will soon be available in paperback.

Frank E. Dicken
Professor of New Testament and Early Christianity
Lincoln Christian University

BOOK REVIEWS

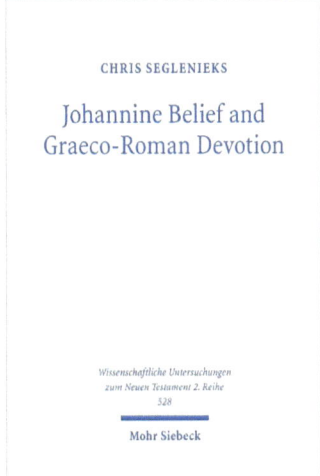

Chris Seglenieks. *Johannine Belief and Graeco-Roman Devotion: Reshaping Devotion for John's Graeco-Roman Audience.* WUNT 2.528. Tübingen: Mohr Siebeck, 2020. Pp. xv + 262.

In this slightly revised doctoral thesis submitted to the Bible College of South Australia, Chris Seglenieks sets out to accomplish two tasks: first, to explore and 'offer a comprehensive description' (p. 1) of how John's Gospel articulates the ideal response to Jesus; and, secondly, to investigate why the Johannine presentation of that desired response is conceptually so complex and narratively so pervasive. By combining these tasks, the study seeks to capture the multifaceted character of 'genuine belief' in John and to do so against the backdrop of engagement with audience members who are envisaged as belonging to a Graeco-Roman setting and as being encouraged to adopt a response to Jesus that involves significant reshaping of their existing practices of religious devotion.

After a brief but valuable literature review, Chapter 1 offers an outline of the study's approach to audience reception, building on the work, among others, of Bill Salier, the author's doctoral supervisor (in his own published doctoral thesis, *The Rhetorical Impact of the Sēmeia in the Gospel of John,* 2004): the method involves moving from the Johannine text to the implied audience and then from a plausible 'real' audience, via an investigation of their likely first-century Graeco-Roman context, back to the text of John's Gospel. This is followed in Chapters 2-5 by a four-part sequential analysis of the Johannine narrative (chs. 1-4, 5-12, 13-17, 18-21), whereby different facets of the required response to Jesus are identified as well as the development of characters' actual responses to him. Five interrelated, sometimes overlapping, categories of Johannine belief emerge on the basis of this textual analysis (Chapter 6): cognitive (that is, knowing and accepting Jesus as the Messiah and Son of God); relational (involving a close relationship with Jesus based on trust, love and friendship, and one that is to be extended to fellow believers); ethical (a form of belief characterised by a life of mimetic obedience to Jesus); ongoing (in that it involves continued allegiance to and abiding in him); and public (through direct confession of and testimony to Jesus).

Seglenieks then turns, in the final part of the study, to construct what he describes as a composite 'religious repertoire', drawing primarily on evidence from Greece and Asia Minor, to delineate the kind of Graeco-Roman patterns of devotion that an early audience of John's Gospel might have brought to the Johannine text as part of their cultural encyclopaedia. Using the same five categories as those underpinning the study's earlier examination of the Johannine evidence, Seglenieks examines beliefs and practices associated with the Olympian pantheon (Chapter 7) together with the cult of Asclepius, the cult of Isis, and emperor worship (Chapter 8). And while some shared emphases, especially cognitive and relational categories, emerge from the juxtaposition of the Johannine

> **The study seeks to capture the multifaceted character of 'genuine belief'.**

text with certain Graeco-Roman analogues, it is the (additional) category of ritual that clearly dominates various Graeco-Roman expressions of communicating with and experiencing the divine (Chapter 9). Two key factors, it is argued, account for John's reworking of familiar Graeco-Roman patterns of devotion, and this in order to establish the distinctiveness of Johannine belief: the unique identity of Jesus as the definitive revealer of God; and the intensity and closeness of the relationship between Jesus and believers, which is continued through the Spirit and experienced through the text of the Gospel (Chapter 9).

> Undoubtedly takes the study of Johannine belief into significant new directions.

This well-written and coherently argued study undoubtedly takes the study of Johannine belief into significant new directions. The decision to examine not only John's use of πιστεύω but also a range of related verbs (such as following, receiving, remaining, knowing) enables Seglenieks to cast the net widely, and productively, to highlight the breadth of responses to Jesus as well as their interconnectedness within the narrative. Furthermore, by adopting Seymour Chatman's categories of 'story' and 'discourse', the study establishes a helpful distinction between the category of 'acceptable belief' at the story level and 'genuine belief' at the discourse level, that is, in the latter case, the quality of belief that the Gospel's audiences are being encouraged to adopt. Seglenieks persuasively argues that the disciples, despite their limited pre-Easter understanding of Jesus' identity and mission, are thus able to function as models of (progressive) belief for John's audience because the ideal response to Jesus, accentuated at certain points of the narrative (cf. Jn 1:1-18; 20:30-31), can only be experienced in a post-Easter setting.

The one area of enquiry that would benefit from further clarification in this study is how its rich and wide-ranging outline of Graeco-Roman patterns of devotion, particularly as a conceptual backdrop for the Johannine presentation of belief, relates to this Gospel's interest in and relationship with Jewish beliefs and practices. Seglenieks suggests that there are 'no explicit connections drawn [in John] between OT forms of devotion and the way people ought to respond to Jesus' (p. 195), even though some of his selected categories, particularly those connected to the cognitive, relational, and ethical aspects of belief, possess some striking scriptural analogues. One thinks, for example, of the ways in which John evokes the Isaianic motifs of knowledge of and belief in Israel's God (Isa. 43:10; cf. Jn 8:24, 28). It may be the case that Seglenieks is thinking primarily, and specifically, about (the absence of) connections between Johannine devotion to Jesus and Jewish practices rather than about the Gospel's engagement with the Jewish Scriptures, which in many ways is closely aligned to this study's findings regarding John's articulation of the ideal response to Jesus. Seglenieks acknowledges that possible connections with Second Temple Jewish patterns of devotion do warrant investigation (p. 207), something that would undoubtedly lend further weight to his own study as an important contribution to wider questions about the ways in which John's Gospel navigates its engagement with both Jewish *and* Graeco-Roman religious traditions.

Catrin H. Williams
University of Wales Trinity Saint David

Centre for Gospels and Acts Research Volumes

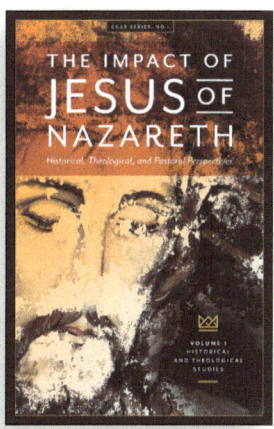 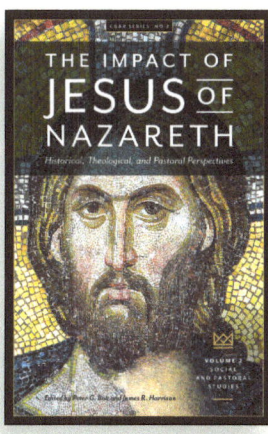 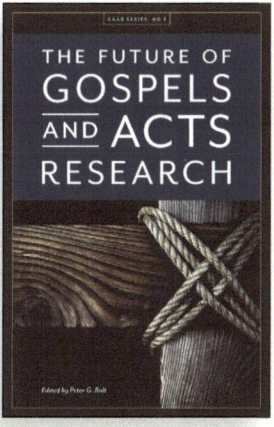 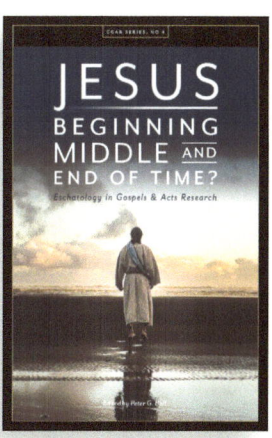

The Impact of Jesus of Nazareth: Historical, Theological, and Pastoral Perspectives
CGAR Series, No 1

Despite his relatively short life and his tragic death, Jesus of Nazareth made a profound impact upon the first-century Graeco-Roman world. Wherever his heritage is celebrated and remembered, Jesus of Nazareth continues to make an impact. The greatness of Jesus of Nazareth was supremely displayed in his moment of greatest weakness on the cross. Those who felt his immediate impact either chafed under his teaching, or embraced it, but rarely did anyone remain untouched by him. The mystery of his salvific death inspires; the power of his resurrection hope sustains; and his impact continues to work its way outwards in manifold implications as his gospel finds a hearing, wherever and whenever that might be.

The Impact of Jesus of Nazareth: Historical, Theological, and Pastoral Perspectives
CGAR Series, No 2

Writing from a variety of perspectives, the essays in these two volumes, explore the impact of Jesus of Nazareth on his own and subsequent times. After Volume 1 collects historical and theological essays, volume 2 moves from the historical and theological, towards the wider impact of Jesus on pastoral practice in our contemporary world.

The Future of Gospels and Acts Research
CGAR Series, No 3

This volume of essays represents a selection of eleven of the papers from the Centre for Gospels and Acts Research 2019 conference, 'Discerning the Trends'. This collection provides a sounding of current Gospels and Acts research. Each essay builds on current research and opens up new questions charting a direction for research in the future.

Jesus: Beginning, Middle, & End of Time? Eschatology in Gospels & Acts Research
CGAR Series, No 4

The Gospels and Acts not only use time, but they also seem to be about time. And back behind those who narrate his story, Jesus not only happened in time, he also thought he was happening to time. *Jesus: Beginning, Middle, and End of Time?* offers seventeen essays, each addressing in their own way, Eschatology in Gospels and Acts Research.

Centre for Gospels and Acts Research Volume 5

**God Beyond Ideology
Rediscovering Theology Through Narrative
(CGAR Series, No 5; Norwest, NSW: SCD Press, 2024)**

Table of Contents

1. Peter G. Bolt, Introduction
2. Greg W. Forbes, Narratival Theology Identified: A Hermeneutical Grid
3. Mary J. Marshall, Revisiting the 'Cup Saying' Debate from a Narrative Perspective
4. Jonathan Thambyrajah, What do Herod and Peter have in Common? Oath-Breaking in Matthew's Discourse and Narrative
5. Timothy P. Bradford, Restoring and Revealing the Human Condition: Matthew's Servant and the Establishment of מִשְׁפָּט / ΚΡΙΣΙΣ on the Earth
6. Peter G. Bolt, Leading Interpreters on a Merry Dance. Ideology, the Underworld, and Herod's Banquet 'Entertainment' (Mark 6:21–23)
7. Andrew Stewart, The Shame of the Son of Man. Honour and Shame in Mark 8:38 And Luke 9:26
8. Jonathan Rivett Robinson, 'All Things Are Possible'. The Narrative Conditioning of Omnipotence in the Gospel of Mark
9. Denise Powell, How Narrative Transforms (part 1): What the Gospel of Luke *Does* to Theophilus
10. Denise Powell, How Narrative Transforms (part 2): What the Gospel of Luke *Does* to Us
11. Danielle Terceiro and Louise A. Gosbell, Feasting with Good Humour? Retelling the Parable of the Great Banquet (Luke 14:15–24) for Children and the Risks of a Comedic Approach
12. James R. Harrison, The Threat of Caesar's Friendship Withdrawn (John 19:12b). The Collision of History, Narrative, and Theology in the Gospel of John
13. Stefano Salemi, Reinterpreting John's Passion Imagery. Contemporary Perceptions of God through 'Christian' and 'Midrashic' Hermeneutics
14. Christoph Stenschke, 'Sovereign Lord, who made the heaven and the earth and the sea and everything in them' (Acts 4:24). God as the Creator in the Acts of the Apostles and its Implications
15. Karen Nivala, Narrative Criticism And Narrative Therapy. Foundations Of A Dialogue

www.ingramcontent.com/pod-product-compliance
Lightning Source LLC
Chambersburg PA
CBHW050747110526
44590CB00003B/108